Regi...

THE ECONOMIC AND SOCIAL DEVELOPMENT OF MERSEYSIDE

CROOM HELM SERIES ON THE REGIONAL ECONOMIC
HISTORY OF BRITAIN
Edited by J.R. Harris and A.J. Sutcliffe

THE ECONOMIC AND SOCIAL DEVELOPMENT OF MERSEYSIDE
Sheila Marriner

The Economic and Social Development of Merseyside

Sheila Marriner

CROOM HELM
London & Canberra

© 1982 Sheila Marriner
Croom Helm Ltd, 2-10 St John's Road, London SW11

British Library Cataloguing in Publication Data

Marriner, Sheila
    The economic and social development of
    Merseyside 1750-1960.—(Croom Helm series on
    the regional economic history of Britain)
    1. Merseyside—Social conditions—History
    I. Title
    942.7'507   HN398.M/

    ISBN 0-7099-0260-3

Printed and bound in Great Britain by
Biddles Ltd, Guildford and King's Lynn

CONTENTS

List of Tables and Figures   vi

Preface   vii

1. Introduction   1
2. Communications 1750–1870   13
3. Ports, shipping and commercial organisation   30
4. Merseyside industries 1750–1870   46
5. Life on Merseyside 1760–1870   70
6. Vicissitudes of trade and transport 1870–1939   90
7. Fortunes and misfortunes of Merseyside's industries 1870–1939   109
8. The managed economy post 1945   126
9. The quality of life from 1870   141

Select bibliography   168

TABLES AND FIGURES

TABLES

2.1	Tonnages carried on the Weaver Nagivation	18
2.2	Distribution of Shares in the Liverpool-Manchester Railway	24
2.3	Traffic on the Liverpool-Manchester Railway	25
4.1	British Alkali Production	61
5.1	Merseyside Population 1801-71	72
5.2	Parish of Liverpool 1856-66	85
7.1	Relative Importance of Industry Groups on Merseyside 1939	109
8.1	Employment in Merseyside Industries 1953-63	136
9.1	Merseyside Population 1871-1911	142
9.2	Merseyside Population 1921-71, Numbers	143
9.3	Merseyside Population 1921-71, Percentages	144

FIGURE

1.1	Map of Merseyside	8

Preface

Economic historians have long been interested in regional history as an escape from the generalisations inherent in national studies. It is, however, possible for there to be considerable variation even within a region and this is certainly true of Merseyside. Merseyside includes districts which exhibit very varied characteristics both economically and socially: in some districts commerce and maritime activities predominate, in others manufacturing industries are foremost and in addition there are rich agricultural areas. Equally there are wide variations in the availability and quality of source materials relating to each district and to each activity within the region. A great deal of research has taken place into some areas and aspects of the region's history but the quality and level of academic competence are not consistent for the whole region so that serious problems arise in using material from diverse sources. For some areas within the region there are no definitive histories; for others, especially for Liverpool, there is a wealth of sources. The author has therefore to resist the temptation to deal in greatest detail with those parts of the region that are best documented. Some sources also need careful interpretation especially those of a statistical nature. As there is no single generally-accepted definition of the constitution of 'Merseyside' each statistical source has to be carefully examined to see to which parts of the region it refers. The number of footnotes and references to source material in the book have been limited because the series aims to cater for a very wide readership but the select bibliography aims to provide a guide to the sources used and to those available for further reference.

Another problem that arose in the writing of this history was in attempting to maintain a balance between different aspects of the region's social history. The book was completed at the time of the serious inner city riots in the summer of 1981. These concentrated attention on the gloom, unemployment and misery of the inner city of Liverpool. The attention of the media was concentrated exclusively on a very small part of the region and there was a tendency to identify such conditions with the whole region. Without in any way detracting from the blackness of the inner city problems it is important to try to keep a sense of proportion and to realise that such conditions are limited to a small geographical area within the region. Similarly the deplorable housing conditions in Liverpool in the 1840s spotlighted in the report of the Royal Commission on Large Towns applied only to one part of the region. It is therefore important to try also to highlight the pleasanter aspects of life throughout much of the region.

My knowledge of Merseyside has been built up gradually over many years and in this process I have been indebted to many people. My long years of association with the late Professor F.E. Hyde aroused and encouraged my interest in Merseyside shipping and trade. I have learnt a good deal about Merseyside's economic development from conversations with Mr M. Stammers of the Maritime Museum. My greatest debt is, however, to the two editors of the series Professor J.R. Harris and Dr A. Sutcliffe. Both of them read the first draft and made many useful comments and Professor Harris has given me continual encouragement and assistance. For the map I am indebted to Mr A.G. Hodgkiss of the Geography department of Liverpool University and I have been greatly helped by the staff of the Liverpool University Library and of Liverpool City Library.

Sheila Marriner
University of Liverpool.

Chapter 1

INTRODUCTION

'Merseyside' conjures up strong emotions of love or hate, of
respect or contempt, of admiration or criticism; few people
regard the region dispassionately. Its image is vivid; bubbling
with life, originality and humour; but restless, even turbulent.
To some people it is synonymous with vandalism, with high crime
rates, with social deprivation in the form of bad housing, with
obsolete schools, polluted air and a polluted river, with chronic
unemployment, run-down dock systems and large areas of industrial dereliction. It has attracted a great deal of publicity as a
particularly strike-prone region, a reputation derived partly
from the fact that it has often been in the vanguard of workers'
campaigns, as for example in 1911 when Merseyside labour spear-
headed national protests, in 1919 when its police force made
history by striking and again in the early 1920s when its building
industry precipitated a national strike and lock-out.
    Merseyside has made an apparently disproportionate impact on
national television through Z-cars, the Liver Birds, the Onedin
Line, Ken Dodd's Knotty Ash and documentary programmes about
Kirkby. In sport its soccer players and their fans carry its name
beyond national boundaries; its rugby league teams frequently
feature in national cup finals and to steeple-chasing enthusiasts
it is the home of the Grand National. The Beatles have indelibly
imprinted it in the annals of pop music and the Liverpool Philharmonic has long taken its place amongst Britain's leading
orchestras. As a source of famous comedians its reputation is
unrivalled - Tommy Handley, Arthur Askey, Ted Ray, Jimmy
Tarbuck and Ken Dodd, to name but a few.
    Historically, too, Merseyside is renowned (or notorious) for
many activities: as the birth place of world-famous shipping
companies; as the testing ground for canals and railways including Stephenson's 'Rocket'; as a pioneer in sanitation, urban
health and housing; for its participation in privateering and
smuggling. As late as 1839, a Royal Commission investigating the
need for police forces, singled out the north-east corner of the
Wirral as one of the two most dangerous and lawless areas in the
country, Cornwall being the second one. Fires were lit on the
Wirral shores to lure ships onto the sandbanks, the wrecked
ships were plundered, survivors were robbed and dead bodies
were mutilated in the quest for valuables. Merseyside is also
internationally infamous for its participation in the slave trade,
despite the fact that it contributed some of the most vocal and
active opponents of slavery led by the Rathbones and William

1

Roscoe. And even in the 1970s Liverpool was notorious as
Britain's major port of entry for smuggled drugs from all over
the world.

Famous names associated with Merseyside are legion and are
drawn from all walks of life. Obvious ones are the two famous
prime ministers, Mr William Gladstone (a native) and Sir Harold
Wilson, (MP for Huyton). Handel put the finishing touches to the
Messiah while staying at Parkgate, which John Wesley also frequently visited. Captain Fortunatus Wright, the best-known of
privateers, came from Wallasey. The Merseyside women whom
history records are more frequently remembered for tough rather
than tender characteristics. The grim, ponderous railway bridge
linking Runcorn and Widnes perpetuates the name of a Mercian
princess, Athelflaed or Ethelfleda, who built a fort on the site
of one of its main supports. In eighteenth-century industrial
history, that dominating business-woman, Sarah Clayton, played
a powerful role in the creation of the St Helens coalfield. In the
Wirral, Mother Redcap's name is synonymous with smugglers and
smuggling and Liverpool's Maggie May is a legend immortalised
in popular music. The image of Merseyside womanhood is, however, softened by the humanity and social conscience of reformers
such as Eleanor Rathbone, by the lovely Lady Lever Art Gallery
and by the beauty of Emily Lyon of Ness, more celebrated as
Lady Hamilton.

Merseyside is a region of sharp contrasts – great monuments
to human endeavour literally and figuratively tower above
stretches of drabness and squalor. This is symbolised in Liverpool's building in the twentieth century of two cathedrals: Giles
Gilbert Scott's massive Gothic edifice in red sandstone for the
Anglicans and Frederick Gibberd's radically non-traditional
steel and concrete Roman Catholic cathedral. Though at opposite
ends of the architectural spectrum, and built by the followers of
two faiths who until relatively recently feuded with each other
they are at least symbolically linked together by Hope Street.
Meanwhile, the strong body of non-conformists scaled the heights
of human endeavour by contributing eminent intellectuals and
social reformers rather than monumental buildings.

The diversity of religious faiths in Merseyside is partly a
reflection of the geographical sources of its population. Large
numbers of Irish, Welsh and Scots have been attracted into the
area by economic opportunities or driven to it as refugees from
poverty and unemployment in their home lands. Lesser, but by
no means insignificant, numbers of foreign-born immigrants
came in, notably from China, the West Indies and Africa. English
migrants, too, were in evidence, coming especially from other
parts of North-West England, from Devon, Somerset and Cornwall
and from Middlesex and London. Amongst the English immigrants
were many sons of landed gentry and of the middle classes seeking
to build their fortunes in trade, fortunes which some then proceeded to take away in part from Merseyside to invest in landed
estates in other parts of the country.

In addition to those who came to settle permanently or to stay
for lengthy periods there were many who passed through the
ports, pausing only for a few days or weeks - Irish on their
way to other parts of England in search of work, seamen of all
nations and, during the nineteenth century in particular, people
from all over Europe bound for the New World. Liverpool became
Europe's greatest emigrant port, as many as 200,000 emigrants
passing through in some years during the mid-nineteenth century.
   Anyone, however, who wishes to learn more about Merseyside's
history must be struck by the lack of a unique definition of its
geographical boundaries. There appear to be not one but many
'Merseysides' and the confusion grows year by year with the
introduction of names such as 'Greater Merseyside', 'the Mersey
Belt' and 'the Mersey District'. Today there is an administrative
area called the Metropolitan County of Merseyside but historically
the term 'Merseyside' has been applied to many different permu-
tations of urban and rural districts according to the purpose
for which a definition was required. Some writers have adhered
to strictly geographical criteria embracing the land on both sides
of the Mersey estuary. Many have concentrated on the economic,
commercial and industrial links which determined the mutual
development of the port facilities around the estuary and the
industrial hinterland. Other definitions have been adopted for
the purpose of the Census of Population, for the Merseyside
development area, for the travel-to-work area, for the marketing
region, for the Merseyside Passenger Transport Authority, for
social services, pensions and hospital boards, for the supply
of water, gas and electricity. Some definitions combine Merseyside with North Wales (e.g. the Merseyside and North Wales
Electricity Board) and Liverpool is often jokingly referred to
as the capital of North Wales.
   How can such a multiplicity of definitions arise? The answer
must be that such a region is not uniform and monolithic. It is
a living, changing, organism built out of a series of sub-regions
which are not themselves discrete, self-contained units. At any
moment, they overlap each other and sometimes only part of a
sub-region is orientated towards Merseyside - the rest is pulled
in other directions, frequently towards the Manchester region.
Over time, the sub-regions themselves have changed both in
size and in character.
   In a short book of this nature it is not appropriate to devote
too much space to technical arguments about boundaries but
rather to adopt a flexible definition and a pragmatic approach.
This involves taking a central core of urban and rural districts
and accepting that on the periphery are areas which at some
times and for some purposes fall within Merseyside's sphere of
influence but which are also subject to strong pulls in other
directions. In this way it is possible to include sub-regions
which made important contributions to Merseyside's development
in one or two respects only; which have economic ties but which
may lack social or administrative cohesion. In addition attention

can be paid to some which are relevant only for part of the
period and it is possible to vary the depth of treatment of the
component parts according to the topic under consideration.
Unfortunately, this raises intractable problems in finding statistics for comparable geographical units over long time-periods
but this must be accepted as inevitable. Wherever statistics are
used it is necessary to specify carefully the parts of 'Merseyside' to which they apply.

Which then are the sub-regions particularly relevant to a
survey of the economic and social history of Merseyside from
1750 to 1960? Some districts automatically slot into key positions.
Pre-eminence must be attributed to the whole area around the
estuary which provided the important port facilities for river,
coastal and international shipping. To the south lie the Cheshire
saltfields; their development gave a great initial stimulus both to
the improvement of transport facilities and to the expansion of
coal production. The coalfield which responded to this need was
that in south-west Lancashire. Together salt, coal and transport
facilities provided the essential foundations for growth. From
these foundations other developments occurred - chemical production, metal-working, a whole range of port-based industries and
further rapid growth in transport industries.

In general terms these are the key constituents of Merseyside
but there are special problems with the Lancashire coalfield. This
played an absolutely vital role in supplying fuel and energy to
Merseyside's domestic and industrial users and, in turn, their
urgent demand stimulated both the output of coal and the provision of means to transport the coal. The southern and western
parts of the coalfield are firmly located within Merseyside itself
but the central part including Wigan has much stronger ties with
Manchester. The boundary must, therefore, cut across the coalfield and exclude Wigan, and, in addition it largely though not
completely excludes Lancashire's most famous industry, cotton.
Traditionally before 1750 the predominant form of textile manufacture in Merseyside was linen, with cotton production mainly
confined to its fringes and especially to the Manchester area
and to East Lancashire, and yet, by the late eighteenth century
Liverpool had become the port of entry for most of the cotton
industry's raw material, it had a growing number of cotton
brokers and eventually they created a thriving cotton exchange,
and Liverpool was the port through which a high proportion of
the finished cotton goods was exported until the port of Manchester had been developed by the Manchester Ship Canal.

Further south, Warrington is situated on the Mersey and it
has very strong historical ties with the Cheshire chemical industry
but gradually it came more firmly within Manchester's orbit and
so it can only be included marginally within Merseyside. Runcorn
too, is strongly linked both to the chemical industries and to
Widnes, immediately facing it across the Mersey; nowadays it
has become an important part of Merseyside and yet for some
purposes it has, in the past, been excluded from the region.

If we look more closely at the forces responsible for bringing these component parts together to form a region it is possible to see how such discrepancies can occur without destroying the economic unity. Of great importance in determining the direction of development was the Mersey estuary's geographical location in the centre of Britain's western coast. From the Middle Ages it was well-placed for communications with Ireland but its remoteness from the south and east of Britain handicapped its growth during the time when Britain's main overseas connections were with Europe. With the discoveries in the New World and the establishment of colonies, Britain increasingly looked westward. Fishing and the coastal trades in bulky produce such as salt and coal (based on the Mersey and responsible for much of its early development) were increasingly over-shadowed during the eighteenth and nineteenth centuries by longer distance trades with Africa, the Americas and Australasia. These trades carried British manufactures throughout the world and channelled vital foodstuffs and raw materials into the growing industrial hinterland. A complex network of economic inter-relationships developed binding together geographical regions which might otherwise appear to have little in common.

To make this possible Merseyside had to become an important communications centre and yet it appeared to start with serious natural disadvantages. The estuary was inhospitable; as we will see later special measures were needed to cope with the great variations in water levels between high and low tides, with treacherous currents, and shifting sand banks and channels. Inland on the Lancashire side of the estuary were stretches of bog and marshland. Much of the Wirral was wild and dangerous. Of the lands bordering the estuary the site on which Liverpool grew seemed to have the fewest disadvantages. It is not, therefore, accidental that Liverpool became the most important constituent of the region. It was situated on the northern side of the estuary at the point where a natural pool gave shelter for shipping and where the channel was at its narrowest - the estuary widening out both towards the sea and inland. Liverpool was therefore the obvious starting point for ferries to the Wirral as it was much later for railway and road tunnels under the river.

Pride of place in Liverpool's growth must certainly be accorded to its position as a port although by the eighteenth century it also had important craft industries such as watch- and clock-making, the production of delft earthenware and glass and other industries such as copper-smelting. Early in the eighteenth century the Pool was converted into the first important wet-dock in Britain. In the course of the eighteenth century the difficulties of land transport were progressively reduced by the advent of turnpike roads such as those from Liverpool to Prescot and from Wigan to Warrington (both turnpiked in 1726). In any event the limitations to land transport were no longer so important as river navigation systems were developed and as the Mersey became the terminus for canals.

By the end of the seventeenth century it had been possible
for flats and sailing barges to navigate the Mersey as far as
Warrington and by the 1730s they could reach Manchester via
the Mersey-Irwell navigation. The carriage of salt was greatly
facilitated by the Weaver navigation opened in 1732 and in 1757
the Sankey Brook Navigation, England's first industrial canal,
linked St Helens to the Mersey. Then came the Duke of Bridgewater's canal and the Leeds-Liverpool canal - the latter first
stimulating the further development of the Wigan coalfield and
later joining with the Douglas Navigation to allow transport
between the Mersey and the Ribble. Gradually the network was
extended via the Trent and Mersey and the Shropshire Union
canals until the Mersey eventually had access by canal and
river and by coastal shipping to most parts of England.

In the nineteenth century, railways greatly added to the
mobility of passengers and goods, starting with Britain's first
important passenger rail service between Liverpool and Manchester. Long-distance services soon linked Liverpool with all parts
of the country and commuter services increased population movements within the region both for work and pleasure. By the end
of the century there was even a railway under the estuary.

In the twentieth century transport continued to play an important role in the region. As late as 1951, after prolonged attempts
to diversify employment opportunities, transport still employed
twice as high a proportion of the occupied population of Central
Merseyside i.e. Liverpool, Wallasey, Birkenhead and Bebington
as for Great Britain as a whole, and for earlier periods the
divergence from the national average was much greater. There
was some decline in older forms of transport, especially canals,
although an important new canal, the Manchester Ship Canal,
had been constructed in the late nineteenth century. There
was a further extension of road transport including two road
tunnels under the estuary and a road bridge across the river
at Runcorn. Since the 1930s Merseyside has been able to supplement land and water transport with air travel from its own airport at Speke.

As inland communications improved with the building first of
canals and roads and then of railways, increasing quantities of
produce came to the port of Liverpool to be exported; at the
same time, the expanding population and industries of the
hinterland hungrily absorbed more and more food, raw cotton,
timber, wool and other materials from abroad. The volume of
shipping therefore grew rapidly and, with changing technology
the size of ships also increased necessitating the building not
only of more but also of larger docks. Liverpool's dockland
spread northwards to Bootle and Seaforth and southwards to
Garston. Along the docks, port-based industries sprand up both
as an effect and as a cause of further trade expansion: shipbuilding, repairing and maintenance, rope-making, sugar-refining,
oil-crushing, milling and tanning. A little further inland, secondary industries developed to convert some of the output of these

industries into such products as bread, biscuits, soap, paints
and sweets and in the centre of the city came the service industries essential to a large port - banking, insurance, broking,
shipping and forwarding agents and produce exchanges.

As well as expanding along the banks of the estuary, Liverpool
also spread inland, eating into agricultural land and absorbing
existing villages in the process of providing housing for its own
growing population, first by private enterprise and then, from
the early twentieth century, also in the form of large corporation
housing estates which were gradually interspersed with industrial
estates. The latter were designed to diversify employment in an
attempt to break the city's dependence on dock, transport and
other service industries by producing new industries such as
car assembly, photographic equipment, football pools, rubber
products, metal safes, cardboard boxes, medicinal preparations,
furniture and many others.

Liverpool must then rank as by far the largest urban centre
within Merseyside. Although located on the north side of the
estuary, it does not mark the northernmost boundary of the
region. The metropolitan county of Merseyside now embraces
Southport, a seaside town some twenty miles north of Liverpool.
Although not located on the estuary, Southport owes a good deal
of its growth to its communication links with the rest of Merseyside first by coach services; then, and more importantly in view
of the very bad state of the roads, by the Leeds-Liverpool canal
which came to within a few miles; canal travel was in turn superseded by rail links from the late 1840s. Southport acted as a
holiday resort, a dormitory for commuters and a haven for the
retired not only from Merseyside but also from Manchester and
from the Lancashire cotton towns.

To the north-east of Liverpool the market town of Ormskirk
and the new town of Skelmersdale form convenient boundaries:
the latter was designed particularly to accommodate excess
population from Liverpool although its natural links have now
brought it closer to Wigan than to Liverpool. Between the coastal
fringe on the one hand and Ormskirk and Skelmersdale on the
other is a rich agricultural area much of which was formerly bog
and which, even now, is heavily dependent on continuous
drainage to prevent flooding. This very fertile area is often
likened to the fenlands of Lincolnshire. A variety of foodstuffs
produced here helps to feed the nearby urban dwellers: cereals,
potatoes and other vegetables, tomatoes, lettuces, poultry. The
area also contains some good grassland for cattle and sheep and
a small part, at Martin Mere, chosen by wild geese as their
natural grazing grounds, has been reserved for the Wild Fowl
Trust.

This area was not, however, exclusively agricultural. Water-
and wind-mills sprang up to mill cereals and, in addition, the
eastern fringe overlapped the west Lancashire coalfield so
mining communities sprang up. The availability of sandstone,
limestone and gritstone led to quarrying as soon as transport

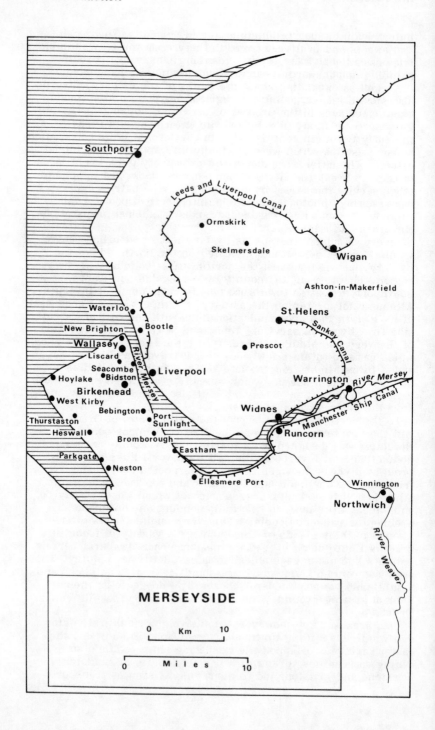

Southport

Leeds and Liverpool Canal

Ormskirk

Skelmersdale

Wigan

Ashton-in-Makerfield

Waterloo

St.Helens

Sankey Canal

New Brighton

Bootle

Wallasey

River Mersey

Liscard

Seacombe

Bidston

Liverpool

Prescot

Hoylake

Birkenhead

Warrington

River Mersey

West Kirby

Bebington

Widnes

Manchester Ship Canal

Thurstaston

Port
Sunlight

Heswall

Runcorn

Bromborough

Parkgate

Eastham

Neston

Ellesmere Port

Winnington

Northwich

River Weaver

MERSEYSIDE

0   Km   10

0   M i l e s   10

was available to carry the stone away, and domestic textile industries were scattered through the area, especially the production of linen based partly on Lancashire-grown flax and partly on imports from Ireland. Craft industries also abounded including blacksmiths and clogmakers.

Due east of Liverpool lies St Helens, whose ties with the Mersey are very strong indeed. It is now synonymous with Pilkington and glass although in the mid-eighteenth century glass-making was more important in other parts of Merseyside especially in Liverpool, Warrington and Prescot. It was only after 1776 that St Helens came to dominate the industry. This town has, of course, other claims to fame, including the Sankey Brook Canal, Beechams' pills and Greenalls' brewery. Its important industries included non-ferrous metals, coal, chemicals, iron-founding, bricks and tiles, rope and paper-making. Here, and also in many other parts of south-west Lancashire, were to be found nail-makers and other metal workers who played such an important role in the early stages of the Industrial Revolution. Of particular significance were craftsmen who made tools, especially files, and the watchmakers whose precision work proved such a vital training ground for the nascent engineering industry.

Such craftsmen were also to be found in Prescot, in Ashton-in-Makerfield, in Leigh and in Warrington. Although as already mentioned the latter town now comes more within the orbit of Greater Manchester its development was, in some measure at least, closely linked to and dependent on the Mersey. Here a mixture of industries appeared including tanning, soap-making, copper and other metal manufacturers, saw-mills, breweries, paper-making, linen weaving and the manufacture of clothing - industries similar to those found in adjacent parts of Merseyside and heavily dependent on Merseyside's transport facilities.

Industrial areas such as these sprang up throughout south Lancashire but they were still surrounded by considerable areas of farmland containing many rural communities and many local industries some of which gradually moved to urban districts. Milling and brewing, for example, occurred widely in the eighteenth century but gradually breweries in urban districts such as St Helens and Warrington grew larger and production became more concentrated. Similarly milling gradually moved towards the ports as imported grain became more important than home-produced. It concentrated in Liverpool and eventually across the estuary in Birkenhead.

On the Cheshire side of the Mersey, too, were rich agricultural areas. Cheshire's famous dairy-farming is particularly important in the south and west of the county but there is some dairying too in north Cheshire and the Wirral (the parts of Cheshire which fall within Merseyside's boundaries). Farms in this area also produce cereals, root crops, grasses and potatoes. Cheshire's particularly significant contribution to Merseyside was, however, its saltfields. The production and trade in salt,

requiring as it did increasing quantitites of coal, stimulated the
development of the south-west Lancashire coalfield and gave an
early impetus to the development of roads, river navigation
systems, canals and shipping to carry both the coal and the
salt. The saltfields also formed the basis for the chemical
industry which was particularly important by the nineteenth
century in Northwich and Winnington with the creation of
Brunner Mond, later to be merged with other firms to form
I.C.I. Before this the chemical industry already had a strong
foothold across the Mersey in Lancashire. The need for alkali
for the soap industry had led to the search for a method of
producing soda from salt by the Leblanc process. Works were
opened for the purpose by James Muspratt in Liverpool in 1822
and then shortly afterwards in St Helens and Earlestown. In
1847, the first chemical factory was opened in Widnes which was
situated at the Mersey end of the Sankey canal, and both
Widnes and its twin town across the river, Runcorn, are extremely important centres for chemical production although they
also have other industries, including copper, asbestos, cement
and tanning.

Until recently, Widnes was generally accepted as part of
Merseyside but Runcorn was excluded. Although they were
linked by a railway bridge and road transporter their ties became much closer with the building of the new road bridge -
the nearest point to the sea at which the Mersey is bridged.
Furthermore Runcorn new town is designed to take excess
population from Liverpool and this greatly strengthens the case
for including Runcorn in Merseyside.

Moving back along the south side of the estuary towards the
sea one comes to Ellesmere Port. Stimulated by excellent transport facilities, industries grew up here to manufacture steel
plates, to mill flour, to make paper and to produce aircraft but
the over-riding significance of this district was to be its position as a centre for oil-refining. From 1922, Stanlow, at the
eastern end of Ellesmere Port, became one of the leading oil
storage and refining centres in the country. Later it was
supplemented by the Queen Elizabeth dock at Eastham and by
an oil terminal nearer the sea at Tranmere but during the 1970s
its prosperity has been threatened by a new oil terminal at
Anglesey which has drawn some business away from the estuary.

Still travelling along the south side of the estuary towards
the sea one encounters Bebington and Bromborough with the
dock system opened by Lever Brothers in 1931. This was strate-
gically well-placed to serve Port Sunlight famous for oils, soap,
margarine and its model village. The village was however preceded at Bromborough by Price's Patent Candle Company's
model village dating from 1853. More recently the Bromborough
Port Estate has been extended to make possible industrial
diversification.

As the Liverpool dock-system spread along the northern side
of the estuary in the late eighteenth and early nineteenth

centuries, shipbuilders who had operated on the sands were gradually pushed out of their former locations and eventually they moved across the river to Birkenhead which became renowned for the great Cammell Laird shipbuilding yard. By the twentieth century, Birkenhead had also become one of the largest flour-milling centres in Europe and it had a vast trade in livestock. Other industries were engineering and brewing. Closely linked to Birkenhead both industrially and along the dock area is neighbouring Wallasey.

The south side of the estuary therefore has its docks and its industries, many of which are port-based but, in addition, much of the Wirral peninsula is residential. It contains extensive dormitory areas and the remains of many once-thriving holiday centres along both the Mersey and Dee estuaries. From the eighteenth century, the fashion for visiting health and watering resorts quickly spread and south Merseyside responded eagerly. The number of such resorts grew rapidly to include Wallasey, New Brighton, Egremont and Seacombe, Liscard, Poulton, Leasowe, West Kirby, Parkgate and Hoylake. Nowadays it seems hard to realise that Eastham was famed for its beauty and known as the Richmond of the Mersey and further along the estuary Runcorn was likened to Montpelier, its air and waters attracting visitors from far afield. During the twentieth century the tourist industry has declined but south Merseyside has retained many beauty spots, open heaths and parklands including Bidston Hill, Thurstaston and Heswall commons, the Grange and Caldy Hills and the Hilbre Islands which are important wild-life centres.

From this brief tour of the region it is possible to gain some idea of both the unifying factors and the great diversity and vivid contrasts. Some industries such as chemical production, tanning and metal manufactures are found in several important centres; equally others, such as cotton manufacture, are notable by their absence. The existence of a range of transport facilities gives the area much of its unity and yet there are disparities even within the transport system. The series of ports ringing the estuary offer facilities ranging from the very modern Seaforth container dock, the grain terminal and oil terminals to large areas of old-fashioned, derelict and deserted dockland including Jesse Hartley's famous Albert Dock – widely regarded as one of the finest nineteenth-century enclosed dock systems in the world. Other extensive warehouse areas which formerly served the docks are also now run-down, abandoned or demolished.

Similarly there are vivid contrasts between new and old industries. Some of the older industries have survived clinging grimly to life or they have been invigorated by transfusions of new technology – viz shipbuilding, glass-making and chemicals; some sections of some industries have died or are dying – viz many former coal-mines which have now reverted to farmland, and paper-making, sugar-refining and milling are rapidly losing ground. By contrast, there are the relatively new industrial estates carved out of former agricultural areas to introduce new industries into the region. There are the new towns of Skelmersdale and Runcorn and large new housing estates such as Kirkby which compare (sometimes even unfavourably) with extensive tracts of older industrial housing and with large areas of better-class private housing and holiday resorts. There are still important agricultural and market-gardening areas which contrast so strongly with the industrial centres and dock systems.

Some parts of the region have serious problems - chiefly endemic unemployment which has proved stubbornly resistant to all attempts to overcome it. The black spots in the region are amongst the blackest in Britain in terms of social deprivation and yet the region also contains considerable stretches of highly-desirable residential areas noted for the affluence of their inhabitants. Despite such great divergencies, the fortunes (and misfortunes) of the various component parts of Merseyside are closely interwoven and it is their economic inter-dependence which gives Merseyside its essential unity.

Chapter 2

COMMUNICATIONS 1750-1870

The key determinant of Merseyside's economic unity is to be
found in its communications and transport facilities. It became
the focal point on which ocean and coastal shipping routes con-
verged to merge with river and canal, road and rail networks.
These facilities not only linked together the component parts of
the Mersey estuary and its industrial hinterland but also gave
them channels of communication with the rest of Britain and with
the rest of the world; at the same time the development of new
transport facilities was both a cause and an effect of the growth
of Merseyside industries. By the period 1750-1800 the economic
growth of the region was already entering a virtuous circle of
expansion in which the growth of one industry stimulated other
industries, called for better transport and was in turn further
stimulated as the new transport facilities became available. At
times it was very difficult to distentangle cause and effect:
businessmen, dissatisfied with existing means for supplying raw
materials or for carrying finished produce to market, set about
improving the channels of rivers, building roads, canals, docks,
fleets of ships and port facilities and later creating railway
networks. Better communications allowed existing industries to
expand and new ones to develop: this increased production then
called forth further improvements in transport to carry even
more raw materials, more manufactured goods and more food to
the growing industrial population. In order to provide new transport facilities investment was needed in rivers and canals, roads
and docks and in the equipment that had to be provided to
create new systems: there was a growing demand for barges
and ships, ropes and sailcloth, pitch and tar, tools to dig canals,
coaches and wagons, stone for walls for canals and docks, bricks
for stations and warehouses, lock-gates, engineering products
of all sorts including locomotives, marine engines, etc. The
growing labour force employed in the building and operation of
transport facilities added to the growing industrial population
and further increased the need for food, clothing, drink,
tobacco, houses etc. so stimulating even more home industry
and more import trades.
  This virtuous circles of growth had started before the opening
of our period and the initiative in setting these processes in
motion came both from Liverpool and from the coal- and salt-fields
of the hinterland where the need for better facilities for the
carriage of heavy produce was already abundantly clear by the
early eighteenth century. Liverpool had been slowly developing

13

since the Middle Ages. The status of borough, conferred in
1207 by King John by Letters Patent was confirmed and extended on several occasions by later kings and Liverpool's freemen
came to enjoy considerable status.[1] There were, however, prolonged disputes over control of the town between the general
assembly of burgesses and the smaller body of leading citizens
who formed the Common Council. From 1580, effective power
resided in the latter body which became highly influential. The
Common Council was however highly undemocratic. Each coun-
cillor continued in office for life. When there was a vacancy new
members were coopted. Furthermore as time went by admission to
freedom of the town was so restricted that by the eighteenth
century most citizens were excluded. The Common Council did
however participate actively in the development of Liverpool's
economic life. In 1672 the value of the municipal estates was
greatly enhanced when the Council leased (and later bought
outright) from Lord Molyneux (the Lord of the Manor) the right
to develop a considerable area of heath and wasteland. As
population grew and as building spread this land became the
site of much of the centre of the town.

From 1680 there was a considerable upsurge both in population
and in industrial and commercial activity. Liverpool's population
which probably numbered 5,000 in 1700, had, by 1750, quad-
rupled to reach some 20,000. One effect of this growth was an
increasing demand for coal for domestic use. Both in Liverpool
and in the hinterland traditional agricultural and fishing pursuits were already being supplemented by new and growing
industries many of which also needed coal. In Cheshire and in
Liverpool the boiling of brine and refining of rock salt called
for coal and this demand stimulated production in the south-west
Lancashire coalfield. Coal was needed for other industries too
including metal working, glass-making, sugar refining and the
production of earthenware. These industries also used the port
of Liverpool to export their salt and coal, metal goods, glass
and earthenware by coastal shipping, or to Ireland or farther
afield to Europe, the West Indies, Newfoundland or the American
Colonies. Liverpool's imports included such commodities as
tallow and hides, Irish linen, iron from Spain and Sweden, wines
from the Mediterranean, Spain and Portugal, cotton, sugar and
rum from the West Indies and tobacco from the American colonies.
To service these trades there was an expansion in the industries
concerned with the building and equipping of ships.

By 1700, however, further general expansion was being
inhibited by poor transport facilities especially by the need to
move more heavy materials and bulky goods such as coal and
salt. Early in the eighteenth century Liverpool's Common Council
became deeply concerned about the need to overcome this bottle
neck in the supply of coal which was causing shortages and high
prices for both domestic and industrial users. The Council therefore began to take the initiative in developing better channels of
communication, first by land and later by water.

Such concern was necessary because nature had been relatively unkind to Merseyside in the grave obstacles she placed in
the way of developing satisfactory means of transport. Shipping
in the estuary and rivers had to combat gales or fog, shifting
sandbanks, treacherous currents, great extremes of tides and
shallow and winding rivers. Even so travel by water was cheaper
and less uncomfortable than overland travel. Considerable
stretches of marshland hindered road-building and the Mersey's
own wide and sandy estuary posed insuperable problems for
early bridge-builders. The nearest bridge to the sea, at Warrington, had immense strategic importance. Defoe called it 'the
stately Stone Bridge which is the only Bridge of communication . . . it is on the great road from London leading to Carlisle
and Scotland and in the Case of War has always been esteemed
a Pass of utmost Importance.'[2]

Overland travel was fraught with many difficulties and dangers.
Apart from such hazards as highwaymen and footpads, at the
beginning of our period there were few roads which had either
drainage or hard surfaces: the exceptions were cobbled streets
in some towns and villages. Generally roads were worn into ruts
and ridges by the wheels of vehicles in dry weather and turned
into rivers of mud in wet weather. The main forms of propulsion
were horse- and human-power. Passengers travelled in coaches,
or horse back or on foot; mail was carried on horseback; farm
animals had to walk; produce was moved in wagons or, if the
terrain was too difficult, by packhorse trains.

The transport of large amounts of bulky and heavy goods was
particularly costly and difficult and yet coal and salt had to be
moved and they were carried by wagons or by strings of pack-
horses with loaded panniers; this type of traffic subjected the
roads, which had never been 'engineered' in the modern sense,
to intolerable wear and tear. The Act of 1727 authorising the
setting up of a Turnpike Trust for the road from Warrington to
Wigan asserted that the existing road 'by reason of many heavy
Carriages of Goods and Merchandises passing through the same
is become ruinous and in many Places almost impassable'.
Several acts were passed to try to reduce the damage to roads
throughout the country by restricting the number of horses per
wagon and the breadth of tyres on wheels but such regulations
tended to increase costs and reduce the amounts carried without
improving the roads.

Turnpikes were one means whereby roads throughout the
country began to be improved during the eighteenth century.
The parishes responsible for road maintenance had neither the
resources nor the motivation for keeping them in a good state
of repair, so the new form of organisation had been developed
whereby turnpike trusts, operating on commercial lines, were
authorised to collect tolls from users in order to build and maintain highways. New technical knowledge also began to be applied
to Britain's roads during the eighteenth century by such road
engineers as John Metcalf, Thomas Telford and John McAdam.

In towns the quality of roads depended materially first on Improvement Commissioners and later in the nineteenth century increasingly on municipal corporations which had to take responsibility for paving, draining, cleansing and lighting them.

Merseyside began to participate in the movement to improve roads though the number of turnpiked roads in Merseyside was small compared, for example, with south-east Lancashire where there were many turnpikes linking the cotton towns. In Merseyside, as we have seen, the pressing need was for coal. Liverpool's coal was carried over the road between Liverpool and Prescot and a major initiative by Liverpool's Common Council was its application to Parliament for powers to turnpike this road. Under the Act which was passed in 1726 the surface was metalled and tolls could be charged to pay for its upkeep. This led to an increase in the supply of coal from the south-west Lancashire coalfield. In 1746 this road was extended to St Helens and in 1753 to Ashton-in-Makerfield and Warrington. The road from Warrington to Lancaster was turnpiked and in 1770 a start was made on the Liverpool-Preston road. On the Cheshire side of the Mersey the need to move salt and coal led to the turnpiking of roads converging on Northwich, and the roads around Chester were improved. Many other small improvements also occurred - roads were straightened to reduce distances, gradients were eased and footpaths and pack-horse tracks were often paved with large stone flags. Many streams and small rivers were crossed by wooden bridges in place of fords and there was a gradual but general up-grading of road surfaces during the nineteenth century.

As roads improved, both goods and passenger services became faster and more reliable and this usually more than compensated for having to pay tolls. Pack-horses were increasingly replaced by wagon services except in relatively inaccessible areas. Carriers advertised regular services to many parts of the country. In the late eighteenth century, for example, there were regular services between Liverpool and Warrington, Manchester, Macclesfield, London, Yorkshire, Staffordshire, Westmoreland, Cumberland and North Wales. In addition, within industrial towns and near to docks the roads were busy with masses of horse-drawn carts of all shapes and sizes.

In addition to carrying goods, wagon services were available to those passengers who wanted a cheap journey. For those who could afford to pay more there was a variety of coach services. As early as 1715 there was a 'Flying Machine' between Liverpool and Kendal. In the 1760s there were services to Manchester, Warrington and London but the latter journey took four days. Gradually stage coach services became much faster - by the 1830s there was a service that took only 23 hours between Liverpool and London - but such journeys were expensive. An inside seat could cost £5 and in addition the passenger had to pay the cost of meals on the way and tips to the guards, coachman, waiters and porters.

Alternative forms of transport were, of course, on horseback or on foot and within towns there were various forms of travel. In the eighteenth century sedan chairs were regularly used in Liverpool until replaced by hackney coaches. William Moss reported in 1796 that in Liverpool hackney coaches were 'numerous, and may be had at any time, to any part of the town and country, except, as in London, in the sudden fall of rain' which could render roads impassable.[3] The fares and regulations were similar to those in London. The charge for up to four passengers was a shilling a mile. The hire of a coach and a pair for a day for four passengers was twelve shillings and sixpence. The charge after midnight was double. Coaches were numbered and registered at the Town Clerk's office and coachmen had to abide by standard rates and to accept the first fare offered unless they were already engaged.

Other forms of horse-drawn transport included post-chaises which were kept at a few inns for wealthier travellers, and private carriages, also for the wealthier. Gigs were not much used in the eighteenth century but in Liverpool there was a heavier vehicle known as a whiskey. The nineteenth century brought a great extension in public transport with the use of horse-drawn omnibuses and trams. From their first use in this country in London in 1829 the idea of omnibuses spread rapidly to other cities including Liverpool. The use of tramways - running horse-drawn vehicles on rails - had long been applied in the coal industry and in quarrying but for passenger transport there was considerable resistance in Britain despite their use in the U.S.A. from 1832. In 1868 an act was passed to allow the building of street tramways in Liverpool for horse-drawn trams and this broke British opposition to the idea and led to something of a 'tramway mania' in Britain.[4]

In view of all the difficulties and dangers besetting over-land travel and the lack of bridges across the estuary it seemed natural to use the estuary, rivers and coastal routes to supplement land travel and to save the wear and tear on roads. Even in the Middle Ages considerable numbers of passengers had to be ferried across the estuary. This function had been performed as required by the monks of Birkenhead Priory and as early as 1318 the resources of the Priory were so over-taxed that they had to provide additional accommodation to house travellers. In 1330 a regular ferry service was established between Birkenhead and Liverpool but this lapsed temporarily with the dissolution of the Priory. Other ferry services were however developed and the river and estuary were increasingly used for the movement of goods. Nature was not, however, very cooperative in providing satisfactory waterways and so as the need for more channels of communication became pressing enterprising individuals had to intervene to improve the channels of rivers and to cut canals.

Before 1750 some important progress had already been made in deepending, straightening and widening river channels. Thomas

Patten of Warrington had worked during the 1690s to make the
Mersey navigable as far as Warrington and in 1719-21 there was
something of a boom in Acts for river improvement schemes. In
1720 an Act of Parliament authorised work to make the Mersey
and Irwell navigable to Manchester. The Patten family again
played a leading role joining Liverpool and Manchester business
interests to promote the scheme. When the Mersey-Irwell navigation had been completed even some very small ocean-going ships
could go as far as Manchester, and barges and shallow boats
could go on to Stockport: this particularly facilitated the movement of increasing quantities of heavy goods such as coal, stone
and timber. As a result the cost of transport between Liverpool
and Manchester was cut to less than a third of its former level.
Later, as the size of ships grew, this route was further improved from 1794 by a canal from Runcorn to Warrington to by-
pass the winding river channel which became very shallow at
low tide.

The 1719-21 boom also included measures to improve the rivers
Weaver and Douglas, although both schemes took many years to
complete. The Weaver Navigation Act of 1721 was the product
of many years of agitation by salt producers for improved transport both of salt and coal. It named the undertakers as John
Egerton of Oulton, John Amson of Leese and Richard Vernon of
Middlewich. They were given powers to make the Weaver navigable between Frodsham Bridge and Winsford Bridge and to make
Witton Brook navigable as far as Witton Bridge. The navigation
to Winsford was opened in 1732 and a further act in 1734 extended
the scheme to Nantwich. In 1757 Liverpool merchants petitioned
Liverpool Corporation claiming that the Navigation was being
mismanaged, and as a result improvements were made in the 1760s.
Some discontent persisted however because the Navigation was
a public trust, the profits going to the county, so that local
landowners had an interest in charging high rates whereas
Liverpool users wanted lower rates.[5] Despite this conflict of
interest the tonnage carried on the Navigation rose significantly
during the eighteenth century apart from some measure of depression in the late seventies.

Table 2.1: Tonnages Carried on the Weaver Navigation

	Tons			
	White Salt	Rock Salt	Coal	All Commodities
1759/60	17,697	22,880	13,297	59,088
1769/70	33,977	32,517	24,330	103,483
1779/80	28,091	40,170	18,102	90,851
1789/90	63,694	47,730	43,602	160,709
1799/1800	106,114	46,206	84,963	247,618

Source: T.S. Willan, *The Navigation of the River Weaver in the
Eighteenth Century* (Chetham Society, Manchester, 1951) pp. 208,
213, 218, 223, 228.

The primary aim of the Douglas Navigation (authorised in
1720 and completed by 1742) was to take coal from Wigan along
the Douglas river to the Ribble estuary from whence it could be
shipped along the coast to Liverpool. Pressure for such a waterway came from Liverpool but it was Wigan coal proprietors who
actually took the necessary measures to make this possible. By
the 1760s possibly as much as half of the south-west Lancashire
coalfield's output was sold via the Douglas Navigation [6] not only
to Liverpool but also as far north as Westmoreland with other
heavy produce such as slates forming the return cargoes.

By 1750, therefore, Merseyside's waterways had already been
rendered more useful by the efforts of merchants, manufacturers
and some landed proprietors who wanted cheaper facilities for
moving heavy bulky produce such as salt and coal, but of course
the potential for river navigation schemes was limited to the
availability of rivers. Other districts also urgently needed water
transport but their needs could only be met by canal building.
In this activity Merseyside was very much a leader: Merseyside
was the location of Britain's first modern industrial canal, the
Sankey Brook; it was closely linked to Britain's most publicised
canal, the Bridgewater, and it became the focal point for many
other canals too.

The Sankey Brook project started as a river improvement
scheme but ended as the first modern British canal. Once again
the motivation was the pressing need for more coal for Liverpool
and especially for salt refining. The turnpiking of the road to
Prescot (1726) had not sufficiently increased supplies to prevent
rising coal prices and so in 1754 Liverpool's Common Council
ordered a survey of the Sankey Brook with the object of making
it navigable. Henry Berry, Liverpool's dock engineer, was
instructed to make the survey to investigate the possibility of
dredging and widening. It transpired that even then it would
have been too small and unreliable, so a ten-mile canal was constructed. Two of the leading proprietors were John Ashton,
who owned the important Dungeon Salt Works as well as being
a Liverpool Cheesemonger and a member of the Company of
Africa merchants, and John Blackburne, who owned a Liverpool
Salt refinery. Both Ashton's and Berry's families lived near
the Sankey, possessing lands around St Helens. Petitions sup-
porting the scheme were presented by many interests: merchants,
owners of salt refineries in Liverpool and Cheshire, brewers,
glass-makers and other traders. The first section of the canal
was opened in 1757 and it was completed in 1761. It connected
the Mersey to the Haydock and Parr Collieries. An Act of 1762
extended it to Fidlers Ferry and in 1830 the canal was further
extended to Widnes. This canal's major importance lay in the
fact that, in conjunction with the Weaver Navigation, a triangular trade developed in salt and coal between the Cheshire Salt-
fields, St Helens and Liverpool. [7] By 1771 it is probable that
some 90,000 tons of coal a year were shipped along the canal of
which 45,000 tons went to Liverpool, 27,000 tons to Cheshire

and 18,000 to Warrington and elsewhere. [8]

The waterway however that attracted the most public attention was the Bridgewater Canal. This originated outside Merseyside but was quickly extended into the very heart of the region. Financed by the Duke of Bridgewater and engineered by James Brindley to carry coal from the Duke's mines at Worsley, first to Manchester and then to the Mersey, the original Worsley canal was authorised in 1759 and opened in 1761. In 1762 a further Act authorised the canal's extension to the Mersey estuary at Runcorn and the Bridgewater Canal was opened in 1767. This canal had several spectacular features that fired the public's imagination: an aqueduct thirty-nine feet high carrying it over the River Irwell; a flight of ten locks to drop it ninety feet to join the Mersey; tunnels to carry it directly into the coalmines - eventually there were some forty-two miles of these tunnels. By 1776 the main complex was complete although there were later additions including the taking over of the Mersey-Irwell navigation. Unlike the other canals, this one did not play a leading role in supplying Liverpool with coal but it tended to fix an upper limit to the price of coal in Liverpool for whenever the price from other coalfields rose above 7s 6d a ton it paid to bring in Bridgewater coal.

In addition to opening new markets for the Duke's coal and to supplying areas short of fuel, the canal also became a mammoth business in its own right. Like many later canal companies, the Bridgewater Company did not restrict its investment to the channel; its warehouses became an important business in themselves; so too were quays and docks for loading and unloading, and facilities for building and repairing barges and flats (sailing barges). The company also acted as carrier. It was highly successful. By the year 1792 the Duke's takings on goods carried between Liverpool and Manchester amounted to £80,000.

The Bridgewater Canal established the technical possibilities, the commercial viability and the modus operandi of canals all over the country - a movement that persisted intermittently until canals were superseded by railways. Even far into the railway era in the late nineteenth century, Merseyside was involved with Manchester in one of the greatest canal ventures - the Manchester Ship Canal. Some of the plans for projected canals failed to materialise but many came to fruition and gradually canals were linked together so that Merseyside was joined into a network radiating throughout the industrially and commercially important parts of England. Of key importance was the Trent-Mersey (the Grand Trunk) Canal authorised in 1766, engineered by James Brindley and completed in 1777. One of the main reasons for this canal was Josiah Wedgewood's desire to be able to carry materials for his potteries by sea from Devon and Cornwall to the Mersey and thence by barge to his works. This canal was highly significant to Merseyside in giving it connections with other waterways: via the Trent Navigation to the east coast; via the Coventry and Oxford canals to the Thames, to Birmingham and the Midlands; via the Staffordshire and

Worcester Canal to the Severn Navigation and the Severn
estuary.

The other vitally important canal to Merseyside was the
Leeds-Liverpool: one of the most adventurous, long distance
and long-delayed projects. Authorised in 1770 it took forty six
years to complete; it suffered changes of route and because it
tried to link together too many places, it had to meander over
long distances. It had to scale high altitudes and was difficult
and costly to build. To economise it incorporated other waterways for part of the route: the Douglas Navigation and the
Lancaster Canal. Eventually it gave Merseyside access to Yorkshire and across to the east coast but perhaps its major importance was the section which joined Liverpool and the Wigan
coalfield; this section was in operation long before the canal
was completed. It was of utmost importance in giving Merseyside
much better access to an important section of the coalfield to
help to ease its dependence on the St Helens' deposits. By 1800
over a quarter of a million tons of coal travelled on the canal
each year making it by far the largest distribution channel for
the coalfield. [9]

Many of the canals were built by merchants, by manufacturers
or by landed interests seeking new outlets for their raw materials
or manufactured produce or searching for cheaper and larger
supplies of basic raw materials: people such as the coal-owning
Duke of Bridgewater, Josiah Wedgewood the pottery manufacturer,
salt and coal producers, etc. The canal companies built and
maintained the channels, provided warehouses for storage and
acted as carriers. Frequently their charges were high, especially
if they had a monopoly, although they were less than the charges
for land transport. Canal engineers overcame many technical
problems relating to each scheme although other difficulties
occurred from lack of co-ordination: for example, although many
canals had junctions with other canals they often differed in
width. The Bridgewater and Trent and Mersey joined at Preston
Brook but the Bridgewater could accommodate wide barges whereas the Trent and Mersey could only be navigated by narrow ones,
hence much produce had to be transhipped and this could be
costly and time-consuming.

Canals were a very important means of transporting produce
during the main period of the Industrial Revolution and they
enjoyed their golden age within our period of 1750-1870. Towards
the end of this period their decline was very much in evidence
as railways displaced them, but before the coming of the railways
they were major highways especially for heavy and bulky produce
and in this respect they linked up with rivers and also with the
very important coastal shipping routes which had been heavily
used long before the era of modern canals and river improvement
schemes. Coastal shipping was a major means of distributing
food, raw materials and manufactured products and of re-
distributing imported produce. From 1660 to the mid-eighteenth
century Liverpool's coasting trade had increased sharply to

supply the region with agricultural produce from North Wales and Chester, with copper and tin from St Ives, clay from Poole and Bideford, herrings from Beaumaris and Greenock, cotton wool from Glasgow and Lancaster, slates from Whitehaven and many other products. Exports by coastal shipping from Merseyside included cheese, salt, earthenware, coal, glass, copperas and lead, a little cloth and re-exports of such products as tobacco, figs, wine, raisins, sugar, pepper, lemons and almonds.

As the industrialisation of Merseyside and Lancashire accelerated after 1750 there was a rise in the volume of manufactured produce from Manchester, Birmingham, Sheffield and Leeds, earthenware from Staffordshire, and salt and coal from Merseyside to be carried in coastal ships. In 1791 for example, 40,000 tons of coal were exported from Liverpool coastwise although exports abroad were even greater, amounting to 57,000 tons. Growing quantities of corn were brought to Merseyside by coastal shipping to feed the population and there was a rise in the re-export of produce from the West Indies, the Mediterranean and the Baltic. By the 1790s the large numbers of small coasting vessels were exerting considerable pressure on the available space in Liverpool's docks and even the building of new docks after 1800 failed to relieve the congestion because the volume of coastal shipping continued to rise too.

In addition to carrying agricultural produce, industrial raw materials and manufactured goods, coastal shipping and, indeed, river and canal boats too carried large numbers of passengers. Because of the problems of land transport, many of the Welsh immigrants into Merseyside came by coastal shipping especially from Anglesey and North Wales; travellers also came from Devon and Cornwall and from North Lancashire and Scotland in coastal boats. In the estuary and on the rivers and canals travellers used ferry boats and barges as people nowadays travel by coach or bus. By the later eighteenth century people went by canal from Liverpool to Manchester or to Wigan or to Southport. On some barges there were facilities for providing travellers with cooked meals; in other cases they stopped for meals or refreshments at inns along the canals or at the terminals.

Ferry services began to link up Liverpool, Seacombe, Woodside, Rock House, New Ferry, Eastham and Widnes and some went along rivers and joined up with canals. There were varied qualities of service according to a passenger's means. By the later eighteenth century there were elegant packet services daily between Eastham and Chester and between Liverpool and Wigan. On the former the fare varied from 3s to 1s 8d according to the quality of the apartments, and the fare for the latter service varied from 2s to 3s. By comparison short cross river services were cheap - the fare for market people and ordinary passengers was 2d but upper class passengers were expected to pay 6d, in this case for the identical service. In addition to the regular scheduled sailings there were many boats for hire for special journeys or for pleasure trips at a cost of about a shilling

for one or two people and two shillings for more passengers.
The facilities for boarding such boats were however negligible
even as late as the 1790s: when boats could not get near to the
piers, passengers - male and female - were carried to them by
the boatmen. Packet services ran farther afield. Until the Dee
became badly silted up there were services from ports such as
Neston and Parkgate on the south side of the Wirral to North
Wales and, of course, services from several ports in Merseyside
to Ireland.

During the nineteenth century the quality of services improved
materially especially with the introduction of steam boats. By
1816 there was a steam packet service between Eastham and
Liverpool and by 1817 a similar service between Parkgate and
Bagillt. In 1817 William Batman applied for permission to build
steps and landing places at Liverpool for a steam service from
Liverpool by the *Etna* which was in fact two vessels joined
together, covered by a deck and propelled by a central wheel.
More and more steam services were developed including an
elaborate system of cross-river services as the Wirral became an
important dormitory area after 1820 and new landing stages
(including floating landing stages to cope with variations in
the tide) were constructed at Liverpool and Birkenhead.

River, canal and coastal shipping contributed significantly
to the development of Merseyside. Together with the forms of
land transport considered above these facilities were the only
ones available during the first half century of the Industrial
Revolution and they managed to cope with the very considerable
demands made on them during that period. Despite their importance, however, they did suffer from very serious setbacks.
Road transport was costly, especially for heavy bulky goods.
Canal, river and coastal shipping were slow: it could take
longer for goods to travel from Liverpool to Manchester than
from America to Liverpool; the journey for cargoes between
Liverpool and Birmingham could last from four to six weeks.
In the summer canals and rivers could lack water and barges
were often in short supply. Few services were regular and
punctual despite advertised timetables. Canals often followed
winding routes in order to pick up sufficient cargoes to make
the venture profitable: the Leeds-Liverpool canal wandered
through considerable areas of Lancashire and Yorkshire for
this reason. Canals built at different times were different widths
and in many instances inadequate provision was made for linking
them together.

As Merseyside and its hinterland grew rapidly in the early
decades of the nineteenth century the increasing pressure for
transport facilities exposed all these weaknesses. In particular
commercial users found their trades limited by the technical
problems and even more seriously by monopolistic practices by
canal companies. Some of the strongest monopolies by the 1820s
were to be found in the control of the waterways between Liverpool, Manchester and Birmingham, but soon the vested interests

were to engineer their own downfall by driving users to develop
alternative facilities, so inaugurating one of the most crucial
phases in transport development in the 1830s, when railways
came of age.

Much of the early pioneering work took place outside Merseyside. There were many tramways built to facilitate the movement
of heavy produce, especially coal and stone, by running horse-
drawn vehicles on rails. Such tramways were very much in
evidence in Lancashire as in the rest of the country. In some
districts there were experiments in the replacing of horses by
steam engines and, as is well known, the Stockton-Darlington
line, opened in 1825, demonstrated the commercial viability of
steam locomotion for goods traffic. Even before this was built,
however, lines had been proposed between Liverpool and both
Manchester and Birmingham. Powerful opposition from vested
interests in canal and road transport and from landowners had
prevented the adoption of these proposals, but gradually the
opposition was overcome and, in fact, the Marquis of Stafford,
nephew of the Duke and chief trustee of the Bridgewater canal,
became the largest single subscriber when, in 1826, Parliament
authorised the building of the Liverpool-Manchester railway.
The capital was to amount to £510,000 to be divided into £100
shares. The subscription contract shows that finance came from
diverse sources but primarily from Liverpool and from the
Marquis of Stafford.

Table 2.2:   Distribution of Shares in the Liverpool-Manchester
             Railway

Place	No. of shares	Percentage
London	844	20
Liverpool	1,979	47
Manchester	124	3
Other	286 $^1/_3$	7
Marquis of Stafford	1,000	23
	4,233 $^1/_3$	100

Source: Figures derived from H. Pollins 'The Finances of the
Liverpool and Manchester Railway', *Economic History Review*
Second Series vol. V, no. 1 (1951), p. 92.

Together therefore Liverpool and the Marquis of Stafford
accounted for some 70 per cent of the shares and Liverpool
supplied nearly 56 per cent of the 308 subscribers.

This was the first railway built specifically to carry passengers
as well as freight and for passengers speed was important, but
in the 1820s most locomotives could barely hold their own against
horses. The directors of the new line decided therefore to hold
a competition to find the best locomotive - a distinction won by

Stephenson's famous *Rocket* at the Rainhill trials. In addition
to the problem of finding a satisfactory locomotive the construction of the line involved overcoming many serious natural barriers:
at the Liverpool end it was necessary to engineer a series of
very deep cuttings through rock; a high viaduct had to be built
to carry the line over the Sankey Valley but most difficult of all
was the floating of the line across the notorious Chat Moss on
bundles of heather and wooden hurdles. The construction of this
line demonstrated that this new form of transport could surmount
even the most serious obstacles.

The line was opened in 1830 to the accompaniment of intensive
national news coverage but the publicity took an unfortunate
twist with the accidental death of the important politician William
Huskisson. Despite this inauspicious start the volume of passengers and freight carried grew quickly.

Table 2.3:   Traffic on the Liverpool-Manchester Railway.

	Passengers	Merchandise	Coal
		Tons	Tons
1830	71,951	1,433	2,630
1831	445,047	43,070	11,285
1832	356,945	159,443	69,396
1833	386,492	194,704	81,509
1834	432,637	210,736	99,337
1835	473,847	230,629	116,246

Source: *Mining Journal*, vol. IX (1839), p. 150.

By the end of the 1830s the Liverpool and Manchester railway
was carrying one third of the freight moved between the two
cities. Users of all forms of transport benefited from increased
competition between on the one hand the railway and on the
other hand the canals and stage coach operators as each period-
ically reduced the charges in an attempt to undercut the other.
The cost of passenger transport was cut by half and the cost
of goods to a third of the former level.

The commercial success of the Liverpool and Machester helped
to popularise the idea of railways, fired the public's interest
and sparked off the building of more lines throughout the country,
many of which were in part at least financed and promoted by
the Merseyside capitalists who came to be known as the 'Liverpool Party'. The group included the Croppers, the Rathbones,
the Horsfalls, the Booths and the Sanders. Both they and
Stephenson had 'long through routes before their minds from
the first'.[10] They played an important role in promoting and
financing lines between the Mersey, Humber, Thames and Severn
and together with other Lancashire capitalists owned a considerable proportion of the London and Birmingham railway. At times
their efforts met with considerable resistance. The breaking of

the water transport monopoly between Liverpool and Manchester
had given added impetus for similar action to break the monopoly
between Liverpool and Birmingham. Opposition was, however, so
intransigent that the promoters had to agree to compromise.
They had to settle in 1833 for the right to create the Grand
Junction Railway. Instead of a completely separate line, this
one was to connect Birmingham and Warrington and then to link
up with Liverpool via the Liverpool-Manchester railway. At the
time this was by far the longest line in Britain and it brought
together the immense industrial potential of the Midlands and
the great port facilities of Merseyside. By 1838 Birmingham was
linked to London, and within Lancashire the Liverpool-Manchester
line was extended to Wigan and Warrington.

Merseyside was quickly covered by a network of lines and
connected up with other parts of Britain. The Liverpool-
Manchester line aimed for speeds of up to 30 m.p.h. which meant
a considerable quickening of travel. Along the lines land was
developed by the building of factories, warehouses and living
accommodation and agriculturalists were able to ship their
perishable goods more quickly to market. Even the fearsome Chat
Moss could now be drained and cultivated. The markets for other
types of produce were also considerably widened: in particular
the distribution of coal was greatly facilitated. The building of
railways themselves, of course, generated a good deal of employment in laying track, building stations and goods yards, supplying equipment and coal and building engineering works such as
bridges. The Liverpool to Manchester line originally terminated
in Crown Street, Liverpool, but was soon extended to Lime
Street. By the 1860s the scale of station building is well illus-
trated by the fact that the iron shed at Lime Street started in
1867 had the largest span in the world (200 ft.) until outstripped
by St Pancras Station. Also in the years 1868-71 the massive
Gothic station hotel was built by the famous architect Alfred
Waterhouse. Bridges, too, became increasingly monumental.
For the first time since the Romans had bridged the Mersey at
Warrington a new bridge was built nearer the sea in response
to the needs of the railway - the fortress-like Ethelfleda bridge
completed in 1868 between Runcorn and Widnes.

Railways were not, of course, completely free of defects: in
the early stages they were often built in short bursts of frenzied
activity causing booms, crises and slumps which disrupted the
national economy. There was also a good deal of wasteful specu-
lation and duplication of some lines; in other cases the short
stretches of line used different gauges and were inadequately
linked up to allow through traffic. The route from Liverpool
to London was, for example, built by three separate companies -
through traffic was not immediately practicable hence there were
delays, costs of transhipment and other costs and inconveniences.

From the point of view of the individual towns and industrial
areas the method of building railways could give rise to serious
problems. The detailed history of railways in the region would

take too long to recount in a short book of this nature, but some
of the problems Widnes encountered illustrate the sort of difficulties that could arise. Widnes' main spurt in industrial growth
began in the 1840s with the expansion in chemical production.
Not being on the direct route between important terminals it
was served by branch railways from St Helens and from Garston
via Widnes to Warrington. During the 1850s and 1860s railway
companies throughout the country were amalgamating and
absorbing smaller stretches of line and as Widnes' two rail links
were taken over by the London and North Western Railway
Company in 1864 one might have expected services to improve.
Instead it became the battleground for competition between on
the one hand the London and North Western Company (which
now controlled all Widnes' rail links) and on the other hand a
joint committee of the Manchester, Sheffield and Lincolnshire
and Great Northern and Midland Railway which built a new line
between Liverpool and Manchester, again with no direct connec-
tion to Widnes. Because some industrial interests in Widnes
claimed that the London and North Western Company failed to
provide them with goods sidings a legal battle ensued to give
the new line access to Widnes and eventually in 1873, after long
wrangles, the Widnes Railway Act gave permission for the building of a new branch line.

As each new form of transport came into extensive use it
naturally affected the prosperity of the older forms of travel.
Rivers and canals had taken much traffic off the roads and then
in turn they were superseded by rail transport, but it is somewhat misleading to draw too clear a distinction between the
different types as they were also interdependent. When passengers wished to travel along canals or rivers they frequently
needed coach services at both ends to link up with barges and
boats. Before the coming of the railway in the 1840s, for example,
the main way of travelling from Liverpool to the holiday resort
of Southport was by the Leeds-Liverpool Canal to Scarisbrick
and then by a five-mile coach journey to Southport. Other coach
services also met packets on the Leeds-Liverpool canal at
Burscough to take passengers to and from Preston or Lancaster.
At Birkenhead an extensive coaching service arose in conjunction
with the ferry, running services to Chester, Bristol, Birmingham,
Shrewsbury and various parts of Wales. The Bridgewater Canal
Company introduced special services for businessmen travelling
between Liverpool and Manchester using a combination of fast
boats and omnibuses. When the Liverpool-Manchester railway
line was opened people from Runcorn had to cross the Mersey
by ferry and then travel from Widnes to Rainhill by omnibus
until the Runcorn bridge gave direct rail access. For Runcorn
travellers who wanted to get to Chester by rail a regular daily
omnibus service covered a four-mile journey to Moore.

Similarly, although industrial buildings congregated along
canals and railways the increasing quantities of produce carried
on them necessitated the use of more and more horse-drawn carts

to carry produce to and from factories, mines or other industrial complexes not immediately adjacent to the transport, and to distribute it on arrival at its destination. Some barges and railways loaded or discharged cargoes directly from or into warehouses or ships but the docks, for example, became increasingly congested with horse-drawn carts.

Coaches and wagons therefore increasingly acted as feeders carrying passengers and goods to water or rail services. Nonetheless the coming of railways in particular was a severe blow to inn-keepers and coaching interests and the effect on canals was very serious for the proprietors whose monopolies were broken and rates were cut. Users of course benefited and it seems unlikely that initially the volume of canal traffic was materially reduced. In the 1840s for example the Bridgewater Canal and Mersey and Irwell Navigation carried more than twice as much freight between Liverpool and Manchester as the railway but because rates had to be cut earnings fell and soon canal companies were in difficulties. The obvious solution was for the railways to take over the canals: for example in 1844 the St Helens Railway bought the Sankey Canal so creating the St Helens Canal and Railway Company. In 1846 the North Staffordshire Railway took over the Trent and Mersey Canal and in the following year the London and North West Railway acquired the Shropshire Union Canal including the Birmingham and Liverpool Junction Canal. In this way the railways were freed from the sort of desperate competition that had previously occurred when the canal companies had slashed their rates in a do or die bid for survival.

Gradually, therefore, railways became the predominant element in a transport system that was still closely inter-connected: road services acted as feeders to canals and railways, and canals were operated in a subordinate capacity by the railway companies. The rail network continued to spread throughout Britain giving passengers and goods rapid and relatively punctual and regular services to most parts of Britain. The greater mobility of passengers and the introduction of cheap excursion fares led to a further expansion of holiday resorts in the region. For the movement of freight, however, the monopoly of canals was partly replaced by the monopoly of railways and throughout the country there were complaints and legal battles continuing into the twentieth century to control the rates charged by railway companies and to prevent them unfairly discriminating between customers. So far as Merseyside was concerned, there was still an alternative form of transport if railways overcharged - namely by coastal shipping. There was, therefore, a tendency for the railways to attract such traffic by lower rates but at the same time charging higher rates on inland routes where no such alternative was available. This type of consideration was also tied in with Merseyside's ocean trades - a ship could discharge its cargo in Liverpool for distribution by rail or canal to the south-east or south-west coast of Britain or it could go on to London, Bristol or Hull and discharge its cargoes there. The efficiency of overland communication and the rates charged, therefore, had a direct bearing on the volume of imports and exports passing through the ports and the aim of the next chapter is to look at Merseyside's ports, shipping and long-distance trades.

NOTES

1. For a fuller account of the early development of the borough see F.J. Routledge, 'History of Liverpool to 1700', in W. Smith (ed.), *A Scientific Survey of Merseyside* (Liverpool University Press, 1953), pp. 94-106.

2. D. Defoe with introduction by G.D.H. Cole, *A Tour Thro the whole island of Great Britain* (Peter Davies, London, 1927), vol. II, p. 668.

3. W. Moss, *The Liverpool Guide* (1796; facsimile edition City of Liverpool Public Relations Department, 1974), p. 9.

4. There was a tramway in London in 1861 but its rails protruded above the road surface and it was scrapped because of objections from other road users.

5. The history of the Weaver Navigation is told in T.S. Willan, *The Navigation of the River Weaver in the Eighteenth Century* (Chetham Society, Manchester, 1951).

6. The effects of the Douglas Navigation on the coalfield are treated in J. Langton, *Geographical Change and Industrial Revolution. Coalmining in South West Lancashire 1590-1799* (Cambridge University Press, Cambridge, 1979), passim.

7. J.R. Harris, 'Early Canal Controversies' in J.R. Harris (ed.), *Liverpool and Merseyside* (Frank Cass, London, 1969), pp. 78-97; T.C. Barker and J.R. Harris, *A Merseyside Town in the Industrial Revolution. St Helens 1750-1900* (Liverpool University Press, 1954), passim.

8. J. Langton, *Geographical Change*, p. 166.

9. Ibid.

10. J.H. Clapham, *An Economic History of Modern Britain: the Early Railway Age 1820-1850* (Cambridge University Press, Cambridge, 1950), p. 387. There is a discussion of the sources of capital for some Lancashire and Yorkshire railways in S. Broadbridge, *Studies in Railway Expansion and the Capital Market in England 1825-1873* (Frank Cass, London, 1970).

Chapter 3

PORTS, SHIPPING AND COMMERCIAL ORGANISATION

Within the complex network of communications created by the mid-nineteenth century, Liverpool inevitably came to dominate not only Merseyside's trade and shipping but also a sizeable share of that of Britain. Liverpool and London vied with each other for the position of Britain's premier port: in general terms London had the edge in imports but Liverpool dominated Britain's exports. By 1857, Liverpool was responsible for forty five per cent of the U.K.'s export trade and also for about a third of her imports.

This battle for national supremacy must not, however, be allowed to obscure the fact that Liverpool was by no means Merseyside's only port. In the eighteenth century the Mersey and Dee estuaries were ringed with small ports and terminals for boats - some expanding, some declining, but between them providing the varied facilities for boats, barges and ships of all sizes which carried a significant proportion of the people, animals and produce transported both within the region and between Merseyside, other parts of Britain and other countries.

During the eighteenth century the facilities for loading and discharging boats were not elaborate. Many boats beached on the sands to be loaded and unloaded from and into horse-drawn carts. Because of the difficulties of navigating the Mersey, the shifting sand banks, strong currents and great tidal ranges, heavily laden ships often anchored in Hoyle lake off the Wirral: there part of their cargoes were off-loaded into barges and the ships, so lightened, could then more easily proceed along the Mersey estuary.

Even by the early eighteenth century, however, Liverpool had already captured a premier position and fired public interest: the 'Pool' had been converted into a dock - the first dock outside London. The initiative for building the Old Dock (as it was later known) came from the town's MPs Thomas Johnson and Richard Norris, the scheme was approved and largely financed by Liverpool's Common Council and Thomas Steers was brought from London to make the survey. The building of the dock was authorised by Parliament in 1709 and ships began to use it in 1715. The demand for dock facilities continued to grow and by the 1730s the dock was seriously overcrowded so an Act of 1738 gave powers for the dock to be extended from $3\frac{1}{2}$ to 4 acres and for the building of a second dock. The second dock (later called the Salthouse because of its proximity to John Blackburne's salt works) was also planned by Thomas Steers though it was most likely finished

by Henry Berry who became Liverpool's dock engineer until
1789. The new dock was completed by 1759 at a cost of £21,000.
   The tonnage of shipping entering the port still outstripped
the dock facilities. It has risen from 14,600 tons in 1709 to
29,200 tons in 1751 and the increase continued. To cope with
greatly increased demand arising from the expansion of overseas trade and coastal shipping, to meet the needs of new passenger services on ferries and rivers and to satisfy the requirements of fishing fleets the size and range of port facilities had
to be greatly extended. One way of dealing with the problem
was by some measure of port specialisation; some became merely
points of call for ferry services; others catered largely for canal
and river traffic; on the south side of the Wirral ports were
especially concerned with passenger and goods services to
Ireland and North Wales; Liverpool dominated overseas trade
though it handled a wide range of other traffic as well. In Liverpool there was growing specialisation in the use of the docks.
The ships using the Salthouse Dock were for example mostly
those engaged in the Irish, French and Mediterranean trades.
The scope for specialisation was further increased by yet another
spate of dock building between 1762-1796. In 1762 Liverpool
Corporation obtained an act to construct the 3 acre North (St
Georges) Dock which was again planned by Henry Berry. The
building of this new dock was subject to delays but eventually
it was opened in 1771 particularly for the use of West Indiamen
and ships trading with North America. The building of two more
docks was authorised in 1785: the Kings Dock of 7 acres finished
in 1788 and particularly connected with the tobacco trade and
the Queens Dock of 6 acres which was not completed until 1796.[1]
   By 1796 Liverpool had some twenty eight acres of docks including five wet docks, five graving docks, three dry docks and
the Duke's Dock which had been built to cater for the Bridgewater Canal traffic. The docks were served by many large warehouses and visitors marvelled at the sight of ocean-going ships
in the heart of the city. The spate of dock-building was however
interrupted by the severe commercial crisis of 1793. Another
act of 1799 gave powers to build two more docks but work was
delayed by the dislocations accompanying the French Revolutionary and Napoleonic Wars. By the turn of the century the existing
docks were seriously overcrowded and another act of 1811 gave
authority for the building of the small Union (later called Coburg)
and the larger Princes Docks. By 1800 the tonnage of shipping
entering the Liverpool docks had rocketed to 450,000 - a fifteen-
fold increase in fifty years. In 1808 as many as 400 ships (average
tonnage 190-200) and 300 barges and flats (sailing barges) were
using the docks at any one time and between then and 1870,
despite short-term fluctuations, the long-term trend in demand
was upwards. By 1855 (two years before the creation of the
Mersey Docks and Harbour Board) 4,096,100 tons of shipping
entered the port compared with 450,000 tons in 1801. This increase was due to the great expansion in the flow of food, raw

materials and manufactured goods within, into and out of the
region; the emigration traffic also reached new heights.

In addition to the increased volume of shipping, changing
ship-building technology necessitated the building not only of
more but also of larger docks and the provision of much more
sophisticated dock, cargo-handling and warehouse facilities.
There were renewed bursts of dock-building in 1813-21, 1830-36
and 1844-64 not only to create new docks but also to engage in
the equally important work of altering, extending and upgrading
older docks to keep pace with additional demands and changing
technology. The Old Dock could not be updated so it was closed
in 1826 and a new Customs House was built on the site. Additional docks catered for special trades and for more advanced
types of ships. The Huskisson Dock, for example, opened in
1852, was intended specially for the timber trade though later
it was used to accommodate larger steamers. The steam-ship
presented a serious fire hazard to wooden sailing ships so
separate docks were used to isolate them. By 1872 over 250
acres of wet docks and over eighteen miles of quay space had
been built. The docks also necessitated the building of miles of
walls, piers, gatehouses and lodges and hydraulic towers to
supply power for handling cargoes.

The construction of Liverpool's docks was accomplished by
a series of enterprising and inventive engineers ranging from
Thomas Steers, Henry Berry and James Brindley to Thomas
Morris and John Foster and to that most famous of all dock-
builders, Jesse Hartley. Hartley came from the West Riding
where he had been trained in bridge building. He was in charge
of Liverpool's docks during the most energetic building period
1824-1860 and the works he planned and executed were massive
in scale and in extent. He used various materials although his
favourite and most distinguished was granite: cyclopean blocks
were fitted together (sometimes in conventional ways but frequently in the random jig-saw patterns which are a notable
feature of much of his work) to produce massive walls and huge
columns; he also used a good deal of structural iron and brick-
work. He is particularly renowned for his famous Albert Dock
complex which Nikolaus Pevsner regards as the 'climax of Liverpool dock architecture' and one of Liverpool's most precious
architectural possessions.[2] The principle for the Dock may have
come from St Katherine's Dock London but when opened in 1845
the Albert Dock was unique. Within the city there had been
battles for over twenty years to establish the idea that warehouses should be isolated from public access - naturally the
private owners of the many warehouses adjacent to the docks
bitterly resisted - but Hartley won. In building the Albert Dock
he used granite, cast iron and bricks. His warehouses, some
of the finest in Europe, were fire-proof, burglar-proof, and
fitted with hydraulic power. The classical dock office, designed
by Philip Hardwick and built in 1846-7 had cast iron columns
and even a cast iron classical pediment.

In addition to providing docks for the increasing volume
and size of ships it was necessary to undertake continual work
on the estuary to ensure the safe operation of ships: providing
such equipment as buoys, lighthouses, charts and pilotage, and
this required a responsible authority for the whole estuary.
Although Liverpool's docks were the most extensive and most
spectacular Liverpool was still by no means the only Mersey
port: the many smaller, less elaborate docklands continually
asserted their right to share the estuary. Such ports as Birkenhead, Widnes, Runcorn and Garston resented Liverpool's domination of the estuary, the strongest opposition coming from Runcorn
and Birkenhead.

To understand how conflict developed it is necessary briefly
to look back well before the beginning of our period. As we have
seen Liverpool's charter was granted in 1207 by King John;
Henry III allowed the burgesses to use the harbour without paying dues to the Lord of the Manor. From this stemmed the great
controversy as to why freemen of Liverpool should be exempt
from the town dues which other users had to pay; the resentment
of other users was compounded by the fact that the proceeds
could be devoted to the needs of the town of Liverpool instead of
being used solely to improve the harbour and later the docks.
This eventually became a very bitter bone of contention. Meanwhile Liverpool itself was subject to the authority of Chester's
customs until 1660 when the London customs authorities decreed
that 'the whole River of Mersey and the Shores on both sides
was and ought to be und'r the care, privilege and Inspection
of the Offic'rs of his Ma'ties Customs att Liverpoole'. Liverpool
could then build a Customs House and dominate the estuary and
river.[3]

The Liverpool docks built in the eighteenth century were
administered by the Common Council of Liverpool. By an act of
1762 all the property created to date in the docks, piers, buoys,
lighthouses etc. was vested in the Mayor, Bailiffs and Common
Council of Liverpool as trustees and in 1811 a corporate body
was set up – the Trustees of Liverpool Docks – consisting of
twenty-one members of the Common Council of Liverpool. Because, however, of growing pressure from other dock users,
from 1825 dock ratepayers were allowed to elect eight members.
Dock users were still dissatisfied especially by their liability
to pay dues from which freemen were exempt and by the diver-
sion of the funds so paid for the benefit of the town rather
than for the docks. A test case challenging this situation confirmed Liverpool's *legal* right to continue to collect but opposition grew steadily from dock users who were not freemen.

Meanwhile the smaller ports were struggling hard for their
independence. Widnes, the Weaver Navigation and above all
Runcorn complained bitterly that dues they paid to cover the
cost of lighting and buoying the Mersey disappeared into the
coffers of Liverpool Council. The dock facilities at Runcorn were
primarily associated with canals: Runcorn became the terminus

for the Bridgewater Canal; then the junction of the Trent and
Mersey Canal with the Bridgewater Canal further expanded the
use of Runcorn and, in 1800, the cutting of the Old Quay Canal
between Warrington and Runcorn for the Mersey-Irwell Navigation brought even more trade. The Duke of Bridgewater had
constructed a dock there for loading and unloading barges and
this was extended as business grew - new docks were built
together with stone piers, quays and warehouses. By the 1820s
Runcorn was a busy port bitterly resentful of Liverpool's
domination. Eventually in 1847, after petitions to Parliament,
Runcorn became a bonded port with its own customs but it still
had to pay dues to Liverpool until 1861 when the Upper Mersey
Dues Trustees were appointed; in 1876 they were replaced by
the Board of Upper Mersey Navigation Commissioners. These
bodies also looked after the interest of other ports such as
Widnes.

Liverpool's other bitter opponent was Birkenhead. In the
same way that the Pool had been converted into Liverpool's
first dock, promoters of schemes to build docks in Birkenhead
concentrated their energies on Wallasey Pool. In the 1820s
there was an elaborately ambitious scheme based on plans produced by the civil engineers, Thomas Telford, Robert Stephenson
and Alexander Nimmo, for a ship canal across the Wirral to bring
ships into docks at Wallasey Pool without their needing to enter
the estuary. The scheme proved too costly and in any event
every proposal for a competing port aroused relentless opposition in Liverpool. Liverpool Corporation even went so far as to
buy up land in the Wirral at a price well above its market value
in order to block the project.

The idea of creating a port at Birkenhead was raised again in
the 1840s. Liverpool had to admit that its docks could not
accommodate all the traffic but it now objected on the grounds
that the plans put forward for Birkenhead would damage the
Mersey navigation by removing the immense scouring power of
Wallasey Pool at ebb tide. Despite Liverpool's objections a
Birkenhead Dock Act was passed in 1844 and work started in
October on plans drawn up by another engineer, J.M. Rendel.
It soon became evident that both the cost and the extent of the
work had been hopelessly under-estimated. Birkenhead had to
ask for supplementary powers to raise additional funds but
eventually, in 1847, the first two docks were opened - Morpeth
and Egerton - together with dock warehouses. Severe economic
depression in the late 1840s however led to heavy unemployment
in Birkenhead and to even greater financial stringency. After
local elections there was an enquiry into the proceedings of the
Dock Commissioners; this showed that the schemes were
seriously overspent and there was a great deal of public
criticism. The Dock Company was in effect insolvent. The gran-
diose plans therefore ended in ignominy; the great rival Liverpool was virtually forced against its better judgement to buy
up the Birkenhead Dock Estate in an insolvent and far from

complete state. This happened in 1855 - the purchase price was
some £1,143,000.

Liverpool appeared to have emerged triumphant from this
battle but success was short-lived: there were many other even
more powerful opponents. There was still determined opposition
from port users in Lancashire, Cheshire and the Midlands who
resented both Liverpool's control and the non-payment of dues
by Liverpool freemen, and this culminated in the creation in
1857 of the Mersey Docks and Harbour Board - the outcome
particularly of the powerful rivalry between Liverpool and
Manchester. The bill to create the Dock Board was promoted by
the business community in Liverpool's greatest rival city,
Manchester. The Manchester Chamber of Commerce and the
Manchester Commercial Association joined forces with the Great
Western Railway. Despite Liverpool's vehement opposition the
bill became law and the Mersey Docks and Harbour Board took
over all Liverpool's and Birkenhead's dock estates and harbour
facilities. Eventually Liverpool received one and a half million
pounds compensation for the loss of the Town Dues. The right
to collect dues and to manage the docks was now vested in the
Mersey Docks and Harbour Board which was controlled by the
dock users.[4]

The Board first met in January 1858. It took charge of docks
and quays, pilotage, traffic, buoys, piers and lighthouses, it
set about completing the Birkenhead estate and continued to
expand and remodel Liverpool's docks. Charges, however,
remained high and the bitterness between Liverpool and Manchester was only dormant - it was to reach boiling point at the
end of the century over the building of the Manchester Ship
Canal.

The development of the region's docks was, therefore, a
continuing process of expansion and adaptation in response to
increasing use, changing demands and new technology and to
the bitter local rivalries between the very commercial interests
whose activities were the *raison d'etre* for the creation not only
of dock complexes but also of the back-up port facilities such
as banking, insurance, produce exchanges, brokers and shipping
agents necessary to service a complex trading system. The
geographical pattern, the scale and organisation of the region's
trade, which constituted such an integral part of Merseyside's
economic life, was also modified as some older trades expanded,
others declined and new ones developed and as the organisation
of trading and shipowning evolved in a changing environment.
The trading pattern included many components of varying
importance: there was the distribution within Merseyside of
Merseyside produce, especially food and raw materials but also
increasing quantities of manufactured goods; Merseyside produce
also had to be distributed to other parts of Britain and to other
countries: as we have seen salt and coal were particularly important but there was a growing diversity of manufactured goods
too. Both foreign produce and British produce from outside

Merseyside was brought into the region: especially important
were increasing quantities of foodstuffs and of raw materials
such as raw cotton, grain, iron and copper ore, kelp for alkali,
timber; in addition, a rapidly increasing volume of manufactured
goods from the rest of industrial Lancashire, from Yorkshire
and the Midlands came into Merseyside to be exported.

Short and medium-distance trades are necessarily considered
in Chapters 2 and 4 in close conjunction with the development
of transport facilities and industry. Long distance trades with
other countries needed facilities for collecting goods for export
but facilities were also needed for the growing re-export trades
and for distributing imported produce through the hinterland.
These trades were also intimately dependent on the development of shipping and commercial facilities and on events in
other countries.

Some of Merseyside's overseas trades consisted of a simple
straightforward exchange of goods between Britain and another
country, but in addition some more complex multilateral trading
patterns appeared whereby British goods were exchanged for
those of a second country which were then used to trade with
a third or fourth country whose produce was brought home.
Many trades also involved the re-export of foreign produce
from Merseyside. Some of Merseyside's trading links with other
countries were well established by 1750. Ireland was the most
obvious trading partner from the Middle Ages: its geographical
location made Merseyside convenient for sending military supplies
to Ireland and peaceful trade developed naturally side by side
with military needs. From Ireland Merseyside received agricultural produce, herrings, flax and linen in exchange for her
own staple commodities salt, coal, copper, soap and alum and
some re-exported foreign luxury goods.

Rather more distant trades such as those with Spain and the
Mediterranean ports involved the import of such commodities
as fruits, wines, copper and iron and among the export trades
cloth was of importance. Salt exports were important in several
trades including those with the Baltic, Denmark, Norway and
Hamburg – a vital return commodity being timber. Salt was also
used extensively by the Newfoundland cod fisheries – the salted
cod brought back was partly consumed at home but some was
also re-exported to the Mediterranean and West Indies. The
West Indian trades had become very important by the eighteenth
century, involving amongst other products the import into
Liverpool of sugar and rum, coffee and dyewoods; until 1800
the West Indies were also Britain's main source of raw cotton
and this came to Lancashire's cotton industry via the Mersey.
After 1801 the U.S.A. became the main source of raw cotton but
already by 1750 Merseyside had long established commercial links
with the American colonies especially through the Virginian
tobacco trade which was established in the seventeenth century.
As the American colonies developed and became independent more
commodities were traded including large amounts of raw cotton

and sugar and a wider range of manufactured exports.

During the eighteenth century, however, both the West Indian trades and trade with North America became inextricably bound up with Merseyside's best known trade - the African slave trade. This grew from the late seventeenth century in competition with London and Bristol. After 1760 Liverpool became the leading British port in the trade and consequently earned a great deal of notoriety. There is little new that one can add to all that has been written about the suffering and loss of life amongst both slaves and crew and about the degrading aspects of the trade. [5] On the credit side it should be noted that there was powerful opposition to the trade by such leading Liverpool citizens as the Rathbones and William Roscoe. From the economic point of view recent work has shown that earlier estimates of the profits were greatly exaggerated. Some large profits were earned but these had to be set off against heavy losses so that average profits were moderate - around eight per cent. It is also a wild exaggeration to claim (as some people have) that the whole prosperity of Liverpool and its hinterland hinged on the slave trade. Merseyside's trading activities were advancing on a broad front during the eighteenth century and the abolition of the slave trade was compensated for by further diversification.

Although the role of the slave trade in Merseyside's development has been over-emphasised it would be equally unwise to under-estimate its contribution. It involved equipping ships with British produce such as copper goods, beads, textiles, iron bars and cooking pots for exchange on the West Africa coast for slaves. This demand constituted a welcome market for these industries. The trade required the building and frequent fitting out of ships, so stimulating shipbuilding and repairing. The slaves were taken to the West Indies or America for sale and the proceeds of sales were either returned to Britain in the form of bills of exchange or else they were invested in such produce as raw cotton, sugar, rum and tobacco for sale in Britain. The slave trade therefore helped to establish Merseyside's trading connections with Africa and to extend the range of her trades with the West Indies and America. The practice of bringing back part of the proceeds in bills of exchange also helped to promote banking and financial organisation.

During the eighteenth and early nineteenth centuries there was a good deal of dislocation of international trade and shipping routes. European wars involving Spain, Holland and France (including the French Revolutionary War) and the War of American Independence closed markets and cut off supplies of raw materials; the seas were covered by privateers who preyed on trading vessels and many ships had to sail in convoy or to be expensively equipped with cannons and additional crew for defence. Merseyside's ships occasionally fell as prizes to privateers but on balance the region gained far more prizes than she lost. Between August 1778 and April 1779, partly as a result of the severe disruption of trade due to the American War of Independence,

Liverpool traders were reported to have fitted out one hundred
and twenty privateers of a tonnage amounting to 30,787, armed
with 1,986 guns and carrying 8,754 crew. Her privateers were
often highly successful and by the early nineteenth century a
considerable proportion of Liverpool's registered shipping had
formerly belonged to other countries.

The most seriously adverse effects of war for Merseyside lay
in the disruption in markets and supplies of produce, especially
those resulting from Napoleon's attempts to blockade Britain by
the Milan and Berlin Decrees of 1806 and 1807, and the dislocations caused by war between Britain and United States in
1812. During the period 1793 to 1816 there were several serious
commercial crises and periods when trade and industry were
disrupted and traders became insolvent – the worst effects
being felt in 1793, 1809–10 and 1815–16. Although these crises
were not solely due to the wars, wartime dislocations, and in
the latter case the ending of war, were major contributory
factors.

The abolition of Britain's slave trade in 1807 therefore
occurred during a period when commerce and traders were
already staggering under the strains arising from Napoleon's
Continental System and the general wartime dislocations. This
may have contributed to the view that the slave trade had been
indispensable to Liverpool's prosperity and that abolition would
result in a serious decline in economic activity. In fact the
trade was far from indispensable to Liverpool but its end,
coinciding as it did with economic depression from other causes,
naturally aggravated the problems of the commercial and
shipping community. Some of the Liverpool merchants who had
been engaged in the slave trade continued to operate illegally
by trading with the colonies of other countries which had not
abolished the trade. Most merchants, on the other hand, had
anticipated for many years that abolition would come and
planned accordingly and, in any event, most of them had a
wide range of other interests. Once the problems associated with
war had been overcome they were able to enter new businesses
by developing their existing connections with Africa and the
West Indies and by seeking out new fields for enterprise.

Gradually the slave trade with Africa was replaced by the
so-called 'legitimate' or produce trades. Progress in this
direction was however very slow even after the monopoly of the
Company of Merchants Trading to Africa ceased in 1821 thus
opening the trade to all comers. It was delayed by political
insecurity, tropical diseases, the difficulty of inland communications and by the fact that the supply to the African coast of
African produce was not as prolific as the supply of slaves had
been. Nonetheless the range and volume of African produce
exported to Britain increased, including such products as ivory,
gold dust, pepper, arrowroot, ginger, ground nuts, gum and,
of particular importance to Liverpool, palm kernels and palm
oil. By 1851 the African Steam Ship Company had been established

to run regular steam services between Liverpool and West Africa and by 1870 it had been joined by another Merseyside company the British and Africa Steam Navigation Company.

Merchants found more immediate compensation for the loss of slaving in the expansion of the West Indian produce trades and in trades with former French colonies. They already had strong, long established trading links with the West Indies involving the import into Britain of sugar, rum and raw cotton and they also found extensive opportunities for extending their established trades with the U.S.A.: raw cotton became extremely important and there was a growing volume of imports into Liverpool of American wheat, rice and flour which swelled to a flood later in the century.

The trade in raw cotton, intimately associated with the Lancashire cotton industry, quickly became a major trade. After 1800 the U.S.A. became Lancashire's major supplier and the port of Liverpool dominated Britain's imports. Between 1820 and 1850 imports of raw cotton into Britain increased from 571,651 bales to 1,749,300 bales: Liverpool never handled less than eighty per cent of the U.K.'s imports and, on occasion, accounted for as much as ninety per cent. By 1850, three quarters of the U.K.'s total imports of raw cotton came from the U.S.A., the remainder coming from Brazil, Egypt and the East Indies. During the early 1860s the trade was seriously disrupted by the American Civil War but, apart from this, raw cotton was firmly established as one of Merseyside's largest trades.

In addition to developing their traditional trading connections, Merseyside merchants found considerable scope for the building of new commercial interests in South America, the Far East and Australia. As the South and Central American colonies were freed from European political control, the opportunities for trade and investment seemed very inviting to merchants whose trades with Europe were still disrupted by war, even though at times these new markets proved to be a mixed blessing. As soon as they were open to general trading there was a mad rush to flood the markets with goods, especially cotton goods, but also with produce such as stoves and hearth rugs for which there was no demand. Markets became glutted and commercial organisation in these new nations was extremely primitive lacking even warehouse facilities to store unsold goods. Goods often had to be dumped on beaches, prices collapsed, produce was stolen or deteriorated. Many of the merchants become insolvent and could not pay manufacturers for the goods exported. Many manufacturers were therefore faced with severe financial stringency and this was a major cause of severe commercial distress in 1810 and 1811. Again in the 1820s many British investors lost their capital in South America but, despite such setbacks as hectic booms and traumatic slumps, British capital continued to flow into these countries and the produce trades continued to grow, especially the import into Liverpool of wool, tallow, hides and dried and salted meat.

Another potentially valuable new trading outlet was the Far

East although again there were many problems to be overcome before its full potential could be realised. The East India Company had a monopoly of most of Britain's trade with India until 1813 and with China until 1834. The removal of these legal monopolies meant that Liverpool merchants could try their luck first in India and then in China exporting textiles and metal goods and bringing back such products as raw cotton, gunny cloth, tea, rice, skins and silk. As in South America the opening of new markets led initially to the flooding of the markets with British goods, prices collapsed and traders were in financial difficulty. In China there were extremely serious problems arising from the absence of established commercial organisation and foreign exchange markets. Western traders had to operate in completely unfamiliar conditions with little or no knowledge of either local conditions or of the language, they had to contend with illness and natural disasters as well as with international war, pirates and civil war. Those who managed to overcome such problems gradually developed large operations with both India and China and (from the 1850s) with Japan too as that country was opened to trade with the west. As Australia was colonised and developed far eastern traders also developed commercial links with that continent taking out manufactured goods, and bringing back wool, grain and gold.

As the range of trading partners grew so too did the supplies of goods for export from Britain. Merseyside's staples – salt and coal – were exported in increasing quantities but there was an even greater increase in the export of such products as soap, glass, soda and other chemicals, cotton goods, Yorkshire iron, Staffordshire pottery and metal and engineering goods of all sorts.

The initiative in developing all these trades came from the merchants, shipowners and manufacturers, and the business community grew in wealth and influence. As in other parts of Britain they became influential in local politics, philanthropy, moral and intellectual pursuits as well as being a major source of the region's employment and prosperity. In the eighteenth century there was little specialisation. In trade as in other respects the eighteenth-century ideal was the 'complete' man who exercised a diversity of skills and knowledge. In Defoe's words Liverpool traders were 'universal merchants'.[6] They each dealt with a range of trades with several countries. Each merchant was likely to own a part share in one or more ship, he would carry out business for other people as an agent, finance his own trade, sometimes help to organise and finance the manufacture of the goods he exported and deal with insurance.

In the later eighteenth century and more especially during the nineteenth century the growing scale and complexity of trade inevitably led to greater specialisation. Some firms specialised in merchanting, dealing perhaps in one or two commodities or with one or two countries; some concentrated on shipowning; some became predominantly bankers and financiers; others engaged in insurance or acted as brokers. In merchanting, for example, the trade in raw cotton was increasingly concentrated in the hands of thirty leading importers. By 1839 they controlled something approaching three-quarters of Liverpool's cotton imports and they included well-known Liverpool firms such as Rathbones, Boltons, Ogdens and Cropper and Company as well as some American companies such as W. and J. Brown and Brown Shipley & Co., and branches of London and Glasgow firms such as Baring Bros. and Dennistoun & Co. There was also specialisation by firms importing timber, wheat, flour, etc.

When such produce arrived in the port it had to be sold and increasingly another specialised class of traders – brokers – took over the work of selling raw cotton, corn, fruit, etc. through the produce exchanges. The job of packing and organising transport and arranging for the shipping documents necessary for goods in transit (especially for exports) also became a specialised job handled by shipping and forwarding agents, and shipping brokers would charter ships. Such specialisation was, however, beginning to occur in other ports as well and in the handling of some produce London began to take the lead. For example, Liverpool merchants importing tea found that they could get better prices and quicker sales by sending their produce for sale by London brokers. This process was greatly accelerated by the spread of telegraphic communications especially after the laying of the transatlantic cable which was successfully completed in 1866.

Banking had also become a specialised business long before 1870. In the eighteenth century banking functions were performed by businessmen as a normal part of their other economic activities. Liverpool's first banker is believed to have been John Wyke, a watch and clock maker and tool factor. In a directory of 1774 two firms called themselves bankers, William Clarke and C. Caldwell & Co., but many traders and manufacturers performed banking functions for themselves and for customers and, if one looks at some of Liverpool's leading bankers between 1774 and the 1820s, one finds them combining banking with a diverse range of other activities. William Roscoe and John Clarke were in the coal trade; Arthur and Benjamin Heywood and Caldwells were general merchants; William Gregson was a merchant, shipowner, privateer, slave trader and underwriter; Thomas Staniforth was involved in the Greenland fisheries; Thomas Leyland in the Irish and Newfoundland trades, the slave trade and privateering; John Aspinall and Son were grocers; Joseph Hadwin was a tea dealer; John Moss was a timber and general merchant, privateer and shipowner; Jonas Bold operated in sugar and slaves and Francis Ingram and Joseph Daltera engaged in the slave trade.

These traders provided banking services such as holding deposits, discounting bills of exchange and remitting money for clients to other parts of the country. In the rest of Britain too the number of 'country banks' grew rapidly in the late eighteenth and early nineteenth centuries though they became notorious for their instability. In Lancashire, however, there was one difference from practice elsewhere: whereas other country banks issued large quantities of bank notes which became worthless if the banks failed, Lancashire banks did not issue notes. Unfortunately this did not protect them from failure: e.g. Chas. Caldwell & Co. failed in 1793, John Aspinall & Son in 1816 and Roscoe, Clarke and Roscoe in 1820; some suspended payments temporarily but recovered again (e.g. Gregson & Co. in 1793) and there were many changes in partnerships and reorganisations of business.

Gradually, however, the scale of banking increased. In 1827 a branch of the Bank of England was opened in Liverpool to extend the circulation of Bank of England notes and also to perform general banking functions and when joint stock banks were allowed by law in 1829, Liverpool's first was the Manchester and Liverpool District Bank, followed in 1831 by the Bank of Liverpool. Gradually private banks were converted into joint stock organisation or absorbed by amalgamation so that banks became larger and more secure and they spread their operations more widely through the establishment of branches.

As business became more specialised there was a growing tendency for firms to join together into organisations representing their special interests. A wide range of trade organisations came into being to cater for special interests: the West India Merchants Association was formed in the eighteenth century; the American Chamber of Commerce in 1801; the Underwriters Association was formed in 1802 as insurance became more specialised. These were followed by such organisations as the African Association, the East India and China Association, the General Brokers Association, the Salt Chamber of Commerce, the Wine and Spirit Association, etc. Many of these associations were represented in the Liverpool Chamber of Commerce established in 1850. With the growth in trade, commerce, insurance and banking Liverpool also acquired its own Stock Exchange which achieved a prominent position amongst provincial stock exchanges and led to the creation of the Liverpool Sharebrokers Association.

Shipowning also gradually became a more specialised activity towards the end of this period. In the eighteenth and early nineteenth centuries much of Merseyside's trade was carried in ships owned locally and registered under the 1786 Act in Liverpool. To the 1830s the typical Liverpool ship was less than two hundred tons. It might be built in Liverpool or bought secondhand. Its building and operation could be financed by several investors because the law allowed the ownership of vessels to be divided into shares but it was customary in Merseyside for each ship to be owned by less than five people.[7] The occupations of the owners were usually that of merchant, ship builder, master mariner, ships chandler and some other maritime pursuit. There were many large and small merchants who owned ships or shares in ships as part of their range of business activities. Even the large merchant houses were usually family firms or partnerships such as the Brocklebanks, John Gladstone, Bibbys, the Tobins, the Rathbones, Cropper, Benson & Co., Charles Tayleur and Sons and Taylor Potter & Co. Such concerns did not describe themselves as shipowners. They used ships in which they had shares to carry their own produce and hired out any surplus space to others. Some owned many ships: John Bibby for example had interests in at least 27 vessels between 1815 and 1835. Others simply owned a few shares in one or two ships. Some shares were also held by people not connected with merchanting or maritime pursuits: they are described as gentlemen, widows, spinsters, farmers, grocers, brewers etc. Between 1815 and 1835 the proportion of such shareholders in Liverpool-registered ships rose from 5 per cent to 14 per cent.[8] Investors in Liverpool ships were also predominantly Merseyside residents though some shares were held by residents of North Wales, Cumberland and Westmoreland. At this time each ship was loaded with goods for export and usually the master was given a considerable degree of authority in selling them abroad. Masters also had to deal with matters such as revictualling the ship, carrying out repairs, replacing crew members and, above all, buying a return cargo or arranging to carry freight for other people.

By and large, therefore, the ownership and the operation of ships were closely associated. In the mid-nineteenth century many changes began to occur and these gradually influenced the structure of the industry. More and more shipowners became specialist carriers and American shipowners influenced the industry. The novel practice established by the Black Ball Line and other American companies of running regular services for emigrants according to time table gradually influenced the operation of British ships. American clippers were also a great technological advance on British sailing ships and Canadian ships were much cheaper to buy than British because of better timber supplies and lower building costs.

Britain, however, rose to these challenges from North America. American superiority in timber supplies was counteracted by the increasing use of metal, first to protect and strengthen ships and then to replace timber in shipbuilding. Merseyside participated in these developments: it became a centre for the sheathing of ships with copper: then ships began to be built on iron frames and eventually with iron plates. Furthermore wind power was increasingly replaced by steam-propulsion though, in the early stages, the very heavy coal consumption meant that steam inevitably had to be limited to short journeys or as a supplement to sails.

Early advances in the use of steam were therefore ferry and coastal services with some ships venturing further afield to Ireland. From an early stage the increasing size of such ships called for larger capital outlay so that it was quite common to find steam ships owned by joint stock companies rather than by individuals or partnerships. As early as the 1820s several joint stock companies came into being to operate steam services between Liverpool and Ireland including the Dublin Liverpool Steam Navigation Company, the Liverpool Belfast Steam Navigation Company, the City of Dublin Steam Packet Company and the Mona and Liverpool Steam Packet Company. The general use of steam ships on longer journeys necessitated the building of more efficient marine engines, an activity in which Merseyside also participated, and this together with a growing worldwide network of coaling stations gradually extended the use of steam. By 1870 Liverpool's total tonnage of shipping was nearly 1½ million tons and of this, about twenty per cent was steam propelled.

All these changes meant that increased investment was needed in shipping and although there were still many small investors there was a gradual growth of larger, specialised shipping companies particularly for the building and ownership of steam ships. Some later used joint stock company organisation to collect the larger amounts of capital needed but most remained family concerns or partnerships. By the mid-nineteenth century many of the famous names associated with Merseyside shipping emerged such as James Moss, John Bibby, Samuel Cunard, Charles MacIver, T.H. Ismay, W. Inman, W.J. Lamport, George Holt, Alfred Holt, John Holt, Thomas and James Harrison, Alfred and Charles Booth, J.S. Swire, Thomas Brocklebank, the Rathbones, Alfred Jones, Macgregor Laird, Alexander Elder and John Dempster.

By the provision of cheap fast services Liverpool shipowners wrested the emigrant trade from American lines after the mid-1850s. Between 1861 and 1900 about a third of all European emigrants to the United States went via Liverpool. In 1870 there were still many sailing ships in use - in fact the clipper could compete quite successfully on some routes. There were also large numbers of small ships which sailed irregularly picking up cargoes wherever they could, but by 1870 organised shipping lines providing regular services of steam ships were well-established in Merseyside.

The period 1750 to 1870 was therefore one in which there were many advances in transport and communications, in the provision of dock and port facilities, in the financing and organisation of commerce and shipping. Intimately bound up with these developments was the growth of industry in Merseyside and its hinterland and this is the subject of the next chapter.

NOTES

1. For a more detailed account of the early development of the docks see F.E. Hyde, *Liverpool and the Mersey: the Development of a Port 1700-1970* (David and Charles, Newton Abbot, 1971), passim.

2. N. Pevsner, *Lancashire: the Industrial and Commercial South* (Penguin Books, Harmondsworth, 1969), pp. 146, 166.

3. J. Touzeau, *The Rise and Progress of Liverpool from 1551 to 1835* (Liverpool Booksellers Company, Liverpool, 1910), pp. 258-9.

4. The history of the Mersey Docks and Harbour Board has been recorded in S. Mountfield, *Western Gateway: A History of the Mersey Docks and Harbour Board* (Liverpool University Press, 1965).

5. The most recent history is R. Anstey and P.E.H. Hair (eds), *Liverpool, the African Slave Trade and Abolition* (Historic Society of Lancashire and Cheshire, Occasional Series, 1976).

6. D. Defoe with introduction by G.D.H. Cole, *A Tour Thro the whole island of Great Britain* (London, 1927), vol. II, p. 665.

7. F. Neal, 'Liverpool Shipping in the early Nineteenth Century' in J.R. Harris (ed.), *Liverpool and Merseyside* (Frank Cass, London, 1969), p. 160.

8. Ibid., 162.

Chapter 4

MERSEYSIDE INDUSTRIES 1750-1870

The reasons for Merseyside's industrial structure are so complex that it is not always possible to find a single convincing explanation for the establishment of a particular industry. Local raw materials such as salt and coal played a role in moulding part of the region's industrial structure but then as industries based on these resources expanded and diversified their output they had to import other materials by river, canal, coastal shipping or from abroad. Other industries grew up specifically to process imported materials such as sugar and tobacco. Some industries were scattered throughout the region but then eventually settled in one or two main centres, whereas others started in one locality and then spread to new ones. Liverpool's shipbuilding and later some of its milling migrated to Birkenhead; salt processing extended from Cheshire to Liverpool and then back along the Mersey. The centre of chemical production underwent a series of shifts during this period and glass-making migrated from several centres to concentrate primarily in St Helens. Both within and between industries there was a great deal of flexibility, adaptability and change; existing businesses expanded, made new products and used new processes: a Warrington sail-making firm for example changed over to wire products and soap-makers might move into glue manufacture but, in addition, new businesses were created to produce an ever-widening range of products in the chemical and metal industries and in the use of new materials such as rubber.

Industrial development during this period was of course taking place against the back-drop of the Industrial Revolution: it is customary to consider that this movement gathered momentum during the second half of the eighteenth century, accelerating into the nineteenth century. It is also customary to regard Lancashire as one of the key constituents of the revolution. In the first phase of the industrial revolution there was rapid growth in some major industries: the mechanisation of the cotton industry; a great expansion in the consumption of coal for a variety of purposes including its substitution for charcoal in iron production and its use as fuel in steam engines; to meet the demands of other industries for mechanisation engineering became important and hand in hand with these developments went improvements in transport. Within this broad framework Merseyside had a stake in improved transport, in coal, metal-working and engineering and a marginal involvement in cotton. As industrialisation proceeded other industries such as chemical production, copper, glass, pottery, soap (all major Merseyside industries) became an integral part of the process.

1750-1800

A significant proportion of the industries that were already present in Merseyside in 1750 were amongst those which, in the country as a whole, showed strong signs of capitalist organisation before the conventionally-accepted beginning of the Industrial Revolution - coal-mining, copper, glass, ship-building, soap-boiling, sugar-baking, pottery, salt-boiling. Even so as late as the beginning of the nineteenth century Merseyside still retained strong agricultural and craft sectors. A high proportion of the population was occupied on the land and in industries organised on a domestic and workshop basis. Many people combined work in agriculture with part-time work in a craft. At this stage it was Liverpool, Warrington, the south-west Lancashire coalfield and the Cheshire salt-fields that exhibited the clearest symptoms of industrial development; there were a few pointers to the future in the district that was later dominated by St Helens but as yet there were few indications of the fate that awaited Widnes, Runcorn and part of the Wirral.

A glance through directories for the early nineteenth century shows just how large were the groups of people in each district regularly ministering to the needs of the local population (even in small and medium-sized conurbations) rather than engaging in the key industries. In directories one finds that most localities were equipped with blacksmiths, wheelwrights and ironmongers, with boot and shoe or clog and patten makers, drapers, hosiers, milliners and hat-makers, hair-dressers, tailors and stay-makers; with tallow chandlers, curriers, sadlers, leather sellers and sometimes tanners; with timber merchants, cabinet makers, joiners, plumbers, painters, stonemasons, brick-layers and sometimes brick-makers; they had physicians, surgeons, veterinary surgeons as well as seedsmen, gardeners and nurserymen; food, drink and entertainment were supplied by corn millers, flour dealers, bakers and confectioners, grocers and tea dealers, butchers, maltsters, brewers and coopers in addition to wine and spirit merchants, hoteliers, and inn and tavern keepers; there were booksellers and some printers.

The larger conurbations, notably Liverpool and Warrington, also boasted attornies, auctioneers, bankers, insurance offices, land and building agents and surveyors. In addition, in these larger towns there was a growing provision of luxury goods. In 1796 William Moss describes shops in Liverpool for the sale of china, trinkets, 'valuable curiosities both natural and artificial . . . paintings and engravings, musical instruments'. [1]

The distribution and sale of locally-produced goods and of produce from farther afield occupied considerable numbers of people in shops, fairs, markets and in hawking produce from

door to door. Most towns had general markets once or twice
a week and some had specialised ones as well. Warrington had a
linen market for example, Prescot a cattle market and Wigan a
cloth market. Liverpool had a general market, one for potatoes,
another for pigs, another for cattle, a corn market, a hay and
straw market, a fish market and one for provisions, vegetables
and butter. In addition to markets fairs were held once or more
a year in towns such as Warrington, Liverpool, Wigan, Ormskirk,
Neston and St Helens.

Many of the locally-produced commodities were agricultural
for this was a very important industry throughout the region.
The coastal plain between the Ribble and the Mersey had a warm,
damp climate and the parts that had been mossland and marsh
were mostly reclaimed by 1800. The formidable Martin Mere was
drained by the enterprise of Thomas Eccleston of Scarisbrick
who employed Gilbert, one of the Duke of Bridgewater's stewards,
to produce some of the finest farmland in the country for oats
and wheat, cabbages, peas and above all potatoes to feed the
local urban populations. In 1796, Moss reported that in Liverpool
one could find a wide range of vegetables 'earlier, in great
perfection and abundance, and cheaper than in any other part
of the Kingdom'. [2] Sheep, cattle and poultry were also reared
nearby. Very fertile land around Warrington too yielded large
supplies of vegetables and fruit but these were consumed more
in the Manchester area than in Merseyside. From the Middle Ages
Cheshire had been renowned for its agricultural production
and this continued to be an important occupation: Cheshire
cheeses were exported to London; cattle, pigs, hides, butter,
tallow and lard were produced in abundance and apples, oatmeal,
malt, flour and potatoes were shipped along the Dee and Weaver.
In the Wirral potatoes were grown especially near to West Kirby
but apart from a small amount of grazing land there was a great
deal of waste and marshland still waiting to be reclaimed in 1800.

Throughout Merseyside (as in the rest of the country) horses
were extremely important both for agriculture and as a major
means of transport. Oats and corn were produced to feed them
and the growing urban horse population reciprocated by supplying dung, shipped by canal from Warrington, Chester and other
towns as manure for market gardeners and potato growers.
Horses also gave employment to blacksmiths and to harness and
leather producers. As a by-product of cattle-breeding and
dairying, Cheshire agriculture produced skins and hides both
for export and to be tanned using local oak bark. In fact curing
and tanning were already very important in Warrington in 1750;
as other towns also developed the industry both hides and
tanning materials were increasingly imported to supply the
tanneries.

The locally-produced grain was processed in the forest of
wind-mills scattered throughout the windier parts of the region.
Some water-power was used where rivers were suitable and a
few mills were operated by the tide in Liverpool, Wallasey Pool

and Bromborough but wind was also a source of energy in the
Lancashire plain, in Liverpool and in the Wirral. By the late
eighteenth century wind-mills were so numerous in Liverpool
as to be a serious nuisance - many had to be demolished to
provide sites for new commercial and industrial buildings. Both
water and wind-mills were not, of course, confined solely to
grinding grain; they also ground dyewoods and medicines and
provided power for paper-making and iron-slitting. The skills
necessary for their construction and equipment proved useful
to the nascent engineering industry.

Brewing was yet another agriculture-based industry. Many
households brewed their own drinks and in addition a multitude
of small breweries, widely dispersed throughout the region,
helped to quench the thirsts and drown the sorrows of local
inhabitants. In 1796, Moss referred to about forty breweries
in Liverpool alone but he added the warning that their ale was
of such poor quality that 'that necessary, native and wholesome
beverage' had to be imported from the surrounding countryside.
There was, however, one ray of hope: a newly-established
porter brewery in Scotland Road promised 'to furnish as good
a quality of liquor as the London Breweries'.[3]

Nearby Warrington already produced good quality ales and
distilled gin and St Helens had a number of breweries. The size
of breweries was already increasing by 1800: some owned
taverns and leased them to landlords to sell the brewery's beer.
As the scale of brewing increased local barley supplies had to
be supplemented by imports from Scotland and even from the
Baltic. Hops came from Chester Fair and from Worcester.

Another activity based initially on locally-produced materials
was the linen industry. Linen was one of the region's important
domestic industries although local supplies of flax had to be
augmented by imports from Ireland. Although linen production
was widespread it was not transformed into a generally mechanised factory industry and, unlike more eastern parts of Lancashire, textile manufacture did not play a dominant role in
Merseyside's industrial evolution. There was a smattering of
textile crafts: a little silk manufacture at Ormskirk and Southport developed by a Macclesfield industrialist; there was some
production of cotton yarn, velveteens, calicoes and muslins
in Warrington where, it is claimed, the first application occurred
in Lancashire of Boulton and Watt's steam engine for cotton
production. Despite this initiative, several attempts to establish
cotton manufacture elsewhere in the region - Liverpool, St
Helens, Prescot, Ormskirk and North Meols - either failed or
had only desultory results.

The outstanding exception to the lack of success of textile
production in the region was the production of sail-cloth in
Warrington - and on a small scale in other places such as St
Helens and North Meols. Warrington became so important that
it was supplying half the British Navy's total requirements
before the industry began to decline steeply early in the

nineteenth century.

This is one of many important instances of the mutual inter-dependence between industry and transport. Warrington's sail-cloth producers found their markets in the growing demand for sails for coastal and sea-going vessels and for the Mersey 'flats' (barges with sails used on rivers and canals). The fishing industry also contributed to the demand. Fishing had long been important to the region: there was a valuable fishery in the Mersey near Warrington where salmon, smelts and sparling abounded before river pollution occurred. So cheap and plenti-ful were the local salmon that it is said that in the late eighteenth century clauses were inserted in the apprentices' indentures to ensure that masters did not require them to eat salmon more than twice a week.

The sea, like the river, also provided excellent fishing and fishing villages were dotted around the Wirral coast and north of Liverpool at North Meols (Southport). At Southport fishing thrived to the end of the eighteenth century: cockles and shrimps were a speciality and it was possible to buy turbot, soles, mackerel, cod, skate, pilchards, herrings, flukes and even sturgeon. Liverpool's fish market was well stocked by fishing fleets from around the estuary with shoals of herrings, shrimps, prawns, cod, flatfish and crabs as well as salmon and fresh-water fish from the river. Liverpool's atmosphere was polluted by herring curing and by the whale-oil industry.

Fishing was one of several sources of the growing demand for boats and ships - a demand which met a response from the long-established ship-building, ship-repairing and other ship-related industries such as roperies, anchor smithies, block-making and the production of pitch and tar. At times war also intensified demand: there was great activity during the American colonies' revolution and the French wars. Frigates and other naval vessels were built in addition to merchant ships by impor-tant ship-builders such as Humble and Hurry, Rathbones, Peter and William Quirk, Hind and Son, Fisher and Co. and Leather and Co.

As Britain's timber supplies declined, wood had to be imported from the Baltic, America and Africa but the actual ship-building facilities required in the eighteenth century were quite primitive. Ships were built on stretches of firm sloping beach, the hulks being propped up with timber. The tools were simple - cutting tools, a saw pit to cut timbers and a steam-chest to bend them. Calking tools and materials and pitch and tar made the hulls water-tight and preserved the wood. Increasingly towards the end of the eighteenth century the hulls of ocean-going ships were further preserved by being covered with copper sheathing supplied by the region's copper producers. The expansion of ship-building on the Liverpool side of the estuary was however beginning to be limited as ship-builders were displaced from their traditional stretches of beach by new docks which gradually forced them to move further south along the estuary.

The growing fleets of ships and barges made possible the carriage of more and more heavy bulky raw materials and finished products for the salt, coal, glass, pottery, soap and metallurgical industries – the first two industries, salt and coal, were Merseyside's key growth points in the mid-eighteenth century both industrially and commercially and their mutual development was intimately bound up with the improvement of transport facilities.[4] In Cheshire salt had long been obtained from brine, and after 1670, with the discovery of rock salt near Northwich, there was increasing rivalry between producers using brine and those refining rock salt. The industry's greatest problem was the cost and difficulty of transport especially overland by pack horse between the wiches and Frodsham Bridge. Brine had to be treated at its source and the white salt was then usually carried to Liverpool, but it was cheaper to move the rock salt and refine it nearer to the coal supplies so saving part of the cost of transporting coal. From the 1690s therefore, rock salt was processed in works at Frodsham Bridge, in Liverpool (Blackburnes works) and at Dungeon (Sir Thomas Johnsons works). This necessitated transporting the rock salt but this was cheaper than bringing coal all the way from Prescot and Whiston to the saltfields. An even more important move to reduce the difficulties and cost of transporting coal, rock salt and white salt was the pressure from 1699 for a Weaver Navigation scheme which was eventually approved in 1721. When opened in 1732 this navigation facilitated a considerable expansion in the salt industry. In 1732–3 shipments of salt on the Weaver amounted to nearly 15,000 tons. Twenty years later they reached nearly 28,000 tons.[5] The figures in Chapter 2 showing the amounts carried on the Weaver indicate the growth in output during the rest of the century.

Meanwhile as we have seen during the eighteenth century there was a growing need for coal in other parts of Merseyside both for domestic consumption and to meet the needs of brewing, pottery- and glass-making, sugar refining, copper smelting, wire-drawing and other coal-using industries. The coalfield that responded to all these demands was that in south-west Lancashire. The boundary of Merseyside cuts across this coalfield: the north (basin of the Yarrow) and centre (basin of the middle Douglas) including Wigan lay outside Merseyside; the south and west (the basins of Ditton and Sankey Brooks and the mossland west of the Billinge/Ashurst ridge) were within it.[6] There had been mining in this coalfield since the sixteenth century and by the 1690s the coalfield's output was possibly around 28,000 tons a year. Pressing demands for fuel, especially from the salt producers and from Liverpool, and improved communications by the Liverpool/Prescot turnpike and the Weaver Navigation encouraged increased production. By the 1740s total output had probably reached 78,000 tons a year; this came predominantly from the south and west of the coalfield to meet Merseyside's needs with some 8,500 tons going from

Prescot and Whiston to Cheshire along the Weaver navigation.
The rest of the century witnessed further rapid expansion first
with the Douglas navigation and the Sankey Brook Canal and
then with even more rapid growth after the building of the
section of the Leeds-Liverpool Canal to Wigan. By the 1770s
total output had probably reached 220,000 tons of which some
75 per cent went via the Sankey Canal, and by 1799 it had
expanded to 680,000 tons, of which a quarter of a million tons
were carried on the Leeds-Liverpool canal.

The industrial revolution of this period is often associated
with a growth in capitalist organisation. Coal production tended
to be a capitalistic industry before the industrial revolution.
The size of collieries varied but before 1740 there were a few
large collieries in the south west some producing 5,000 tons a
year. In the second half of the eighteenth century several
powerful coal owners competed fiercely with each other[7]: for
example, Sarah Clayton, the famous woman industrialist
developed the Parr collieries; Jonathan Case extended his
workings eastward from Huyton towards St Helens; John Mackay
developed Ravenhead where the British Cast Plate Glass
Company and the Ravenhead copper works set up in 1776 and
1780 consumed quantities of coal. Trade depression during the
War of American Independence destroyed several of the larger
businesses in the St Helens region, including that of Sarah
Clayton. When trade and coal production expanded again an
increasing number of coal-masters replaced the small group
that had dominated the industry but even so by the end of the
century there were some very large collieries each producing
over 30,000 tons a year. Increased output was partly dependent
on improved transport but it was also partly dependent on
improvements in mining technology with a growing use of steam
drainage, the building of wagonways and railed roads, with
'longwall' mining in the Sankey basin and the 'Lancashire
System' (combining longwall and pillar and stall) in Orrell.

During the eighteenth century there were close connections
between the salt and coal industries. As a culmination of improved river navigation, canals, turnpikes and the growth in
Liverpool's export trades, a triangular trade developed between
the coalfield, the Cheshire saltfields and Liverpool. Liverpool's
major saltworks (Blackburnes) was moved to Garston in the
1790s but Liverpool entrepreneurs increasingly gained control
of the Cheshire industry because they were dissatisfied with
irregular supplies reaching them for export. In 1784 most
Cheshire salt works' proprietors lived in Cheshire: by 1804
two-thirds lived in Liverpool. Around the turn of the century
they also began to acquire coal mines to reduce their dependence
on coal masters. After 1800 some St Helens coal masters replied
by acquiring salt-works. By 1830 every coal proprietor in and
around St Helens was also a salt works' proprietor.

Copper smelting was another Merseyside industry whose
development was intimately bound up both with coal production

and with improved transport facilities. From their first introduction into Britain in the sixteenth century the copper and
brass industries, like coal, had shown capitalist tendencies
and so foreshadowed the types of organisation that other industries were later to adopt: they were organised in fairly large
units which combined together on occasion to engage in restric-
tive practices; their main raw material, copper ore, was imported
from outside the region - in the case of Merseyside mostly from
Anglesey, and their finished products served markets throughout Britain, in Europe, in Africa and in the East and West
Indies. During the eighteenth century new markets were opened
through the use of copper and brass for a growing range of
articles such as buckles and buttons, locks, toys and door
furniture and, in the later eighteenth century, the industry's
sheets were attached to ships to protect their timbers.

Copper production was present in Merseyside before 1750. In
1719 a copper works was established at Bank Quay, Warrington
by Thomas Patten. His coal and ore were carried along the Mersey
to Warrington. After 1750 the industry spread: in 1767 Charles
Roe and Co. of Macclesfield set up a works in Liverpool to smelt
Anglesey copper and to produce copper and brass articles for
the African slave trade. Soon afterwards the Warrington Company
set up a works at St Helens primarily to gain access to cheap
coal. The Parys Mine Company, dominated by the copper magnate
Thomas Williams, set up a smelting and refining works on the
coalfield at Ravenhead in 1779. [8] Thomas Williams also bought the
Warrington Company's Stanley Works near St Helens in 1785 as
an addition to his copper empire and both his Stanley and
Ravenhead works either sent refined copper to Liverpool for
sale or they sent it to the Company's other mills. By the early
nineteenth century Thomas Williams' empire had waned and at
the same time South Wales was moving into the predominant
position in Britain's copper industry so the importance of
Merseyside copper declined, although the industry did not die
out in the region, as we shall see, it was later to develop very
close links with the great new chemical industry.

Several of Merseyside's other industries also needed transport
facilities for heavy and bulky materials and produce including
soap, pottery and glass manufacturers. Soap-makers needed fat
and alkali - the latter was largely obtained from kelp imported
from Scotland and Ireland. By the end of the eighteenth century
soap production in Liverpool and Warrington was expanding to
the point at which Merseyside was about to overtake London
to become the country's leading soap producer but this put
increasing pressure on the supply of natural alkali which was
also being consumed in increasing quantities by Merseyside's
glass industry - it was this joint demand from soap and glass
that helped to give birth to the chemical industry.

Glass production has been established in Merseyside before
1750. There were glass makers in the Bickerstaffe area in the
seventeenth century; by 1700 there were glass houses in

Warrington, Liverpool, Thatto Heath, Sutton and Prescot.
Although Liverpool and Warrington expanded their glass production it was St Helens that was becoming the main centre of
the industry. Under French influence a cast plate glass factory
was established in Ravenhead in the 1770s; in 1792 the crown
glass firm Mackay West and Co. started at Eccleston and by
1800 the St Helens district was producing most types of glass
other than flint glass.

Pottery manufacture was widespread in Merseyside in the
eighteenth century relying heavily on materials brought in by
water especially Cornish clay. By 1760 Liverpool had some
twenty factories producing earthenware, delftware, porcelain
and salt glaze for which the port gained a very high reputation.
Some famous names associated with Liverpool pottery were those
of William Chaffers, Seth Pennington, Samuel Gilbody, William
Reid and the Herculaneum Pottery Company. John Sadler and
Guy Green achieved such skill in their new process for printing
pots and jugs that for a time Josiah Wedgewood sent his Queens
ware to Liverpool to be printed.

Liverpool's pottery reached its zenith in the eighteenth
century but other parts of Merseyside had their potteries too:
coarse earthenware goods were produced in Prescot; in St
Helens earthenware mugs, stoneware bottles, sugar moulds
and drips were made and there was a pottery at Parkgate in
the Wirral.

A notable feature in Britain's industrial development in the
late eighteenth century was the increasing output of iron goods
of all sorts and this was both a cause and a consequence of the
far-reaching technological changes in iron and steel production
that are associated with names such as the Abraham Darbys,
John Wilkinson, Henry Cort and Benjamin Huntsman. At Coalbrookdale, in the Midlands, Yorkshire, Derbyshire, Wales and
Scotland the industry was revolutionised and larger works
poured out increasing quantities of cast and wrought iron.

Merseyside lay outside the mainstream of this industry's
technological revolution but on the other hand the whole region
was strewn with businesses, old and new, large and small, which
fashioned the increasing quantities of cheaper iron and improving
qualities of steel into a rapidly diversifying range of products.
Already there were many skilled metal-workers in the region.
Blacksmiths had traditionally dealt with a whole range of metal
goods such as horse shoes and metal tyres for wooden wheels.
The mill-wrights who equipped the region's multitude of mills,
were highly skilled in installing machinery of all sorts. The
heavy iron industry was not much in evidence in 1750 but rapid
development occurred after that date. By the 1780s there was a
steam-powered slitting mill at Bidston Moss and by the 1790s a
steam-powered rolling and slitting mill in Liverpool. Several
ironworks were established including that outpost of Coalbrookdale in Liverpool later known as the Phoenix Foundry. As
Coalbrookdale exported iron pots and kettles through Liverpool

a warehouse was built in the port in 1758 and run by George Perry. Then to meet the growing demand for pots a foundry was erected in Liverpool. After Perry's death the foundry was first taken over by Joseph Rathbone and then, in 1793, by William Fawcett who engaged in a lucrative cannon-making business for ships needing to defend themselves or wishing to engage in privateering during the French Wars. Other iron-works included the St Helens Foundry established in the 1790s which amongst other activities made iron pots for the Africa trade, and close to the margins of the region the Carr Mill Forge and the Haigh ironworks.

In Warrington there was a growing output of tools such as shovels and spades. Some of the region's most important metal products, however, were small products some of which called for great skills: files and other small tools, watches and clocks, locks and hinges, nail-making, wire-drawing and pin-heading. Watch- and clock-making were extremely important craft indus-tries in Liverpool, Prescot and Warrington and they spread to other parts of south-west Lancashire such as Ormskirk. Parts for watches and clocks were often made by farm workers in their own homes. Through this industry precision skills were diffused throughout the region. There was a thriving export trade in watches, clocks, watch cases, springs and other parts: they went to London and abroad.

The intricate skills learned in this industry were also applied to making other precision products such as chronometers, sextants and other navigational aids for ships and, perhaps even more importantly, these industries themselves required tools. In addition to the invention of specialised equipment such as a wheel-cutting machine for watchmakers invented in Liver-pool in the seventeenth century, there was an urgent demand for multi-purpose, small hand tools such as files, pliers and nippers and these were produced in very large quantities both for local use and for export. Lancashire had already earned a considerable reputation for such tools as early as 1700 and in the later eighteenth century, Lancashire files made from high quality Sheffield steels, were reputed to be the best in the world. One of the best known business histories (by the late T.S. Ashton) records the activities of a Warrington file-maker, Peter Stubs.[9]

The craftsmen who made both clocks and also the tools for the clock and watch industries were highly skilled precision workers who provided a nucleus of labour for the developing engineering industries although the size of the supply of such skills was totally inadequate in face of the explosion in demand towards the end of the eighteenth century and in the early nineteenth century. The main age of steam lay ahead but the growing mechanisation of industry and the beginnings of steam engineer-ing were already in evidence by 1800. In the coal industry steam engines were beginning to be used to pump water from mines. The first recorded Newcomen engine in a Merseyside mine was

erected for the Case family near Prescot. From the 1740s steam
engines were operating in the St Helens coalfield and by the end
of the eighteenth century most important collieries had installed
them. Steam power spread to other industries too: cotton was
not one of Merseyside's leading industries but a Boulton and
Watt steam engine was installed in the Peel, Ainsworth cotton
factory in Warrington in 1787. By 1800 Liverpool and St Helens
had steam-powered mills. At the Ravenhead Plate Glass Works
a Boulton and Watt engine drove polishing machinery and the
Parys Company's copper works at St Helens had an illegal steam
engine made by infringing Boulton and Watt's patents. Steam
power was used in Liverpool for rolling and slitting iron and
in St Helens for grinding corn.

Many other industries were also present in Merseyside: some
were based on imported materials such as sugar-baking in
Liverpool and Warrington and tobacco processing. Tobacco,
imported through Liverpool gave rise to snuff manufacture and
also to the production of clay pipes in Liverpool and the surrounding countryside. In urban areas printing was a growth industry
and in some districts there were speciality industries - Ormskirk for example had many hat makers and in Liverpool there
were furniture and coach-makers. In fact, by 1800, Merseyside
had a broad industrial base made up of a diverse collection of
crafts and skills from which further development could occur.
Coal-mining, brewing, ship-building and a wide range of metal
and engineering industries were ripe for expansion: new demands
and new technology could easily spark off rapid development.
Also present in the region, and awaiting a catalyst to set off
a chain reaction of growth, were the necessary ingredients for
an important new industry - chemical production. Raw materials
such as salt and coal were accessible; the demand for alkali
for soap- and glass-making and for bleaching materials for the
textile industries could provide the incentive; scientific interest
and knowledge were being diffused through the region, experiments were occurring and there was some small scale production.

Throughout eighteenth-century Britain there was a great wave
of scientific interest and scientific knowledge was disseminated
to the industrial and commercial classes through philosophical
societies, like the Birmingham-based Lunar Society, through
books and periodicals, lectures and through institutions such
as the non-conformist academies. Efforts to educate the artisan
classes in scientific and industrial subjects culminated later in
the creation of Mechanics Institutes. This intellectual ferment
affected Merseyside in common with other parts of the country.
Amongst the academies for non-comformists Warrington's held
a pre-eminent position and Liverpool had its Literary and
Philosophical Society. The names of industrial chemists
associated with the region in the eighteenth century include
Mathew Turner of the Warrington Academy, Joseph Priestly,
the Aikin Brothers, Thomas Bentley (Josiah Wedgewood's
partner) and Dr James Gerrard, a Liverpool surgeon who, in

the 1780s, was making sal ammoniac, sulphuric acid, Glauber salts and alkali. Even more significant was the arrival in Liverpool, also in the 1780s, of a Frenchman, Bourboulon de Boneuil, who set up a company at Garston to develop a sulphuric acid works. His firm was the first in Britain to combine the manufacture of soda and chlorine bleach although many other people were also experimenting. This firm only lasted a few years but its workers spread new ideas to bleachers. As yet, however, Britain was more favourably placed than France for supplies of natural alkali and the great impetus to chemical production did not come until the 1820s.

1800-1870

During this period Merseyside became more industrialised although that did not mean the abandonment of such occupations as fishing and agriculture: a good deal of land was reclaimed and farmed in the Wirral and in Cheshire farming continued to thrive. Agricultural produce was distributed by canals, by ferry and coastal shipping, by pack horse, and later by railways. The rich agricultural coastal plain of Lancashire continued to produce food and there were many food-producers around the growing urban centres supplying them with milk, vegetables, etc. At Fearnhead near Warrington a Liverpool shipowner, James Cropper, set up an experimental agricultural school.

Gradually, however, in some parts of the region serious battles developed between farming and manufacturing interests - especially due to the pollution from chemical works which damaged crops and animals as well as humans and polluted rivers, killing the fresh-water fish. The industrial revolution during this period was characterised by the wider application of power to industrial processes and to transport, by further innovations in mineral-fuel technology and by the development of engineering. All these elements were present in Merseyside's industrialisation but here a further ingredient appeared which not only had significant immediate effects but which also contained the germs of the post-1870 stage of industrialisation, namely the chemical revolution.

We have already seen its beginnings in the late eighteenth century - not at that time large enough to be impressive but in this period the chemical industry was firmly established in Liverpool, St Helens and Runcorn soon spreading to Warrington and Widnes and on to the Cheshire saltfields. Between 1800 and 1870 'heavy' chemicals predominated - first alkali derived from salt by the Leblanc process for the glass and soap industries and bleaching materials for the linen and cotton textile industries and, increasingly, sulphuric acid - unglamorous aspects of an industry associated with devastating pollution and most of whose products had no appeal whatsoever to the general public. None of Lancashire's alkali producers thought their products were

worth displaying at the Great Exhibition of 1851. And yet new
chemical technology acted as a catalyst for other industries and
increasingly determined those other industries' costs, technology
and potential growth rates; chemical exports also materially
assisted industrial growth in other countries.

The immediate stimulus to chemical manufacture in Merseyside
early in the nineteenth century was provided by the urgent
demand from the soap, glass and textile industries for improved
supplies of alkali and bleaching materials. To 1820 the bulk of
the alkali used in Merseyside was obtained from kelp, the ashes
of seaweed, imported from Scotland and Ireland. London soap
boilers on the other hand preferred to use Spanish barilla and,
when the duty on barilla was reduced in 1822, Merseyside soap-
makers feared that their rival producers would have a competitive
advantage. As it happened, it was Merseyside soap-boilers who
were, themselves, about to gain a great advantage for in 1822
James Muspratt came to Liverpool from Dublin, he settled in the
soap-making district and he began to produce soda on a large
scale using the Leblanc process.

The Leblanc process of soda manufacture from salt had been
patented in France just before the French Revolution and
sporadic small-scale attempts had occurred in Britain to develop
this method but Muspratt was the first manufacturer to produce
soda on a large scale in Britain and he is often regarded as the
'father' of the British heavy chemical industry. He had already
been much occupied in chemical experiments and production in
Dublin making hydrochloric acid and prussiate of potash before
starting production in Liverpool. His output was avidly consumed
by soap-boilers and, glass-makers also needed large amounts of
alkali. In 1828 Muspratt was joined by J.C. Gamble but there
were bitter complaints in Liverpool about pollution from the
works, and because of pressure from Liverpool Corporation
Muspratt and Gamble transferred their business to St Helens.
Later Muspratt moved to Widnes leaving Gamble producing in
St Helens which became an important centre of chemical production. By 1871 there were thirteen chemical plants in and around
St Helens, (in Parr, Ravenhead, Sutton and Gerard's Bridge).

Merseyside was an ideal site for chemical manufacture: salt
and coal were available locally and transport facilities were
adequate to bring in other materials such as brimstone or pyrites
from North Wales, Ireland and Spain and limestone from Derbyshire and North Wales. Excellent transport facilities also facilitated
the distribution of chemical products to local industries and for
export. The success of Muspratt's business stimulated other
entrepreneurs, including soap and glass-makers, to enter
chemical production. Soap-making spread along the Mersey with
the growth of firms such as Hudsons of Liverpool; Crosfields
in Warrington; John and Thomas Johnson, Hazlehursts and Hayes,
Ollier & Co. in Runcorn and many others. At St Helens Crosfields
started to make their own alkali; in Runcorn, Hazlehursts and
Johnsons both began to produce vitriol, and the Runcorn Soap

and Alkali Co. was formed.

From 1830 natural alkali had been eliminated from Merseyside soap production. This reduced costs and in fact Merseyside soap makers gained rapidly on their competitors. Because of the need to import materials soap was essentially a port industry, some eighty per cent of England's output being made in ports, especially on the banks of the Mersey, the Thames and the Tyne. In 1851 England's soap output totalled 81,570 tons. Of this 28,590 tons (thirty five per cent) was made in Liverpool, Warrington and Runcorn, 26,170 (thirty two per cent in the London area) and 4,780 tons (six per cent) in Newcastle and Gateshead. On average, Merseyside firms were larger than those in competing regions and they had considerable cost advantages. Local production gave them cheap alkali, their wages were lower than London's and they used imported palm oil in place of London's more expensive tallow. The import into Liverpool of palm oil rose from 55 tons in 1785 to 30,000 tons in 1841. Soap prices could therefore fall at a time when real wages were rising. Consumption per head rose from 5.9 lbs. a year in 1801 to over 10 lbs. in 1851 and domestic demand was further stimulated by the repeal of the excise tax on soap in 1853. Merseyside was particularly well-placed to meet the growing demand from the Lancashire textile industry and also from Ireland. Of 6,000 tons of soap exported from England in 1851 between seventy and eighty per cent went through Liverpool and a high proportion of this went to Ireland.

Glass-makers also benefited greatly from the improved supplies of alkali which lowered their production costs and they too began to make their own alkali especially in the St Helens area - the British Plate Glass Co. and the Eccleston Crown Glassworks both began to produce saltcake in the 1830s, the Union Plate Glassworks followed suit in the 1840s and later Pilkingtons set up their own chemical works.

Many consumers of alkali, therefore, started to supply their own needs but, in addition, specialist firms were created to produce alkali, bleaching materials and other chemicals in St Helens, Liverpool, Runcorn and Warrington. Then in the mid 1840s a very important new growth point appeared for chemical production, namely Widnes. In the 1830s Widnes was a collection of hamlets. According to the 1841 census of population the chief occupations were tool-making, watch-making, the cutting of files, wire-drawing, sail-making, the sale of beer and agriculture. Battles were, however, taking place between transport interests which put St Helens at a relative cost disadvantage. Widnes on the other hand could acquire coal through its access to railways and to an extension of the Sankey Canal, and salt from across the estuary via the Weaver navigation.

The comparative cost advantages of this site for chemical production attracted the attention of the so-called father of its chemical industry, John Hutchinson, who opened his works there in 1847 and Johnson McClellan of Liverpool who started to

produce borax and tartar salts there also in 1847. Suddenly
Widnes began to act like a magnet attracting outstanding scien-
tists and inventors from Britain and abroad - men such as
William Gossage, Henry Deacon, Holbrook Gaskell, James
Muspratt's sons, and later J.T. Brunner and Ludwig Mond. In
1851 William Gossage, a soap manufacturer, who had also experimented with the production of soda, sulphuric acid and copper
manufacture, came to Widnes and devised a process that cut the
cost of soap from 6d per pound to 2d per pound. By the end
of this period he had become one of the largest soap manufacturers in the North of England exporting as much as 15,000
tons of soap a year. He also produced soda and other chemicals.
In 1853 Henry Deacon and Holbrook Gaskell started to produce
soda and James Muspratt's sons also set up business in Widnes.

Other chemical products also began to be made in Widnes. In
the 1840s James Muspratt had experimented (unsuccessfully)
with the production of artificial fertilisers after encountering
the famous German chemist Justus von Liebig at the British
Association meeting held in Liverpool in 1837. Other manufacturers, however, took up the challenge and in 1861 the Lancashire Manure Co. opened a factory in Widnes. Then, too, in
both Widnes and St Helens chemical and copper production
drew closer together. Alkali producers, needing sulphur,
imported much of their supplies from Sicily. The price of
Sicilian sulphur however rose sharply so alkali producers
switched to obtaining their sulphur from copper pyrites - and,
of course, copper producers also obtained sulphur as a by-
product of their own copper production. Thus, for example,
Lamberts Copper Works was established in 1850 in Widnes to
use pyrites after sulphur had been extracted and later its name
was changed to the Widnes Alkali Company; and in St Helens
the Bridgewater Alkali Works built in the early 1850s also
demonstrated the close inter-dependence of alkali and copper
production.

By 1873 Widnes had some twenty chemical factories, a copper
works, a soap factory and two iron works. The chemical factories
were operated on a moderately large scale. Hutchinson's and
Gaskell, Deacon's each employed 500 men and Muspratt's had a
work force of 240. The chemical industry as a whole in fact
made considerable progress during this period and developed
sizeable export markets especially in America. Sixty per cent
of Britain's total output of soda was exported and between
thirty and forty per cent of her total output of bleaching
powder was exported. Liverpool was the main port for such
chemicals. Nationally the production of alkali was particularly
concentrated in Lancashire and North-East England: of 83
works using the Leblanc process in 1864 some 36 were in
Lancashire and 20 in North-East England. Some indication of
the relative outputs of the two regions can be seen from the
following table although Haber's heading 'Lancashire' also
includes some production in the Midlands, Wales, Southern

England and Ireland and his heading 'Tyneside' includes
Scotland.

Table 4.1: British Alkali Production

| | 000 tons | | | |
| | 1852 | | 1878 | |
	Lancashire	Tyneside	Lancashire	Tyneside
Bleaching Powder	3.1	10.0	77.1	27.9
Soda Crystals	12.2	28.8	47.7	123.2
Soda Ash	37.1	35.1	120.9	87.1
Caustic Soda	not available		98.8	2.0

Source: L.F. Haber, *The Chemical Industry during the
Nineteenth Century* (Oxford University Press, 1958) p. 59.

The greatest problem, however, associated with chemical
production was severe pollution due to the escape of hydrochloric acid fumes and the dumping of large amounts of waste
which was washed into streams and filled the atmosphere with
a smell like rotten eggs. Naturally, local inhabitants objected
and at a very early stage Muspratt was driven to leave Liverpool. Around St Helens there were continuous complaints and
farmers and landowners sued manufacturers for damage to
their land, crops and animals. In Widnes, John Hutchinson bought
up as much land as he could as dumps for his own waste and
he leased tracts as dumps for other manufacturers. Here, however, the chorus of protests steadily increased and one of
Hutchinson's incidental enterprises, the Widnes Gas and Water
Company, came under severe public censure for the pollution
of its water.

The battle over pollution was long, hard and often bitter but
at least manufacturers and industrial chemists could not be
accused of not trying to find solutions both by experimenting
with alternative ways of making soda to replace the Leblanc
process and also by trying to find commercial uses for the
pollutants. The alternative process most favoured was the
ammonia soda process which, after decades of unsuccessful
attempts by many inventors, was eventually successfully
developed in 1863 by a Belgian chemist, Ernest Solvay. In 1872
Ludwig Mond acquired the rights to work this process in
Britain and together with Brunner set up Brunner Mond which
was to play a key role in Britain's chemical industry after 1870.

The other approach to pollution was the conversion of hydrochloric fumes and sulphur into by-products and again there was
widespread experimentation over a considerable period. Several
successes were registered. William Gossage, the soap manufacturer, produced the Gossage tower to condense acid fumes.
Another solution was to use the hydrochloric acid to produce
bleaching powder for which there was a long-term demand
from cotton producers and a new and growing demand from

paper producers as new technology in paper-making led to the use of esparto grass from the 1860s. David Gamble devised a way of producing bleaching powder in St Helens but it was Widnes that became Britain's largest producer of bleaching powder.

Continuing complaints about pollution brought government intervention. There was an enquiry by a House of Lords Committee[10] and, to meet this challenge, Hutchinson had organised the Widnes Alkali Manufacturers' Association in 1859. In 1863 the government acted – the Alkali Act compelled manufacturers to ensure that 95 per cent of the hydrochloric acid they produced did not escape.

The period to 1870 was an eventful one in the industry's development. Although at this time it was largely ancillary to other industries, producing for other manufacturers rather than making consumer goods itself, the foundations were laid through these and many other experiments for the great proliferation of new chemical products and processes after 1870. The endless battles against pollution resulted in more by-products and in the Solvay ammonia soda process which was soon to oust the Leblanc process. Other experiments were taking place in the use of electrolysis in place of heat and from these the electrochemical industry was to emerge; there was evidence of the beginnings of the great blossoming in pharmacology; a few experiments were taking place in the production of chemical fertilisers in Widnes and in the processing of Peruvian guano in Wallasey. There were even during this period some experiments in coal-tar chemistry in which Germany was later to predominate.

The initial stimulus to chemical production came, as we have seen, from the needs of soap and glass manufacturers. Although some glass manufacture continued in towns such as Warrington where flint, watch, bottle and crown glass were made, by 1830 Merseyside's glass industry was largely concentrated in St Helens where the plate glass-works at Ravenhead loomed large over the industry though two new competitors opened up in the 1830s – the Union Plate Glass Company and the Manchester and Liverpool Plate Glass Company. In 1826 the St Helens Crown Glass Company (later to become Pilkington Bros.) was created to produce window glass and during the course of the nineteenth century St Helens was to displace North East England as Britain's main producer of window glass largely through the exertions of Peter Greenall and the Pilkingtons. By the 1860s there were only two other important British producers of window glass – Chances of Smethwick and Hartleys of Sunderland although there was growing competition from imports of Belgian glass. The manufacture of flint glass was established in St Helens on a smaller scale and after the middle of the century the output of bottle glass began to expand. By 1867 William Pilkington claimed that St Helens made two thirds of Britain's plate glass, one third of her window glass and one tenth of her bottle and flint glass.

The chemical industry's development was, however, not only closely bound up with that of the industries consuming its output; also important were the industries supplying its raw materials, especially salt and coal. The Cheshire saltfields' main markets were chemical producers and export markets and their output rose from 150,000 tons in 1800 to a million tons by 1870. The coal industry had far wider markets - demand escalated because of the needs of salt and soap boilers, glass, copper and chemical producers, the metallurgical industries and steam engines in factories, mines, locomotives and steamships. The appetite for coal was seemingly insatiable and extensive deposits were still available both inside and immediately outside Merseyside's boundaries in the south-west Lancashire coalfield.

By 1800 the links between coal, salt and Liverpool enterprise were already strong: as we have seen Liverpool salt entrepreneurs had acquired coal mines and St Helens coal proprietors began to acquire salt works in Cheshire. The two industries were very closely inter-connected to the 1830s but then their interests began to diverge again. By 1845 less than 200,000 tons of the 700,000 tons of coal transported from St Helens down the Mersey by canal and rail went to salt works. The total output of the South-West Lancashire coalfield rose steeply. By the mid 1840s it had probably risen to about a million tons a year, as a result of the extension of existing works and the sinking of new pits. This output was consumed by Merseyside's heavy industries, by salt works and by export markets.

The most important part of the coalfield was now the Wigan section which was linked to Liverpool by the Leeds-Liverpool Canal. Later in the century railways superseded the canal. By 1850, the counties of Lancashire and Cheshire were producing just under ten million tons of the U.K. annual output of sixty five million tons and by 1870 Lancashire's and Cheshire's output amounted to 14.7 million tons out of a U.K. output of 110.4 million.

The links between copper production and the chemical industry have already been mentioned. Nationally South Wales had moved into the forefront of copper production but Merseyside's industry continued to thrive in St Helens, Runcorn, Widnes and Wallasey and, in addition to smelting and refining, the range of products increased to meet the needs of other industries including such things as rods and plates for steam locomotives, copper-covered rollers for calico printing and brass pans.

The output of metal goods of all sorts continued and many new metal and engineering products were added to the range of Merseyside's output. The long-established watch and clock industry continued especially in Prescot, although in Liverpool output began to decline after 1850 in face of foreign competition. The production of files and small tools such as vices, chisels, gauges and pliers continued to thrive and although tools assisted in the mechanisation of other industries, tool-making itself was not

mechanised because, as yet, mechanical methods could not
achieve the great accuracy that was necessary. The vigorously
growing engineering industries in South Lancashire constituted
a very important market for tools of all sorts.

The production of traditional products such as iron cooking
pots continued unabated but in addition there was a considerable
growth in heavy metal goods, engineering products and shipbuilding. Iron foundries were located throughout the region in
Liverpool, St Helens, Warrington, Runcorn, Widnes, Birkenhead
and Wallasey. In the early years of the nineteenth century the
demand for cannon was still pressing and throughout this period
the development of ports and shipping necessitated a supply of
heavy anchors, chain cables, metal bollards, the metal parts of
capstans, pitch boilers etc. Wire was needed for many purposes
and new uses were developed especially in Warrington where
wire-weaving replaced the declining sail-cloth industry and
wire was used for all sorts of winding cables for collieries,
cranes and ships and for wire meshes for purposes such as
mattresses and chairs. One of Warrington's leading firms in
this sphere was Rylands. In 1856 this firm supplied material
for the first (unsuccessful) Transatlantic Telegraph Cable;
in 1863 it created the Warrington Wire Company to produce
its own rod to replace supplies from Shropshire and Staffordshire and soon afterwards a mill was added to produce sheet
iron.

The demand for nails was still pressing as in the eighteenth
century: as building accelerated in the region so too did the
need for nails, although after 1830 hand-made nails were displaced by machine-made ones. Building also called for a growing
supply of both structural and decorative metal work and for
metal equipment. All sorts of buildings contained metal in place
of wood, partly for increased strength and partly in the hope
of reducing fire risks. Warehouses were constructed with metal
frames – the crowning glory of this type of construction in
Merseyside being the famous Albert Dock complex, but there
were many other iron-framed and columned warehouses too. ·
The Liverpool Sailors Home included structural metal, columns,
galleries and rails. Many commercial buildings such as the
Albany and Oriel Chambers had iron balconies and other iron
components and under the influence of John Cragg, owner of
the Mersey Iron Foundry, Thomas Rickman designed churches
containing structural iron-work, iron windows, fences etc.
Between 1813 and 1821 he built St Michaels in the Hamlet,
Liverpool, St Georges in Everton, and St Mary's of Birkenhead.
On a humbler plane it was possible to buy prefabricated iron
buildings though these were not architecturally designed. The
catalogue of an iron-works at Garston includes a wide variety
of standardised metal buildings for export ranging from huts
and small bungalows to sizeable churches. Structural metal was
also needed for building stations, factories and bridges. Building also created a market for small metal goods such as window

frames, pipes and gutters, fences and gates, iron ranges and gas ovens and door fittings and, part of the elegance of the Georgian era in house-building stemmed from wrought iron-work - especially balconies and railings.

The development of engineering was extremely important during this period as the mechanisation of industry and transport called for machinery of all sorts, stationary steam engines, steam cranes and locomotives. Merseyside's pioneering role in the development of railways led inevitably to the local production of railway equipment - there were engine-works in Birkenhead, Warrington and nearby in Newton-le-Willows. Perhaps even more important were the developments in marine engineering and ship-building. In terms of tonnage the wooden sailing ship pre-dominated to 1860 but, from 1800, Britain's shipbuilding industry was faced with growing competition from Canadian and U.S. builders who enjoyed lower costs and far superior timber supplies. Many of Britain's ships were imported - by 1835 about half of Liverpool's registered ships had been built in North America. Many other ships had been bought new or second hand from other British ports so that Liverpool's shipbuilding industry was subjected to severe competition. Its output was very erratic varying between 1800 and 1835 from as low as 610 tons in 1808 due to wartime dislocations to over 6,000 tons in 1835.[11] The number of shipbuilders also varied from some 16 in 1805 to 24 in the early 1830s at which time Liverpool probably built a little over 5 per cent of the U.K.'s total output of ships.

There were also many small builders scattered along the estuary, rivers and canals and the industry particularly began to develop in Birkenhead. From Merseyside's point of view the most important developments were experiments in building iron ships and in the use of steam propulsion. There were many early attempts to produce marine engines; for example as early as 1816 the Coalbrookdale Foundry in Liverpool, which was at that time producing cannon and equipment for West Indian sugar mills, turned to the production of marine engines, but pride of place in Merseyside's shipbuilding history at this time must be accorded to Lairds shipbuilding yard at Birkenhead (now Cammell Lairds) which played a leading role in switching shipbuilding from timber to iron and from sail to steam. Experiments in steam propulsion had taken place in Britain in the eighteenth century but even in the early nineteenth century steamships were largely confined to sheltered waters and to relatively short journeys on lakes, rivers and coastal services. One of the important experi-menters on Merseyside was William Laird who established a boiler works on the edge of Wallasey Pool in 1824. Soon afterwards he added a shipyard and in 1828 he was joined by his son, John. They concentrated on iron ships and especially on ships which could be dismantled for delivery to relatively inaccessible customers and put together again on arrival at their final destination. In 1833 they built an iron paddle-wheel vessel, the *Lady Lansdowne* for the City of Dublin Steam Packet Co. -

it was sent to Ireland in pieces and put together on Loch Derg.
Two others were built for the East India Company's exploration
of the River Euphrates - the parts were shipped to Syria, carried
across the desert by camels and reconstructed on the banks of
the Euphrates by engineers, ship-builders, joiners and other
craftsmen sent for the purpose. For many years virtually every
ship built by Lairds was experimental as they increased the
size of ships, and developed new equipment such as screw
propellers. By 1840 they had constructed some thirty-two iron
vessels and they were responsible for the first iron vessels
used in India, China, South America, the U.S.A. and Egypt.
From the 1850s the transition in Britain to iron and steam was
more rapid and Lairds were well placed to expand their building
on the basis of their very considerable technical know-how.
Amongst the most famous of their ships at this time was the
Alabama, the celebrated Confederate war-ship and blockade-
runner during the American Civil War.

Although Laird's yard became Merseyside's pre-eminent shipbuilder and marine engineer it was by no means alone. Other
yards and marine engineers appeared on the south side of the
estuary to build and repair ships - for example, the Canada
Works Co. Ltd. which began as an engineering firm and built
steam locomotives before turning to shipbuilding; Clover,
Clayton & Co. primarily engaged in ship-repairing; Cochran &
Co. and Taylor & Co. specialised in steam yachts, launches
and barges. On the Liverpool side of the estuary the building
of docks had engulfed many former shipyards. The numbers
of ocean-going ships built in Liverpool steadily declined to
1860 but on the south side of Liverpool the building of smaller
boats thrived and further inland along the estuary and along
the canals and rivers were a multitude of small boat builders
and repairers. The building of coasting vessels was important
at Runcorn and the Bridgewater Canal Company built and
repaired its barges there; small boats were built at Widnes;
Warrington had an early shipyard for building iron-boats; the
Weaver was lined with small boat builders and some small boats
were built at St Helens, Parr and Newburgh.

Another branch of the heavy metal industries that grew
quickly from the mid-nineteenth century in Merseyside was the
production of galvanised iron sheets using Staffordshire iron,
foreign spelter and hydrochloric acid from St Helens and Widnes
chemical works. In this line Merseyside quickly became one of
Britain's leading producers - just after the end of this period,
of eleven new galvanised sheet works built in Britain 1876-81,
five were in Liverpool and one in Warrington.

The fortunes of Merseyside's other staple eighteenth-century
industries varied a good deal during the period 1800-1870.
Warrington's sail-cloth industry suffered a rapid decline and
Merseyside's pottery industry experienced a somewhat slower
running down. In Liverpool the industry had passed its peak
by 1800 but there were some surviving potteries and some new

ones in other parts of the region. In St Helens the industry
held its own producing pipes, tiles and stoneware; one Wallasey
pottery specialised in flower pots and drain pipes and the
Seacombe Pottery made earthenware, stoneware, coloured
printed ware and later Parian ware. Rope-making continued
although some rope-makers turned to wire ropes and cables in
addition to or instead of their traditional product - for example
Garnock, Bibby of Liverpool and B.B. Glover of St Helens.

The refining and processing of sugar and tobacco continued
to thrive - the latter in Liverpool and the former in Liverpool,
Warrington and Wallasey and brewing remained a very important
occupation although it was increasingly concentrated in large
units in St Helens, Liverpool, Runcorn, Ormskirk and the
Wirral. The tanning industry around Warrington, Liverpool
and Runcorn, originally based on local hides, skins and tanning
materials now expanded rapidly to process imported hides with
imported tanning materials and the milling industry too switched
increasingly to imported grain.

Early in the nineteenth century supplies of grain were
restricted by the French Wars and the 1815 Corn Laws which
prevented import until the price of home-produced grain reached
80s. a quarter. During the period when the Corn Laws were in
force, two-thirds of the grain processed was home-produced
although supplies were increasingly coming from the Isle of Man
and Ireland. After the Repeal of the Corn Laws and with the
growing colonisation and cultivation of virgin lands abroad, the
flow of imported grains gradually swelled into a torrent and
included maize for animal feed as well as grain for human consumption. As supplies of imported grain exceeded home supplies
milling concentrated more and more in the ports especially in
Liverpool and Warrington and, increasingly, in Birkenhead. The
size of mills steadily grew and steam-power began to replace
wind- and water-power although windmills on the hill-tops held
their own better than those on the plains and there were some
interesting experiments in combining more than one source of
energy. At Bromborough Pool, for example, the Ellis family
had mills which utilised a combination of tide-, wind- and steam-
power. After 1860 steam-power predominated and processing
was concentrated more and more in a small number of large mills.

Amongst the industries considered in this chapter there were
few that did not have connections with the building industry
either as suppliers of materials or because they needed industrial
and commercial buildings of all sorts and houses for their
workers: indeed building became one of Merseyside's more
important industries. Mention has already been made of the
growing use of metal for building purposes, but, of course,
many other components were needed too: the glass industry
supplied windows, the pottery industry made tiles, pipes and
stoneware; Welsh slate quarries provided roofing; lime kilns
and cement works were needed and there was an enormous demand
for bricks. There were extensive brickworks in St Helens,

Runcorn, Rainford and the Wirral and smaller ones throughout
the region. For prestige buildings and for many large structural
works stone was needed and there were plentiful local supplies
of some types: there were stone quarries at Runcorn, Bebington,
Bromborough and Eccleston. The engineer Telford praised
Widnes' stone in 1817 and at Woolton and Rainhill there were red
sandstone quarries. Jesse Hartley the famous dock builder had,
however, to venture beyond the boundaries of Merseyside to
find the great blocks of granite that were such a notable feature
of his dock walls, piers and lodges. Despite a growing use of
structural metal, timber remained a major building material,
and both for building and for other purposes supplies had
increasingly to be imported because of the decline in home-
produced timber. Great timber yards appeared throughout the
region and special docks were built in Liverpool (the Brunswick,
and then the Canada Docks) to handle imports. Birkenhead also
participated in the import trade.

The assembly of all these components into buildings was largely
undertaken by small building firms created, for the most part,
by men who had started their working lives as bricklayers or
stonemasons, millwrights, carpenters, joiners and cabinet
makers. Especially in and around Liverpool and the Wirral Welsh
immigrants played a disproportionately large role in supplying
building skills and many Irish immigrants became unskilled
labourers. The typical builder of small houses started as a
craftsman, he saved a small sum, acquired a plot of land and
started to build. Large estates were broken into building plots
and later land companies were formed to sell land and in some
cases to make advances to builders although much larger
supplies of capital came in the form of loans and mortgages
arranged by solicitors. Some working class houses were built
for businessmen who could only find a labour force by supplying
housing but many houses were built by speculative builders
for rent. From the mid-nineteenth century building societies
were formed to enable artisans to buy their own houses and
throughout, many larger houses for the middle and upper classes
were either built to order or for sale.

For much of the period 1800-1870 there was a shortage of
houses in most areas because of the rapid growth of population
in urban centres. Generally speaking therefore the building
industry was prosperous and was hard-pressed to cope with
the demands made on it as we shall see in the next chapter and
this was partly responsible for the fact that Merseyside had
the dubious claim to fame as the home of the original 'Jerry'
builder. The Liverpool firm of Jerry Brothers, Builders and
Contractors, was responsible for many hurriedly-built poor
quality houses with showy exteriors and their name became
applied to this type of building.

NOTES

1. W. Moss, *The Liverpool Guide* (1796; facsimile edition City of Liverpool Public Relations Department, 1974), p. 96.

2. Ibid., pp. 12-3.

3. Ibid., p. 96.

4. The importance of coal and salt to the region is shown in T.C. Barker, 'Lancashire Coal, Cheshire Salt and the Rise of Liverpool', *Transactions of the Historic Society of Lancashire and Cheshire*, vol. 103 (1951), pp. 83-101.

5. T.S. Willan, *The Navigation of the River Weaver in the Eighteenth Century* (Chetham Society, Manchester, 1951), pp. 39-40.

6. These are the divisions adopted in J. Langton, *Geographical Change and Industrial Revolution: Coal Mining in South West Lancashire 1590-1799* (Cambridge University Press, Cambridge, 1979) pp. 36-7. The output figures quoted below are from ibid., pp. 93, 154.

7. T.C. Barker and J.R. Harris, *A Merseyside Town in the Industrial Revolution. St Helens 1750-1900* (Liverpool University Press, 1954), passim.

8. The history of Thomas William's activities in Merseyside is told in J.R. Harris, *The Copper King. A Biography of Thomas Williams of Llanidan* (Liverpool University Press, 1964).

9. T.S. Ashton, *An Eighteenth Century Industrialist. Peter Stubs of Warrington 1756-1806* (Manchester University Press, 1939).

10. *Report of the Select Committee of the House of Lords to Inquire into Injury from Noxious Vapours*, *Parliamentary Papers XIV*, 1862.

11. F. Neal, 'Liverpool Shipping 1815-1835', M.A. dissertation, University of Liverpool, 1962, p. 62.

Chapter 5

LIFE ON MERSEYSIDE 1750-1870

The creation of large industrial and commercial complexes
involved massive investment in the building of factories,
foundries, glass, chemical and soap works, mills, warehouses,
docks, shipyards, stations and all the paraphernalia of modern
industry and transport. It was also inevitably accompanied by
a rapid build-up in the number of workers of all sorts - manual,
clerical, managerial and entrepreneurial; at the same time the
quality of life for this growing population was materially influenced by industrial and commercial development - both for
good and for bad.

When, however, one tries to produce information about the
growing population it is very difficult to discover satisfactory
statistics to show the extent, the distribution, the exact timing
and the sources of population growth. Before the first census
of population in 1801 estimates of population were very hit and
miss and even within the period 1801 to 1871 there were changing
methods of census-taking, changes in the bases of enumeration
and in tabulation. Different results are obtained by using
registration districts, or administrative areas or ecclesiastical
parishes. Several industrial towns only came into existence
late in the period growing on the basis of villages or hamlets.
Even by apparently taking the same units for successive censuses
one is liable to find that the boundaries of those units have
changed over time: to take one obvious example, the 'Liverpool'
of 1801 was a different geographical area from the 'Liverpool'
of 1871. Migratory movements are also inadequately charted: it
is not possible to make even moderately satisfactory calculations
about migration until 1841.[1]

Because of all these qualifications it is best *not* to treat
population statistics as very exact figures or to place too much
emphasis on totals at any one time but rather to use them to
indicate the most important trends in the population of Merseyside's main constituent parts. Table 5.1 shows clearly the very
rapid upward trend in population in the region and in particular
the numerical predominance of Liverpool and its immediate environs
(West Derby). Together they accounted for between sixty and
seventy per cent of the region's population. Liverpool had been
growing fairly rapidly even in the eighteenth century. According
to one estimate the population increased from about 20,000 in
1750 to around 54,000 in 1790. At the time of the first census
in 1801 it was recorded as 77,653. By 1861 it had nearly reached
270,000 but its rate of growth was falling off and by 1871 it had

been overtaken by West Derby. On the Wirral, Birkenhead
was the most important growth point especially after 1841. Its
population rose from under 500 in 1801 to nearly 11,000 in 1841
and it rocketed to nearly 43,000 in 1871. Together with its
neighbours Tranmere and Wallasey it accounted for nearly
four-fifths of the Wirral's total population in 1871.

Merseyside's other towns also grew but at varying rates and
on different time-scales. Warrington experienced a moderately
steady threefold increase between 1801 and 1871 from just over
10,000 to around 30,000. The growth of the town of Runcorn
(which was only part of the registration district in Table 5.1)
showed a ninefold increase from 1,379 in 1801 to 12,444 in 1871.
Widnes (including Farnworth, Appleton and Cronton) grew
slowly from 1801 to 1851 (1,063 to 3,211) but then the population
rose to 6,905 by 1861 and to 14,359 by 1871, well over a fourfold increase in twenty years. The figures for St Helens present
greater problems because for some time the town's population
statistics were not recorded separately from those for Windle,
Parr, Sutton and Eccleston. It seems likely, however, that the
population may have numbered around 4,000 in 1821. It probably
doubled between 1831 and 1845 and doubled again between 1845
and 1870 to reach around 25,000.

Where did all these people come from? Natural increase
accounted for some growth. In the 1860s for example the rate of
natural increase in central Merseyside accounted for a little under
half of the population growth - the remainder being due to
immigration. There was, in fact, a great deal of population
movement both within the region and from other regions. Waves
of migrants from rural areas within Merseyside surged into the
towns; town-dwellers moved from one town to another or from
town centres to suburbs and dormitory areas. Other people
came from outside the region - from all over north-west England,
from Cornwall, Devon and Somerset, from Middlesex and London;
there were strong movements from North Wales and Scotland
but by far the largest flood of immigrants came from Ireland,
especially during the potato famine of 1845-7.

In 1861 nearly half of Liverpool's population and over sixty
per cent of Birkenhead's could be classed as immigrant (i.e.
born in another county or country). In Liverpool nearly a
quarter of the total population was Irish, four per cent Scottish
and two and a quarter per cent from North Wales. Of Birkenhead's total population, fourteen and a half per cent were Irish,
nearly five per cent Scottish and four and a half per cent from
North Wales. Many of these migrants settled in national groups -
Irish Catholics were found in heavy concentrations in Birkenhead for example and in the Scotland Road district of Liverpool;
Irish Protestants in Kirkdale and Everton; the Welsh in Everton,
Toxteth and Wavertree. Many of the Irish immigrants however
only stayed near the port for a short time before re-emigrating
to the U.S.A. in search of better opportunities or moving inland
to industrial towns in search of work. From the early 1830s

Table 5.1: Merseyside Population 1801-71

Registration District[1]	1801	1821	1841	1851	1871
Cheshire			Thousands		
Runcorn[2]	11.4	16.2	22.9	25.8	30.5
Wirral[3]	9.4	12.2	31.8	57.2	102.9
Lancashire					
Liverpool	77.7	119.0	223.0	258.2	238.4
West Derby[4]	12.0	32.4	88.7	153.3	342.9
Prescot[5]	20.7	28.2	43.7	56.1	92.6
Ormskirk[6]	18.5	25.6	35.0	38.3	59.3
Total	149.7	233.6	445.1	588.9	866.6
Cheshire			Percentage		
Runcorn	7.6	6.9	5.2	4.4	3.5
Wirral	6.3	5.2	7.1	9.7	11.9
Lancashire					
Liverpool	51.9	50.9	50.1	43.9	27.5
West Derby	8.0	13.9	19.9	26.0	39.6
Prescot	13.8	12.1	9.8	9.5	10.7
Ormskirk	12.4	11.0	7.9	6.5	6.8
	100.0	100.0	100.0	100.0	100.0

Source: *Census of Great Britain 1851, Census of England and Wales 1871.*
1. These are the 'Superintendent Registrar's' Districts.
2. Budworth, Daresbury, Runcorn and Frodsham.
3. Neston, Eastham, Woodchurch, Wallasey and Birkenhead. In 1871 Birkenhead, Tranmere and Wallasey were separated from Wirral and called the 'Birkenhead District'. For comparative purposes the figures have been re-combined here.
4. Toxteth Park, Everton, Walton, Crosby, Litherland, West Derby and Wavertree.
5. Includes Hale, Much Woolton, Huyton, Farnworth, Prescot, St Helens and Rainford.
6. Bickerstaffe, Aughton, Halsall, Formby, North Meols, Tarleton, Scarisbrick, Ormskirk and Lathom.

St Helens had a growing Irish settlement living virtually in isolation from the rest of the community and, as the chemical industry grew, Widnes drew extensively on Irish labour. In all areas the Irish tended to gravitate towards the heavy, unskilled labouring jobs in building, digging and manufacturing.

The rapid build-up of population in the region necessitated the pouring of vast amounts of resources into housing. By 1870

sprawling conurbations had eroded rural areas, swamped
villages and intruded into the coastal regions with their attractive holiday resorts and clusters of fishermen's cottages. Liverpool, already a moderate town in 1750, continued to sprawl
inland and along the estuary like a giant octopus swallowing
whole villages and hamlets. Warrington grew into a large manufacturing town. Sizeable new industrial towns sprang up such
as St Helens, Runcorn and Widnes and dormitory areas multiplied
rapidly. In the process Merseyside became notorious for its
pollution.

The growth of dirty, smelly industries and lack of sanitation
in working-class areas created serious problems and attracted
widespread publicity especially after 1820 when the rate of
population growth, and hence of building, accelerated rapidly.
Lower working-class housing generally became bad and Liverpool
in particular achieved a great deal of adverse publicity in the
reports of the Commissioners who investigated the health of
towns in the early 1840s. They branded Liverpool as one of the
worst towns in the country for over-crowding, cellar dwellings,
unhealthy courts and insanitary streets. Some 130 years later
Liverpool was once more singled out as an area with some of
the most appalling housing conditions in Britain.[2] In some other
parts of Merseyside too conditions were indeed grim by 1870:
soot, chemical fumes and mounds of poisonous waste shrivelled
trees and natural vegetation, damaged crops, poisoned animals,
eroded buildings and caused bronchial and sinus complaints
amongst human beings. Widnes earned the title of the dirtiest
and ugliest town in England and Runcorn was described as a
town covered by a 'murky cowl'.[3] The river became dank and
foul, its banks slimy with sewage and chemical effluvium: it
was often said that anyone falling into the Mersey would be
poisoned before he drowned.

Such conditions blighted the lives of large numbers of the
working classes and publicity was focussed on the worst
features. Many commentators ignored the beautiful country
districts, the extensive estates of attractive villas and comfortable dormitory towns, the public parks and Georgian and
Regency squares, the model villages, the new towns and garden
resorts. The area has also a legacy of lovely manor houses and
halls, some oustanding civic, commercial and industrial buildings
and a wide range of church architecture. Certainly Merseyside's
black reputation from the mid-nineteenth century is in stark
contrast to its popular image in the late eighteenth and early
nineteenth centuries when it was renowned for its beautiful
health resorts, scenic views, fresh breezes and sea bathing.

Around the estuary and along the coast attractive resorts
catered for the national fashion for sea bathing confirmed by
George III's patronage at Weymouth. At the northern extremity
of Merseyside at South Hawes in the parish of North Meols, an
inn, called South Port, was built in 1798 to cater for sea bathers
and from this Southport developed quickly as a favourite bathing

place with pure unadulterated water and mild temperatures.
Soon a mile of beach was lined with bathing huts and, nearby,
were warm and cold indoor sea-water baths. As the fishing
industry declined along this part of the coast fishermen eagerly
turned to providing trips for tourists in pleasure boats. From
a population of under 2,000 in 1801, the resort grew so rapidly
that by the 1820s it was the third largest watering place sur-
passed only by Brighton and Great Yarmouth. It catered
initially for the better-off holiday makers, the retired and other
well-to-do residents drawn not only from Merseyside but also
from Manchester and the Lancashire cotton towns. In the words
of Robinson's *Southport Guide* (1849) it was a 'quiet place of
repose . . . convenient to our unhealthy manufacturing towns,
where for a while the founders of wealth and prosperity of the
country may cease from their labours and regain vigour of mind
and body'. Gradually it acquired all the appendages of a seaside
town – a promenade, a theatre, a pier and a Winter Garden and,
by 1871, its population had grown to over 18,000. Between
Southport and Liverpool other sea bathing centres sprang up
at Crosby, Waterloo and Seaforth and a mere three miles north
of Liverpool lay the village of Bootle where 'genteel company
resort for sea bathing and sea air'. [4]
Although it had to be admitted that in Liverpool itself there
was a handful of offensive occupations, notably the preparation
of whale oil, which caused obnoxious smells, and the boiling of
salt, which generated large quantities of soot, William Moss
regarded these as isolated exceptions. [5] He praised Liverpool
for its 'pleasant and salubrious situation', for the circumstances
which 'conspired' to make it 'very healthful', for the cool and
refreshing sea breezes which 'in hot weather, render it a
desirable retreat from the interior of the country at those
seasons, aided by the salutory recreation of sea-bathing'. [6]
From 1796 sea-bathing was supplemented by public sea-water
baths and there were also cool, temperate and warm baths
supplied with fresh well-water by the steam engine of an
adjoining cotton manufactory. According to another guide,
Kaye's *Stranger in Liverpool*, the 'sweet, romantic dell, well
known by the name of the Dingle, a favourite pleasure resort'
lay further inland along the estuary and between Garston and
Hale there was 'beautiful and picturesque scenery'. [7] Eighteenth-
century Widnes also became a pleasant river resort for local
inhabitants and by the early nineteenth century Runcorn was
attracting longer-distance tourists with its mild climate, salt-
bathing, 'salubrious situation . . . and air impregnated with
health' and 'beautifully romantic and picturesque scenery'. [8]
Moving back along the south side of the estuary towards the
sea an attempt to develop a resort at Ellesmere Port fizzled out
after 1801 because of the commercial development accompanying
Telford's completion of a tidal basin at the entrance to the
Ellesmere Canal. Not so nearby Eastham, which was famed for
its beauty and magnificent woods: Liverpudlians came by ferry

boat to enjoy the scenery and fresh air. The ferry boat also
played its part in the rise of other resorts along the estuary
especially after 1815 when steam ferries increased in number
and reliability. From the mid-century cheap rail fares gave
another great boost to the tourist and day-tripper industries
throughout the region. Gradually the south side of the estuary
was lined with resorts - Rock Ferry, Seacombe, Egremont,
Wallasey and New Brighton from whose promenades, parks and
piers, visitors and residents alike could enjoy the air and
the river scenery.

Across the Wirral on the Dee estuary sea-bathing, fresh air
and magnificent panoramic views of Wales awaited visitors to
the small ports earlier developed to cater for sea travellers to
North Wales and Ireland, a traffic which had started to decline
with the silting up of the Dee. By the early nineteenth century,
Neston, the largest town in the Wirral with a population of
3,596 had inns for travellers and gaming parlours, coffee houses,
assembly rooms and a theatre to amuse travellers awaiting favourable winds. The important eighteenth century port, Parkgate,
already celebrated for sea-bathing, also became a fashionable
resort and Hoylake (now linked with West Kirby) developed
first as a bathing resort from 1792 and then added other holiday
attractions as its role as an embarkation port for Ireland declined.

In addition to meeting tourists' needs there was growing
pressure for living accommodation for people of all classes who
worked in the region's trade, industry and transport systems.
In 1750 housing and living conditions were quite reasonable by
contemporary standards. Much of the region was rural, the two
largest conurbations being Liverpool and Warrington. Warrington
was described by Defoe as a large populous 'old built Town, but
rich and full of good Country Tradesmen' and of Liverpool he
said 'there is no town in England, London excepted, that can
equal Liverpoole for the fineness of the Streets, and beauty of
the Buildings; many of the Houses are all of Free Stone, and
completely finished; and all the rest (of the new part I mean)
of Brick, as handsomely built as London it self'. [9]

Early in the eighteenth century it was customary for Liverpool's merchants and wealthy citizens to live in the centre of
the town and similarly, as manufacturing towns developed,
manufacturers initially lived in close proximity to the source
of their income; the Patten family, for example, played a leading
part in developing both the copper industry and the Mersey-
Irwell navigation and in 1750 Thomas Patten built his beautiful
home, Bank Hall, in the centre of Warrington - some 122 years
later it was sold to Warrington Corporation to become Warrington
Town Hall. Somewhat lower down the social scale, tradespeople
usually had their shops or warehouses below or adjacent to their
homes and large numbers of craftsmen's workshops were incorporated in their houses - often on the top floor with continuous windows to catch the maximum light.

As population grew and wealth increased the upper and middle classes tended to move out of the centre of town first into pleasant suburbs where attractive villas and expensive mansions were built by the wealthy merchants, manufacturers, shipowners and brokers and comfortable houses for the white collar workers. The density of urban building was modified by squares and gardens. The urban congestion was not yet bad enough for the epidemics and lack of sanitation, so characteristic from the 1820s, to detract from the pleasures of the sophisticated social life in towns. The eighteenth-century development of elegant classical houses which epitomised Bath, Edinburgh and parts of London appeared on Merseyside too though on a slightly different time-scale.

The boundaries of Liverpool spread outwards in concentric circles, many excellent houses being built in the environs, spilling over into pleasant villages such as Everton, Derby, Knowsley, Childwall, Woolton and Wavertree. Toxteth Park was a favourite residence for merchants and traders, many of whom had elegant houses, and by the mid-nineteenth century the handsome mansions of Everton were clearly visible across the Mersey. Gradually omnibus services allowed commuters on a somewhat lower income scale also to travel to such dormitory areas as Childwall, Allerton and Bootle. The environs of Liverpool also spread northwards. Seaforth was created by Sir John Gladstone's Seaforth House built on the shore in 1813, other Liverpool merchants and some manufacturers such as the chemical producer James Muspratt following his lead. Then between 1830 and 1870 Great Crosby became an important residential area, the sea-front at Waterloo being a favourite site for houses of the wealthy.

Improved transport, however, was luring people much farther afield. Steam ferries turned much of the Wirral, with its hilly terrain offering excellent situations for houses, into a gigantic building site. Dormitory areas and retreats for the retired were interspersed between and merged with holiday resorts. From 1830 railways further extended the travel to work areas on both sides of the river and eventually as far north as Southport.

Much of the building was haphazard and unplanned but there were some notable attempts to plan estates and whole towns and even to provide a precedent for twentieth-century garden cities. From 1820 Southport was developed as a garden seaside resort, a dormitory area for Liverpool and Manchester and a haven for the retired through the deliberate actions of the main landowners, the Heskeths and the Bolds who refused to allow any industrial pollution. Handloom weavers were tolerated; cotton mills were banned. Streets were wide, tree-lined and planned on a grid system; leases restricted builders to detached or semi-detached houses, all with gardens and open spaces. The sandhills and undeveloped land around teemed with wild-life and birds, and the town was described by the

Hon Mrs Catherine Winter as 'a city of green lanes'.[10]
Similarly Birkdale, which adjoined Southport (and was eventually
amalgamated with it in 1912) was planned by surveyors and
landscape gardeners to attract the wealthy merchants and manufacturers from Liverpool and Manchester.

The outstanding example however of town planning in
Merseyside was Birkenhead, designed to emulate Bath and
Edinburgh. The census of 1811 recorded only 463 inhabitants;
the population rose to 31,000 by 1851 and to nearly 43,000 in
1871 with a further 21,500 in nearby Tranmere. This was due
primarily to William Laird, a Liverpool merchant who bought
land in the Wirral in 1824 with the specific intention of building
a new town to rival Edinburgh and nearby, at Wallasey Pool,
he established a yard for building boilers from which sprang
the great Cammell Laird shipyards. By the late 1840s part of
Laird's vision for the town had materialised. His great and
dignified square, Hamilton Square, was complete and a beautiful
park had been laid out by Joseph Paxton the celebrated landscape gardener. Contemporaries waxed lyrical about these
developments. W.W. Mortimer claimed that 'never were works of
immense public utility, grand in conception and admirable in
design commenced with greater spirit and energy'.[11] Stately
mansions and magnificent streets appeared on green fields. In
1845 the *Edinburgh Journal* called Birkenhead 'one of the
greatest wonders of the age'. Its rapid creation was due to
'the hugeness of the power created by the industry and wealth
of this country'. Its wealth was drawn largely from Liverpool
and the *Edinburgh Journal* went on to say that if it were ever
completed 'the banks of the Mersey will present the greatest
monument which the nineteenth century has erected to the
genius of Commerce and Peace'.[12]

Such eulogies were, however, somewhat premature. Some
broad, regular streets were built and Paxton's park - the first
park laid out at public expense - had a considerable influence
on the development of Britain's public parks but his plans to
simulate Nash's housing development around Regents Park in
London only partially materialised and much of the rest of the
town's planned layout was abandoned to jerry-builders and
haphazard development. The plans had been too ambitious
and funds ran out.

Another attempt by a Liverpool merchant to build an extensive residential and seaside resort also met only with partial
success. In 1830 James Atherton chose an excellent site on the
North-East corner of the Wirral. The land rising up from the
shore offered sites for beautiful villas with excellent views of
the Mersey, the sea and Wales. Wide roads were planned and
excellent transport facilities by road, by steam ferry and later
by railway. New Brighton was designed as a high class watering
place but it too fell far short of expectations. Some less ambitious
developments, however, succeeded. In 1846 William Laird bought
200 acres of land on an eminence at Eastham to be laid out as

Carlett Park where pleasant villas could be built with lovely
gardens in a woodland setting and with good views of the river.
Rock Park at Rock Ferry and Clifton Park, Tranmere, became
favourite sites for handsome villas. Oxton, Bebington, Poulton
cum Seacombe, Egremont and Liscard were also dotted with
pleasant houses, many with good views of the river. On the Dee
side of the Wirral, large houses appeared in the holiday resorts
of Neston and West Kirby and the village of Caldy, which had
been very ragged, was extensively upgraded when Mr R.W.
Barton employed an architect and builders in the 1830s and 1840s
to rebuild or improve every single house.

Much of the wealth for these developments was generated by
Liverpool's commerce and industry but other industrial areas
also played some part. Sarah Clayton, the important St Helens
coalowner laid out Clayton Square (then on the outskirts of
Liverpool) as a home for herself in the eighteenth century. In
the nineteenth century Thomas Beecham escaped from the grime
of St Helens emulating the many Lancashire industrialists who
built villas in Southport. Many chemical manufacturers lived
initially in or near Widnes before spreading into Appleton and
Rainhill and some Northwich salt producers acquired luxury
homes in nearby Hartford.

Unlike the middle and wealthy classes, the time and cost of
commuting were beyond the means of manual workers. They had
to live within walking distance of their work and as docks,
industries and transport systems grew they could only be housed
close to their work by very high-density building, leading to
gross over-crowding and insanitary conditions. Liverpool was
beginning to experience some problems by the late eighteenth
century but for most of Merseyside overcrowding problems
did not surface on any large scale until after 1820. Before then
the more immediate problem was the serious lack of investors
willing to provide working-class houses for rent. Would-be
employers often had to build houses in order to acquire a labour
force. St Helens, for example, was little more than a village in
1750: coalowners had to provide houses or lodgings; the Parys
Mine Company built houses for its workers and agents and so
did the Ravenhead and Eccleston Glass Works. In the nineteenth
century the Birkenhead Dock Company had to build 350 dwellings,
often referred to as cottages but actually claimed to be the
first working-class tenements in England. In the 1850s the
London firm, Price's Patent Candle Company, started to build
a model garden village at Bromborough. By 1857 there were 76
cottages there.

Such workers were fortunate. The rate of building gathered
pace from 1820 in Liverpool and Warrington and in parts of
Birkenhead. The mining and industrial town St Helens was now
growing rapidly and by the mid-nineteenth century Widnes and
Runcorn needed a growing labour force. Problems began to
occur widely; altough many speculators built working-class
houses there was insufficient investment to meet the whole

demand for low-rent houses. Many of those built were of very
poor quality, many were built back to back, they were overcrowded in unplanned streets and lacked fresh air, water,
sewerage, paving and drainage.

All this has been vividly chronicled in the reports of the
commissioners appointed to inquire into the Health of Towns in
the early 1840s: they particularly put Liverpool under the
microscope. [13] They found that many poor quality houses had
been thrown up both within the town and also on undrained
land beside stagnant pools outside the official boundaries.
Within the parish of Liverpool were some 35,000 houses and
4,000 warehouses, factories and workshops, averaging 24
buildings an acre. Within the other townships in the municipality
were another twelve or thirteen thousand houses. The excessive
density of population was only equalled by Nottingham. Roads
were narrow, houses were crammed along tiny courts and alleys
with inadequate ventilation. In the Parish of Liverpool nearly
half the population lived in courts or cellars. In 1841 Liverpool's
surveyors estimated that 68,345 people lived in courts. Another
estimate gives a figure of 45,000 people living in cellars (some
of which were in courts). From 1 July 1844 the Corporation had
legal powers to ban cellar living but cellar dwellers were evicted
at a time when there was no alternative accommodation at a price
they could afford - newly built house rents were too dear for
them. More families had therefore to be crammed into existing
houses. Many thousands of people also resorted to lodging houses
some of which housed up to 20 people in a room three or four
yards square, sleeping on shavings or straw for a penny a night.

In all working-class areas sanitation was totally inadequate.
The Commissioners of Sewers had spent over £100,000 on new
sewers and paving but this was in better class districts. From
1842 the authorities could insist that *new* houses were equipped
with privies but in existing houses water closets, refused access
to drains, could only be discharged into cess-pools, and cess-
pools were often located so that they could only be emptied by
carrying the contents through houses. Many hundreds of courts
and alleys had no drains at all and were extremely damp. 'In
the number and the undrained condition of courts, Liverpool
appears to have an unhappy pre-eminence and to surpass all
other towns, bad as many of them are.'[14] One witness said that
he welcomed violent storms and heavy rain 'for these are the
only scavengers that thousands have had to cleanse away the
impurities in which they live or rather exist.'[15] Public scavengers
did not clean courts at all and they only cleaned streets about
once every three weeks, hence they were in a filthy condition.

Fires were also a great problem especially in warehouses
containing cotton which was easily ignited by the careless use
of naked lights and by porters' pipe-smoking. Until well into
the nineteenth century water supplies were totally inadequate
both for fire-fighting and street-cleansing. The two water
companies only provided domestic supplies. For other uses water

had to be pumped from docks and canals and steam engines
could take up to twenty minutes to raise enough steam to pump
water for fires. For domestic supplies charges were high - it
was claimed that the Corporation could have supplied water at
one-sixth of the price.

Amidst the welter of disadvantages Liverpool enjoyed two
advantages - plentiful supplies of cheap domestic coal (although
many tenants used doors and other woodworks as fuel instead)
and the provision of ample bathing facilities: cheap baths at the
north and south ends of the town, public baths for rent at
Georges Dock and a floating bath moored in the river opposite
Princes Pier. Despite these advantages consumption and typhus
were endemic: epidemics of cholera were frequent and there
were severe scarlatina epidemics in 1848 and 1857. Child mortality reached staggering heights: in 1844 of every 100,000
children in Liverpool nearly 50,000 died before the age of ten
and the principal causes of this unhealthiness were the very bad
housing conditions.

Immigration was often blamed for Liverpool's abnormally bad
conditions, especially Irish immigration. It was claimed that
many of the 60,000 Irish in Liverpool were so dirty in their
habits that English workers refused to live near them. Like the
Irish, however, many others, destitute and unemployed, came
from nearby manufacturing towns in such poor health that they
were very vulnerable to illness. There were also large numbers
of European migrants passing through the port and a large
population of sailors who transmitted diseases. In fact the
Commissioners reported that Liverpool had an 'incredible migratory population' and that the high death rate should be attributed
more to this factor than to the indigenous population. [16] These
same factors also contributed to Liverpool's abnormally high
illegitimacy rate. In Lancashire, one in thirteen of all children
born in 1830 was illegitimate and twelve per cent of these were
born in Liverpool alone.

In Merseyside's growing industrial towns similar problems
began to appear though on a smaller scale and at a somewhat
later date. When Liverpool's slums were spreading rapidly in
the 1820s, Widnes was still quite rural and in Warrington there
were gardens in the centre of the town, many surrounding
tanyards, factories and warehouses. True the streets were
inadequately paved, cleaned, lighted and policed, there was
no satisfactory fire-engine house; in 1831-2 Asiatic cholera
raged through Warrington and the problems gradually intensified.
St Helens had been, in effect, a country town in 1800 but by
the 1850s its industrial expansion also brought pollution,
inadequate sanitation and outbreaks of cholera. Accommodation
was scarce, dingy and monotonous and many lodging houses
were opened. Widnes' worst problems arose from the 1850s
particularly as its chemical industries expanded. To house the
workers brought from St Helens and Ireland cottages were
thrown up quickly in dingy rows. The town became impregnated

with chemical fumes, smoke and refuse. With no public sewer for a population of about 10,000 by 1865, little wonder that typhoid and small-pox raged.

From the eighteenth century attempts were made to remedy some of the worst evils of urbanisation by private acts of Parliament which empowered Improvement Commissioners to pave, light, cleanse and drain streets, to widen them, to demolish some buildings and to police towns. But each town needed a separate act and each act contained provisions specific to that town. The powers were generally inadequate and the timing varied considerably. Liverpool had the first of a series of Improvement Acts in 1786, Warrington in 1813, Birkenhead 1833, St Helens 1845, Southport 1846, Runcorn 1852. Other acts dealt with supplies of water and gas, again on a piecemeal basis, but fortunately the emergence of such deplorable conditions led to general acts too. The Municipal Corporations Act of 1835 helped some districts by creating more effective town councils for the existing boroughs and also for some newly developing industrial towns. Public Health legislation was extended by the 1848 Public Health Act which set up local Boards of Health. There was also a great deal of activity directed towards improving conditions in Liverpool. In 1846 there was an act for paving, sewering and draining the town and on 1 January 1847 Liverpool set a national precedent by appointing as its first Medical Officer of Health Dr W.H. Duncan, a lecturer at the Royal Infirmary School of Medicine. Dr Duncan had long been a critic of Liverpool's deplorable sanitation and he now started a vigorous campaign to rid the town of insanitary dwellings. In 1848 the Borough Engineer was asked to prepare a report on sanitation and to submit a scheme for sewering the whole town. Also in 1848 the Town Council bought out the town's two water companies and set about extending the supply. From the mid-1850s Liverpool at least had an abundant supply of clean water.

Despite continued efforts however there was a great backlog of old houses in need of attention. In 1864 the City Engineer estimated that there were still 3,173 insanitary courts comprising 18,610 houses with an average of over six people to each house. One fifth of Liverpool's population still lived in these courts compared with nearly half the population in the 1840s. A further act of 1864 therefore gave the Medical Officer of Health power to ask the Grand Jury of the Quarter Sessions to order the demolition of houses unfit for human habitation – that was far in excess of the powers of most local authorities. In 1870 there was still much to be done but some important improvements had taken place in drainage, water supplies and supervision of house-building standards.

Until the creation of the Peelers in London from 1829, the problems of law enforcement were considerable both in town and country. The watchmen employed in towns to keep order at night were generally old and inefficient; constables were often part-time. Merseyside had a reputation of lawlessness. Smuggling was

rife in the Wirral; in country districts highwaymen and footpads
were a constant threat to travellers and as late as the 1820s
they even infested the outskirts of Liverpool. In ports sailors,
particularly privateers' crews, were rowdy and indisciplined.
Throughout the area drunkenness was common amongst all
classes. Labour disputes and religious feuds escalated into riots
which were quelled by the military.

Riots were precipitated by many factors - some profound,
some apparently trivial. In 1775 a serious riot in Liverpool by
unemployed sailors in the Africa trades was subdued by a
detachment of the Royal Regiment of Dragoons but only after
the sailors had set fire to merchants' and shipowners' houses
and used cannons, other firearms and cutlasses to try to
destroy the Exchange. In 1811, patrons of Liverpool's Theatre
Royal rioted over a change in the running of the theatre. In
1812 Luddites broke machines in various parts of Lancashire.
In 1839 riots by English and Irish labourers on the Birkenhead
and Chester Railway were put down by soldiers. During the
revolutionary activity common throughout Europe in 1848, armed
societies were formed in Merseyside especially by Irish navvies
in Birkenhead - a force of a thousand special constables un-
covered several caches of arms but there were no actual riots
at this time. Shortly afterwards however Catholic rioters in
Birkenhead protested when magistrates condemned the papal
establishment of an English hierarchy and episcopate and
Protestant counter-demonstrations followed. In 1862 the so-
called Garibaldi riots in Birkenhead, ignited by events in Italy,
again brought clashes between Catholics and Protestants.

In Liverpool there was great bitterness between Irish
Protestants and Catholics and frequent riots and disturbances
on St Patrick's day and on the anniversary of the Battle of the
Boyne. In the Liverpool area non-Irish workers tended to be
relatively conservative; many skilled operatives, shipwrights
and seamen had the vote as early as the eighteenth century.
They were pre-eminently royalist, anti-Jacobin and anti-
Catholic and in the nineteenth century the Protestant Irish
Orangemen allied with them. The Catholic Irish were much more
militant but out-numbered. In 1875 Picton predicted that Liverpool's Town Council would always be Tory because of the anti-
Catholic feeling - a correct prophecy until 1955 apart from a
three-year interlude following the 1892 election.

Because of this conservatism Owenite Socialism took very
little hold in Liverpool despite a visit by one of Owen's friends,
John Finch. There were a few Chartist demonstrations but
Liverpool was only marginally affected and the authorities held
several Chartist trials in Liverpool because they felt these would
not spark off any public reaction. In St Helens too Chartism was
virtually non-existent.

Labour organisation in Merseyside therefore particularly
took the form of societies, clubs and later unions. Before the
Combination Acts of 1799-1800 (designed to stamp out unions)

there were already trade societies. In Liverpool, for example, there were several connected with the shipping industry, especially for shipwrights and joiners and there was a Fire Engine (i.e. Steam Engine) Society in the St Helens district at least as early as 1776. The creation of friendly societies was boosted by the Friendly Society Act of 1793 which also unintentionally led to the formation of pseudo-unions, ostensibly limited to giving their members funeral and other benefits but also engaging in industrial action. In the eyes of employers (and very often in practice as well) labour unrest was tantamount to rioting. Some unions were relatively strong; military intervention was needed to quell the more violent strikes that occurred even before the Combination Acts were repealed in 1824. The rioting by unemployed sailors in Liverpool in 1775 had been more or less spontaneous but the strike of colliers in the St Helens coalfield in 1819 was well organised and a Liverpool master shipbuilder claimed in 1821 that the shipwrights' society was so powerful that it could and did limit the amount of work per day done by each of its members. Other examples of organised craftsmen included the St Helens glass-bottle makers (from at least 1825), Liverpool house painters (1820), typographical workers (1821) and steam-engine makers (1824).

The main weakness of these societies lay in their narrow occupational and geographical base: they attempted to enforce a closed shop against workers from neighbouring towns, even against those from rival unions in their own town so that employers could and did bring in other workers to break strikes or used the unemployed as strike-breakers.

The repeal of the Combination Acts allowed such societies to engage in overt industrial action and new unions were formed especially by skilled workers such as boilermakers, carvers and gilders, coopers, potters, shoemakers, chemists, iron-founders, carpenters and other craftsmen in the building trades. Nationally seven building trades unions merged to form the Builders Union and Merseyside members joined the battle between building workers and employers which ended in this Union's destruction in 1834. The individual unions however survived and the strong Stonemasons Union in Liverpool and Birkenhead started the battle for a 9-hour day in the 1846 building strike. Throughout Merseyside building unions were active and often successful because the urgent need for houses and industrial buildings strengthened their bargaining power.

Many more broadly-based unions appeared from the 1840s: some covered wider geographical areas, for example millwrights, miners, British Crown Glass Makers and Flint Glass Makers; others united workers in allied trades, for example the Amalgamated Society of Engineers which came to fruition in 1851; yet others were federations of unions of different trades either national (for example the National Association of United Trades of the Protection of Labour) or regional (e.g., the Liverpool Trades Guardian Association). The latter association formed in

1848 by fourteen trade societies to protect unions against
employers invoking the criminal law, eventually became the
Liverpool and Vicinity United Trades Council (1868) after various
name-changes.

On the whole, unions of the period from the 1840s to 1870
behaved with moderation, concentrating on friendly society
activities. Although unionism was gathering strength amongst
the non-skilled workers on Merseyside as elsewhere in the
country as yet there was little to indicate the extent to which
Merseyside workers were later to spearhead violent and bitter
confrontations between labour and employers which, on occasion,
were to verge on a complete collapse of public order. During
this period they were rather concerned with improving their
members' standards of living within the existing society.

For many of the people in the lowest social strata, however,
unions could not provide any answers at all. For those on very
low wages, for the unemployed and for people who for a variety
of reasons could not look after themselves, there was of course
poor relief similar (with slight variations to suit local conditions)
to that for the rest of the country. From 1601 there was provision
for relief for the main classes of poor, especially the aged and
infirm, lunatics, orphans and widows. From 1723 this had been
supplemented by the creation of work-houses in each large town
or by union workhouses for smaller districts. The Speenhamland
system which was well-known in southern England for relieving
workers who were in employment but were earning very low wages
was not extensively used in Merseyside especially around
'prosperous Liverpool'; [17] it was however used to assist some
hand loom weavers in parts of Merseyside such as Warrington.
The problems of long-term unemployment and under-employment
were not as serious in Merseyside at this time as in the south -
unemployment tended to be more limited and short-term though
some outdoor relief was paid in some cases to able-bodied workers
either to supplement very low wages (especially for large
families) or through rent payments to prevent families becoming
an even greater burden on the poor rates by being rendered
homeless. Practice varied between parishes: some spent between
ten and twenty per cent of their outlay on housing whereas
those such as Liverpool and Warrington with large work-houses
gave less rent relief to the able-bodied. A good deal of outdoor
relief was however given to the aged and infirm, to widows and
deserted wives. Table 5.2 showing the numbers of people and
types of expenditure for the parish of Liverpool indicates that
between a quarter and a third of Liverpool's expenditure was
on outdoor relief.

For some of the workshy and for some of the able-bodied
who genuinely could not find jobs there were work-houses
throughout the region and the number of their inmates increased
during this period with increasing population and industrialisation. In the 1790s, for example, Liverpool had under 1,200
people in the work-house but by the 1860s the number had grown

Table 5.2: Parish of Liverpool 1856-66

	(1) Total Poor Rate Expenditure £	(2) Outdoor Expen- diture £	(3) (2) as % of (1)	(4) Nos. in receipt of Relief	(5) Nos. in Work Houses	(6) Nos. in Industrial Schools
1856	103,458	29,686	28.7	9,819	2,279	891
1857	110,758	31,893	28.8	10,870	2,182	942
1858	106,296	29,976	28.2	10,457	2,213	904
1859	109,067	30,863	28.3	10,680	2,041	824
1860	113,017	32,158	28.5	10,825	2,125	606
1861	109,570	36,222	33.1	13,052	2,356	728
1862	131,115	40,442	30.8	13,290	2,713	949
1863	131,878	36,947	28.0	12,946	2,871	1,049
1864	135,717	33,478	24.7	11,191	3,175	1,191
1865	156,551	37,399	23.9	11,571	3,539	1,355
1866	164,893	41,061	24.9	12,459	3,588	1,372

Source: 'Miscellaneous Returns' in *Act for the Administration of
the Laws Relating to the Poor of the Parish of Liverpool*
(printed for the select vestry of the parish of Liverpool, 1867).

to over 3,500. In the work-houses the able-bodied were set to
work on spinning, weaving, knitting, silk- and lace-making,
on gardening or raising livestock, on making clothes, coffins
or nails or on repairing roads. In some workhouses inmates
could earn bounties which were given to encourage hard work
and efficiency. But workhouses were not only for the able-
bodied. Some were primarily homes for the aged and infirm and
all accommodated large numbers of non-workers including in
addition to the aged and infirm, lunatics, widows and orphans.
Children were often taught to read and write, to help the
women to carry out domestic duties and when possible they
were trained for work. Finance was provided by the parish
which set up the workhouse or in the case of smaller parishes
each had to pay the cost of maintaining those of its paupers who
were accommodated in the union workhouses.

On the whole the workhouses in Merseyside were better run
and more humane than those in some other parts of the country
with overseers relieved of day to day administrative duties by
salaried governors or governesses but even so life was not easy
either for the staff or inmates. There was strict economy in fuel
for heating and rules for behaviour included bans on swearing
and drinking. Inmates had to be clean, decent and obedient
and there was a code of punishments for those who did not toe
the line. Perhaps to impress moral virtues on the inmates there
were provisions for attendance at church by adults and at

Sunday School for children.

So far as the rest of the inhabitants of the region were concerned religion more frequently had a different effect. Several
references have already been made to the role of religious
antagonism in stirring up unrest. As Merseyside's population
was built up by immigration it is not surprising that there was
a considerable mixture of religions and these stamped themselves on the nature of the region, leading not only to the
building of churches but also considerably influencing the
educational facilities. Anglican churches were of course
scattered throughout the region. Roman Catholicism was partly
indigenous; for example St Helens grew in an area dominated
by Roman Catholic landowners but the Roman Catholic component
of the whole region was greatly intensified by Irish Catholic
settlers in Liverpool, the Wirral, Widnes and to a lesser extent,
other parts of the region. The many Welsh settlers retained
their non-conformist faiths and some also clung to their own
language; some Scottish immigrants built their own places of
worship and throughout Merseyside there was a scattering of
synagogues for the Jewish settlers. From the seventeenth
century the Presbyterians, Quakers and Baptists were strong
in Warrington for example; they were later joined by Congregationalists and, after several visits by John Wesley, by
Methodists. John Wesley particularly recruited converts in the
newly developing industrial towns in Merseyside such as St
Helens and Widnes as he did elsewhere. In Runcorn too there
were Wesleyans, Calvinistic and Primitive Methodists, the United
Free Methodist Church, Congregationalists and Welsh Presbyterians.

Educational facilities were closely though not exclusively
linked with religion. In 1750 the provision for education was
quite limited. There were some grammar schools such as Merchant
Taylors at Crosby and others at North Meols and Liverpool.
There were some educational charities such as the Bluecoat
Schools in Warrington (1711) and Liverpool (1718) and others
were established later, such as the Liverpool School for the
Blind founded in 1791.

As the industrial revolution proceeded many children worked
a six-day week and so, from the third quarter of the eighteenth
century, Sunday schools tried to teach literacy and numeracy to
working children in Merseyside's industrial areas as elsewhere
in England. Probably the earliest in Merseyside was Warrington's
(1777). By 1800 there were Sunday schools in Liverpool and
Runcorn, St Helens' started in 1806 and Southport's in 1818.
Various religious authorities contributed to the Sunday School
movement and also to the creation of day schools. Again Warrington was a leader: in 1788 a charitable day school was started by
the Unitarians. Each religious group with a large enough flock
created its own schools. The religious schools' movement polar-
ised into the two national schools societies - the National Society
of the Church of England and the British and Foreign Schools

Society of the non-conformist churches and this movement was
strengthened by government subsidies from 1833. In addition
there were some factory schools such as those of the Ravenhead
Plate Glass Works, the St Helens Crown Glassworks and the
British and Foreign Copper Company and, for technical training, Mechanics Institutes were established throughout the
region. For those who could afford the fees there were many
private day and boarding schools.

At the level of higher education there were colleges for
training teachers such as Warrington Training College and
perhaps the most famous educational institution within the area,
the Warrington Academy opened in 1757 as a scientific and
literary centre for non-conformists who were legally debarred
from the older universities. Both students and subscriptions
came from all over Britain and from abroad and the Academy
numbered amongst its brilliant members Joseph Priestly, the
eminent scientist, John Taylor, an outstanding Hebrew scholar,
Dr William Enfield and Dr John R. Forster, a German naturalist.
Warrington boasted the best printing press in Lancashire to
produce their works and from 1760 a circulating library served
the academicians; this library was later incorporated in the
municipal library formed in 1848 - claimed to be the first library
to be supported by local rates.

Warrington therefore excelled in its education facilities but
other parts of Merseyside also had libraries and cultural institutions. A library started by John Fell in 1715 gradually expanded
in St Peters Church in Liverpool. In 1769 the Academy of Arts
was instituted in Liverpool and in 1798, the Athenaeum News-
room and library. The Royal Institution was started in 1814, its
new premises in Colquitt Street being opened in 1817 by William
Roscoe. Another Liverpool library, started by a group of literary
people, was located in Lord Street by 1787, and in the Lyceum
in Bold Street by 1803. Patronised by William Roscoe and the
Rathbones, it formed the basis for Liverpool's public library.
The William Brown Library and Museum were built in the late
1850s.

In addition to other libraries in Merseyside (for example,
Southport had a public library by the 1820s) there were many
newsrooms, often located in the more respectable coffee houses
and taverns which served as sources of information, as meeting
places for business people and as centres for entertainment.
Merseyside in fact abounded with entertainments of all sorts.
Lack of space prevents detailed treatment of the whole area but
some indication of the favourite amusements can be gleaned by
paying special attention to Liverpool.

Until lack of sanitation and over-crowding became serious
from the 1820s life in towns was generally considered attractive
although not in the same class as the more fashionable towns
such as Bath. William Moss said that most of the inhabitants were
kept there by work or business and escaped to live in pleasanter
places as soon as they could. He also said that Liverpool had an

unusual society - one of general harmony and sociability but one 'unclouded by those ceremonies and distinctions that are met with in a more polished life.'[18] Nonetheless balls and suppers were held in the Assembly Rooms in the Exchange until it was destroyed by fire in 1795: the function was then taken over by a Lord Street Hotel. Concerts were given in a public concert room in Bold Street, and Ranelagh Gardens (the site of the Adelphi Hotel) boasted a pavilion with orchestral and vocal entertainments, firework displays and strawberry gardens. There was a music hall and theatres - by the mid-eighteenth century London companies visited Liverpool performing Shakespeare amongst other plays - and there were also strolling players. By the late eighteenth century Liverpool had a circus in Christian Street for equestrian performances.

A favourite pastime was walking and there were many public walks and promenades. In the centre around St John's Church were eleven acres which were later to form the site of St Georges Hall. There were St James Terrace, the Ladies Walk, Everton Terrace, Mount Pleasant, and parades along the river front - Kings Parade, Georges Dock Parade, Princes Dock Parade and North Dock Parade. The piers of the dock entrances were also open to the public. Close by were pleasant rural walks and, after the establishment of steam ferry services, it was estimated that up to 20,000 people would cross the river on a Sunday afternoon to walk in the Wirral.

Sporting entertainment also abounded - cricket, cock-fighting, dog-fighting, bull- and bear-baiting and, very popular, archery. There were regattas and boat races. Within easy reach were horse races. There was a trial and training course at Leasowe by the mid-eighteenth century, races on the sands and marshes at Crosby and the first Grand National was run in 1839. Nearby at Southport there was greyhound racing by the 1830s. Billiards and tennis were played and skittles and bowls were very popular, often being attached to taverns. Drinking was popular amongst all classes in the inns and taverns and, for the lower classes, the ale houses. Drunkenness was rife - chains had to be fixed around the docks to stop drunks falling in but there was also a hospital specialising in reviving those who fell in despite the chains. Snuff-taking was popular and tobacco was extensively smoked especially in locally-produced clay pipes.

Other areas of Merseyside enjoyed similar recreations - in inns, taverns, alehouses; there were assembly rooms, theatres and music halls in the larger towns such as Warrington and Southport and there were also some local specialities - for example, the Widnes Boat House Inn, known as Snig Pie House, was famed for its eel pies and Southport was renowned for its sea-food such as shrimps and cockles.

The picture of life on Merseyside is not therefore one of unrelieved gloom. Although there were many black spots, life for many people was comfortable and pleasurable. The worst conditions were experienced by considerable numbers of the lower working classes who were concentrated in Liverpool and in the growing industrial towns. For craftsmen, white-collar workers, the middle and upper classes and for the workers in villages and rural areas life ranged from luxurious to tolerable, and for all classes entertainments were so abundant as to attract large numbers of tourists to the region.

NOTES

1. There is a helpful discussion of such problems in R. Lawton (ed.), *The Census and Social Structure* (Frank Cass, London, 1978).

2. Department of the Environment, *Inner Area Studies, Liverpool, Birmingham and Lambeth* (HMSO, London, 1977).

3. C. Nickson, *History of Runcorn* (Mackie, London, 1887), p. 1.

4. W. Moss, *The Liverpool Guide* (1796; facsimile edition, City of Liverpool Public Relations Department, 1974), p. 124.

5. Ibid., p. 107.

6. Ibid., p. 109.

7. Quoted in W.W. Mortimer, *The History of the Hundred of Wirral* (E.J. Morten, Manchester, 1972), p. 189.

8. C. Nickson, *History of Runcorn*, pp. 176-7.

9. D. Defoe with introduction by G.D.H. Cole, *A Tour Thro the whole island of Great Britain* (Peter Davies, London, 1927), vol. II, p. 668.

10. Quoted in F.A. Bailey, *A History of Southport* (Downie, Southport, 1955), p. 205.

11. Mortimer, *History of Wirral*, p. 325.

12. Quoted in ibid., pp. 336-9.

13. The following account is pieced together from the *Second Report of the Commissioners for inquiring into the State of Large Towns and Populous Districts* with Minutes of Evidence, *Parliamentary Papers XVIII*, 1845, passim.

14. Ibid., p. 26.

15. Ibid., para. 97, p. 81.

16. Ibid., p. 93.

17. G.W. Oxley 'The Permanent Poor in South West Lancashire under the Old Poor Law' in J.R. Harris (ed.), *Liverpool and Merseyside* (Frank Cass, London, 1969), p. 30.

18. Moss, *Liverpool Guide*, p. 117.

Chapter 6

VICISSITUDES OF TRADE AND TRANSPORT 1870-1939

To 1870 Merseyside's position in the country's economy rested
essentially on its geographical location: on the fact that it
linked the U.K.'s most thriving industrial areas in Lancashire
and the Midlands with their sources of food and raw materials
and their world markets, especially those across the Atlantic.
Such a situation had already brought into being a complex network of communications and service industries together with a
thriving body of shipping, commercial and industrial interests.
In 1870 the possibility of serious long-term decline must have
seemed remote to the prosperous business, industrial and
shipping communities. They could not have foreseen that the
focus of the U.K.'s commercial and industrial strength would
increasingly move from the North West and Midlands to the
South East and Midlands eventually leaving Merseyside struggling
on the periphery. This process affected the interests of the
region in varying ways. In this chapter we will see how shipping,
trading and transport fared to 1939 and in the next chapter the
fortunes of Merseyside's other industries will be considered.
  Communications still played a crucial role. After 1870 both
goods and passenger traffic made new demands on existing
facilities. There was a considerable expansion of shipping
services and further dock- and railway-building. On balance
canal and river services declined despite some attempts at
modernisation but there were many novel variants on existing
forms of transport: the Manchester Ship Canal, an overhead
and an underground railway, a road tunnel under the Mersey,
a transporter bridge over it at Runcorn and electric tramways
in city streets. Both on the roads and in the air new technology
brought new forms of travel, news speeded under the oceans
along submarine cables and on land telephone systems appeared.
  In shipping and trading the pre-eminence within Merseyside
of the Liverpool/Birkenhead region was already well established
before 1870 despite the multiplicity of small ports. The ever-
growing scale of operation of trade had already led to some
specialisation of function and this movement was now speeded up.
Brokers organised purchases and sales of commodities through
produce exchanges and through the development of forward
markets, and they in turn were supplied with up to date information about crops etc. by submarine telegraphy. Shipping and
forwarding agents packaged goods, arranged for transport
and dealt with the growing intricacies of shipping documents.
To the 1860s insurance had been largely, though not exclusively,

90

the business of individual under-writers and partnerships. The
number of insurance companies had, however, started to grow:
in 1836 for example there was the Liverpool Fire and Life
Insurance Co. (later to become part of the Liverpool and London
and Globe); in 1845 the famous 'Royal' was created by Liverpool
businessmen engaged in international trade; and in 1862 the
London and Lancashire was founded with its headquarters in
Liverpool. Increasingly after 1870 Merseyside's insurance
business was dominated by large companies based wholly or
partly in Liverpool: the British and Foreign, the Albion, the
Thames and Mersey, the Commercial Union and the Union Marine.
Not surprisingly Liverpool firms became particularly important
in handling marine insurance both locally and nationally although
some also undertook fire and life business and some rapidly
extended their overseas connections particularly with America.

Banking companies too participated in the national movement
towards large scale operations: through mergers and amalgamations larger banking companies were created with branch offices.
These banking companies undertook a greater share of the work
involved in financing trade, in arranging foreign exchange
transactions and in paying bills of exchange when they fell due.
Share brokers and the stock exchanges catered for the growing
body of investors in stocks and shares. Shipping companies,
railways and cartowners provided transport, and warehousing
companies provided storage. For example the Liverpool Warehousing Co. Ltd. established in 1895 became the largest organisation of its kind in Europe with 400 warehouses in Liverpool
and Manchester, handling equipment for all kinds of commodities
and a forwarding department to assist exporters.

Such specialisation of function is highlighted by the multiplication of associations and societies catering for specialist
groups. For shipowners there was the Liverpool Steamship
Owners Association; for cartowners the Cartowners Association.
Shipping and forwarding agents, general brokers, underwriters
and commercial travellers each had their own associations. The
creation of specialised produce exchanges for each commodity
brought together the shippers, merchants, brokers and dealers
who were concerned with it: for many years Merseyside's most
important single import was raw cotton and this was handled by
members of the Liverpool Cotton Association which channelled
eighty per cent or more of the U.K.'s cotton imports into the
manufacturing areas of Lancashire. The grain trade was even
more concentrated as a high proportion of imported grain was
actually milled in Merseyside: the Corn Trade Association therefore included millers as well as merchants, brokers and dealers.
Similarly, smaller associations handled such imports as fruit and
tobacco. In fact traders united either according to commodity
(e.g. the Cotton Association, the Corn Trade Association, the
Wine and Spirit Association, the Timber Trade Association,
the Jute Goods Association, the Salt Chamber of Commerce) or
according to geographical links (e.g. the African Association,

the American Chamber of Commerce, the West India Association).
In 1850 many of these bodies had come together to form the
Chamber of Commerce.[1] There were also local branches of professional societies such as Chartered and Incorporated Accoun-
tants and Architects.

Merseyside's established trades in such products as American
cotton, West Indian sugar and Mediterranean fruits and wines
were still very much in evidence after 1870 and so were the
export of cotton piece goods, coal and salt. There was, however,
some expansion of some traditional trades and development of
newer ones. Grain imports from the Americas and Australia
and South Africa, meat from New Zealand and Argentina, fruit
from South Africa and Brazil, tea and rice from the far east,
palm oil from Africa, tanning materials and hides from South
America. To meet the growing demands of the building industry
timber was brought from all over the world - firs from the
Baltic and Americas, teak, mahogany, rosewood, cedar etc. from
Africa and the East Indies. Exports also increased and the out-
flow of machinery, metal and engineering products and chemicals
became more and more diversified.

Human cargoes were still very important - the slave trade had
finished but the emigrant trade now played a vital role in shaping
the development of Merseyside shipping especially between 1870
and 1900. The flow of emigrants, already very much in evidence
before 1870, was further increased by the railway system: for
example, emigrants from such areas as Scandinavia landed in
Hull and were then brought by rail to Liverpool. Between 1860
and 1900, of the five and a half million emigrants from the U.K.
to the U.S.A., some four and three quarter millions sailed
from the Mersey.

By this time steamships were rapidly replacing sailing ships
due to a steady stream of technological improvements involving
the use of more iron and later steel in shipbuilding and to
increases in the efficiency of marine engines which reduced
coal consumption. This changeover to steam particularly affected
the emigrant trades. From 1870 most emigrants sailed in British
steamships rather than in American sailing ships. Their quarters
were often far from ideal but legislation gradually forced shipowners to improve conditions for the poorest, and, at the same
time, there were more emigrants who could afford to pay for
greater comfort. This growing demand was met by passenger
liner companies such as Cunard, Inman, National, Guion and
White Star, and, in fact, one of the most spectacular aspects of
Merseyside's development at this time was the creation of world
famous shipping companies running both passenger and cargo
liners all over the world. Technological change brought an
increase in the average size of ships from two and a half thousand to ten thousand tons between 1870 and 1914. This in turn
was one of many factors making necessary the creation of large
companies with massive capital resources. According to one
estimate the employed capital of just six companies increased

from £1.45 million in 1870 to over £14 million in 1914. [2] Capital
growth of this sort was largely achieved by companies starting
in a small way as one man or family concerns: they then grew
by ploughing back profits and later by absorbing other companies. Few of the big liner companies became public companies
in the nineteenth century and few drew on outside capital until
after the turn of the century.

In addition to liner companies there were joint stock limited
liability companies which were created to build or buy one ship -
so-called 'single ships' companies, and also tramps. Tramp
steamers plied the world picking up cargoes wherever they were
available and many included the Mersey in their itinerary though
Merseyside is usually associated more with passenger and cargo
liners than with tramps. By the late 1870s the Liverpool Steamship Owners Association claimed that it represented thirty per
cent of Britain's total steam tonnage.

The boom in steamship building led to severe competition and
rate-cutting both between British shipping companies and
increasingly with the ships of other countries especially Dutch,
German and American companies and later in the Far East with
Japanese ships. One way of trying to reduce competition and
raise earnings was by organising conferences to control freight
rates or share out business. Many such agreements were made
but they usually only lasted for short periods as new competitors
entered the fray and undercut conference rates so that throughout much of this period most shipowners were faced with problems of how to maintain the earning capacity of their heavy
capital investment. Those liner companies which relied heavily
on the emigrant trades found themselves faced with serious
problems: emigration was seasonal and the volume fluctuated
violently from year to year. Soon there was bitter competition
between the Liverpool companies - in the 1880s the steerage fare
across the Atlantic fell as low as four guineas. There was also
the difficulty of finding return cargoes. Passenger liners could
not easily be converted to bring back corn or cotton on the
return journey. In the late 1870s the National and Guion Lines
tried bringing back carcase meat and even live cattle but there
were insuperable difficulties in ridding the ships of the smell
for the next outward cargo of passengers. Alternative solutions
were for the firms to merge into larger companies or for them
to raise rates by conference agreements which replaced rivalry
between companies. Many attempts were made to control rates
through agreements but they did not last long in face of cut-
throat competition; and Merseyside shipping companies increasingly had to contend with rivals in other British ports (especially
Southampton) and with German and American shipping companies.
In fact Merseyside's emigration boom peaked in the 1880s declining to a mere trickle by 1900: as a consequence several
of Merseyside's passenger lines went out of business and the
surviving ones had to find new outlets for their energies.

For companies running cargo liners there was also the problem of trying to maintain a continuous flow of business and one way of achieving this was by appointing agents or establishing agencies abroad to collect business to fill the liner fleets. For example Holts had agencies in China and Singapore; Harrisons had agents in New Orleans and Calcutta; John Holt set up a large merchanting business in W. Africa and so on. The agents themselves had to range widely in order to get business; thus, for example, Swires (Holts' agent in China) set up a fleet of river steamers to act as feeders to the ocean-going fleet; in New Orleans, Harrisons' agent Alfred Le Blanc had representatives throughout the American cotton belt and wheatlands to arrange for shipments of cotton and wheat in Harrison's ships; in South America Noel West, who was agent for the Pacific Steam Navigation Co. similarly ranged widely to acquire cargoes. An extensive network of such agencies was established throughout the world by Liverpool shipping companies and they played a very important role in helping to keep the large liner fleets occupied. [3]

The liner companies created before the first world war are too numerous to list in full but reference can be made to some of the leading ones which fired the public imagination. [4] Amongst the best-known are those operating on the North Atlantic routes. Thomas Ismay and his White Star Line set new standards of passenger comfort and spurred others to follow. Cunard held the Blue Riband of the Atlantic for a quarter of a century with such famous liners as the ill-fated *Lusitania* and the *Mauretania*. The many Merseyside ships which sailed to the Mediterranean and Near East included those belonging to Bahr, Bahrend, Ellerman and Papayanni, the Glynn Line, the Bibby Line, James Moss & Co. and the Larrinaga Steamship Co. Merseyside was linked to India and the Far East by ships belonging to the Brocklebank, Harrison, Hall, Clan and Bibby Lines and by the Ocean Steamship Company's Blue Funnel Line. Ships of the Beazley and White Star Lines went to Australia and New Zealand. The West Indian and Central and South American trades were served by Lamport and Holt, Harrisons, Booths, Booker and the Pacific Steam Navigation Company. West African trades were served by the ships of Elder Dempster and of the Guinea Gulf and Palm Lines. In addition to this far from exhaustive list of Mersey-based lines, other companies based abroad or in London or Glasgow also ran services from the Mersey - the Canadian Pacific Steamship Co., Furness Withy, Houlder and Houston, the P. and O., the Henderson and Anchor Lines - and frequently these 'outsiders' became members of the Liverpool Steamship Owners Association.

The development of trading and shipping inevitably exerted pressure on dock facilities. Between 1850 and 1913 the value of imports into Liverpool trebled and the value of exports increased fourfold. In 1870 just over 5.7 million tons of shipping entered the Mersey and paid dock dues; the comparable figures for 1900 and 1914 were 12.4 and 19.1 million tons. [5] These long-term

upward trends led to serious complaints about congestion from
shipping in the docks and about lack of sufficient quay space
and warehouse accommodation especially for the trades in bulky
produce such as timber. There were, for example, bitter complaints from the timber merchants and other importers who
concentrated around the Canada and Sandon docks. Further
pressure was exerted by changing technology, especially the
building of the larger iron and steel steamships which increasingly replaced sailing vessels after 1870. Liverpool and Birkenhead, therefore, needed more docks, they needed larger docks
suitable for new types of ships, they needed more quay space,
more warehouses and more sophisticated handling facilities;
furthermore with larger ships, the continuing battle against
currents, tides and shifting channels could only be won by
larger and more efficient dredging equipment.

The Mersey Docks and Harbour Board tackled its many pressing problems vigorously. The new dock engineer who succeeded
the Hartleys (father and son) was George Fosbery Lyster
(1861-97) and under him some seventy three acres of new docks
were built - Langton and Alexandra opened in 1881, Harrington
in 1883, Hornby 1884, Toxteth 1888. In Birkenhead the Low
Water Basin was opened in the 1870s and the Victoria Dock in
1909. In order to speed up cargo handling on both sides of the
river the Board installed more plant and cranes hydraulically
or electrically operated. Extensive new warehousing facilities
were built including special accommodation for grain handling
and storage, large blocks of warehouses for wool storage,
tanks for 12,500 tons of oil in Liverpool's south docks and for
a further 18,000 tons in Birkenhead for the Anglo-American
Oil Co. Ltd. The new tobacco warehouse opened at the Stanley
Dock in 1900 was claimed to be the largest warehouse in the
world. At Birkenhead the Foreign Animals Wharf could accommodate 6,000 head of cattle and 16,000 sheep and cold storage
was available for 3,380 carcases.

In order to deepen the channels and the estuary, and so
reduce delays for large vessels, several new dredgers were
built after 1890; by 1909 some 132 million tons of sand had been
removed from the Bar and sea channels to increase the depth
at the Bar at low water of Spring Tides from 11 feet to 28 feet.

All this new building, upgrading and re-equipping necessitated not only engineering skills but also heavy investment and
the Dock Board frequently had to push ahead in the teeth
of bitter controversey. In the event some twenty per cent of
all U.K. port investment between 1870 and 1909 was in Liverpool
and Birkenhead. By 1914 the Dock Board had spent nearly £32
million on new docks and on improving shipping channels and it
boasted one of the best dock systems in the country. Symptomatic
of its pride and confidence was the completion in 1907 of the
new Dock Offices: these, together with the Royal Liver Building
(topped by the liver birds) and Cunard's classical head office,
made up Liverpool's distinctive and world-famous water-front.

Meanwhile the provision of more and better facilities for
goods traffic did not mean that passengers were neglected:
Georges landing stage, completed in 1847, had quickly become
too small. The Board therefore obtained powers to build the
floating Princes landing stage (completed in 1876) which later
extended for nearly half a mile: it had two hundred pontoons
and several bridges and movable gangways to facilitate passenger movements both for ferries and for passenger liners what-
ever the level of the tide. In the years before the first world
war some 30 million passengers a year used the ferries between
Liverpool and Rock Ferry, New Ferry, Birkenhead, Seacombe,
Egremont and New Brighton. This period was also, as we have
seen, the heyday of the larger passenger liners although there
were a few ominous pointers to the later rapid decline in passenger traffic. By 1900 Merseyside's share of the emigrant trade
had declined rapidly. In 1907 the White Star Line transferred its
express passenger service to Southampton. Cunard was also
complaining about passenger facilities though it did not actually
transfer its large liners to Southampton until after the 1914-18
war. It was already beginning to appear that Merseyside should
concentrate on developing its strength in the commodity trades.

Despite the deteriorating role of passenger services, the
history of the Liverpool and Birkenhead Docks under the Mersey
Docks and Harbour Board is one of substantial progress to 1914
but unfortunately the bitterness and rivalries that had been
such a striking feature of the docks' earlier history were still
very much in evidence. The smaller Mersey ports still resented
Liverpool's predominance which was further challenged by the
deliberate creation of competing port facilities by railway
companies; then too the long-standing Liverpool-Manchester
rivalry erupted once more resulting in the building of the
Manchester Ship Canal followed by a growing challenge from
the Port of Manchester.

By 1938 railways had invested over £60 million in Britain's
ports. In Merseyside the railway's main efforts were concentrated
on the development of Garston's dock alongside Liverpool's
dockland: this had been opened in 1853 by the St Helens Canal
and Railway Company. It grew rapidly as a coal dock. In the
1860s it had been taken over by the London and North Western
Railway. After this company's opening in 1870 of a line to
Wigan, Garston could handle Wigan's coal as well as St Helens'.
Additional docks were opened in 1875 (the North Dock) and 1909
(Stalbridge). The railway company offered to carry cargoes
overland to and from Garston at preferential rates and consequently the port took some fifty per cent of Liverpool's coal
trade and ten per cent of the grain trade. Garston also received
large shipments of timber from Canada, the U.S.A., Scandinavia
and France, of chemicals and ores from Africa, the U.S.A. and
Spain and of bananas imported by Elders and Fyffes.

Of the smaller Mersey ports, Runcorn still struggled to expand:
between 1873 and 1884 some half million tons a year passed

through the port - especially coal, salt and china clay - in fact its prosperity was intimately linked with the fortunes of the coal and chemical industries. Its foreign trade expanded little after 1870 - it was the coastal and canal trades that were important and another Mersey port whose fortunes were inextricably bound up with canal traffic was Ellesmere Port. Ellesmere Port began to grow slowly from the 1860s with the building of shipyards as well as soap works. In 1898 a copper smithy works was set up. There were grain mills on the waterfront and in 1905 the Wolverhampton Corrugated Iron Company established a works there. All these growing industries needed to bring in bulky raw materials and to remove their own heavy finished products so expanding the demand for water transport. The prosperity of both this port and of Runcorn also became bound up with the fortunes of that other great challenge to the Mersey Docks and Harbour Board - the Manchester Ship Canal.

Although the creation of the Mersey Docks and Harbour Board had been regarded as a victory for Manchester over Liverpool Mancunians were still far from satisfied: they complained about dues and congestion and both Liverpool and Manchester interests struggled vainly to loosen the railway companies' stranglehold over the land carriage of cargoes. The Suez Canal had demonstrated the viability of a ship canal and Mancunians were greatly attracted by the possibility of creating their own port for ocean-going ships. In this way they could simultaneously undermine the monopoly positions held by both the railways and the Mersey Docks and Harbour Board. During the early 1880s a group of businessmen led by Daniel Adamson began to plan a ship canal but they encountered serious obstacles. Bitter hostility from Liverpool, from the Bridgewater Canal and from the railways led to several rebuffs in Parliament. It was not until 1887 that the necessary Act gave authority for work to proceed. Even then progress was slow: floods and escalating costs meant that the capital, raised largely in Manchester and nearby mill towns, had to be supplemented to the tune of over £3 million by Manchester Corporation. Eventually, however, the Canal was opened by Queen Victoria in May 1894.

In the early days the Canal did not exert severe competitive pressure on the existing Mersey docks and neither did it undermine the strength of the railway companies. On the contrary the railways made life difficult for the Canal: they were for example slow to link up their services with those of the Canal or to offer special rates for traffic associated with the Canal. Many merchants still found it cheaper to load and unload at Birkenhead using the railways for inland transport though some Liverpool timber, grain and cotton merchants opened branches in Manchester and founded the Manchester and Liverpool Transport Company for the transit trade. The Canal also met opposition from established shipping companies which were slow to alter their services to utilise the Canal so attempts were made to set up new shipping lines that could use it, the most successful

being Manchester Liners Ltd. This company, promoted in
Manchester and London, was registered in 1898 with C. Furness
of Furness Withy providing over half of the capital.[6] The line
was particularly successful in developing the cargo liner trades
with Canada and the U.S.A. Because of opposition the Port of
Manchester grew slowly at first but gradually it was established
and from 1906 it ranked as the U.K.'s fourth port. From Merseyside's point of view one very important aspect of this building
of the Canal was the extension of land available within Merseyside for industrial development. Along the banks new industrial
complexes sprang up especially for the chemical industry and
the refining of oil.

During the 1914-18 war Merseyside's docks were necessarily
mobilised for wartime needs. The Mersey was geographically
well-placed to receive the raw materials, foodstuffs and munitions
that poured across the Atlantic. In 1918 Liverpool handled nearly
thirty seven per cent of the U.K.'s total imports.[7] There were
serious labour shortages in the docks and troops were stationed
there to protect both installations and cargoes. The docks themselves did not suffer direct attack as during the Second World
War, but the shipping community suffered heavy losses of lives
and property through the sinking of some 1½ million tons of
Liverpool-based shipping alone.

At the end of the war there was a hectic scramble in Merseyside as in other ports to replace lost shipping and to cope with
the immediate post-war boom but when the boom collapsed in
1920 the longer-term prospects were not so encouraging. It
soon became clear that operating and trading conditions had
changed materially not only for Merseyside but for the whole of
the U.K. World trade had declined and the U.K.'s competitive
position had deteriorated. The terms of trade certainly turned
in Britain's favour during the 1930s as the prices of raw materials
and foodstuffs fell dramatically and this encouraged more imports,
but this favoured London rather than Merseyside for London was
Britain's leading import, Liverpool was the leading export port.

With regard to imports, between 1924 and 1938 London accounted
for around forty per cent of Britain's imports whereas Liverpool's
share fell from around twenty-two per cent in 1921 to as low as
eighteen per cent in 1938.[8] Overall, Liverpool lost heavily to
London in the import trades during the depression period and
did not fully regain her share afterwards though if we look at
some individual import trades we find varied fortunes. In raw
cotton imports Liverpool's share of the U.K. trade fell from
eighty per cent pre-war to below sixty-five per cent in the mid
1930s - particularly due to further encroachments by Manchester.
By 1926 the tonnage of goods handled by Manchester had reached
some six million and by 1937 it had risen to seven million. On
the other hand Liverpool's share of U.K. imports of raw wool
increased from twenty per cent pre-war to nearly thirty-five
per cent in the late 1930s and her share of U.K. imports of
oilseeds also increased. Perhaps the worst feature, however,

with regard to imports was the erratic nature of several of the
trades. In the import of raw rubber, for example, Liverpool
had handled over fifty per cent of U.K. imports pre-war: in
the inter-war years her share varied from five per cent to
thirty-nine per cent. In the import of wheat Liverpool's share
fluctuated between eighteen and twenty-six per cent and her
share of sugar and tobacco imports also fluctuated widely. One
import trade which she did dominate, however, was the import
of tin ore: between eighty and ninety-five per cent of the U.K.
imports came through Liverpool.

With regard to exports Liverpool managed to retain her share
accounting for about one-third of U.K. total exports throughout
the inter-war years. Only in 1938 did London manage to overtake Merseyside as an exporter. There was, however, a change
in the composition of exports: a relative decline in cotton and
other textiles and an increase in metals, machinery and chemicals.
Despite the fact that Merseyside retained its position in the U.K.
exports the situation was far from satisfactory. Its relative
position was maintained but as U.K. trade generally declined it
was a question of holding a steady share of a decreasing total.
The hinterland from which the supply of exports came was very
depressed for much of the inter-war years. Then, too, during
the inter-war years cheap mass transport by tramp ships became increasingly important and Merseyside's facilities were
tailored more for valuable liner cargoes than for this type of
trade. Merseyside's position as an entrepot port also declined
and there were further falls in its passenger services, highlighted by the transference of the large Cunarders to Southampton.

The region's shipping companies were therefore having to
operate in increasingly unfavourable conditions and at the same
time they faced severe competition from foreign mercantile
marines as other countries heavily subsidised their fleets for
nationalistic reasons. Throughout the world there was a serious
excess of shipping capacity and this reached crisis proportions
during the depression. Although there were some improvements
in technology, such as some changeover from steam to diesel
power there was little temptation for shipowners to embark on
heavy capital expenditure in the unfavourable environment of
cheap coal, falling trade and excess carrying capacity. The
shipping community's confidence was also seriously shaken by
the spectacular collapse of the Royal Mail Group of companies
which included several important Merseyside companies.

Groups of ships and even whole companies had changed hands
pre-war: they were moved about like pieces on a chessboard.
After the war this movement continued through mergers and
takeovers. In 1919, for example, Cunard had bought the Brocklebank Line and in 1935 Alfred Holt & Co. acquired control of the
Glen and Shire Lines. At a national level Lord Kylsant had built
up his extensive shipping empire, the Royal Mail Group. This
included several Merseyside lines: as early as 1910 he had taken

over Elder Dempster and reorganised it into Elder Dempster &
Co. Ltd. which itself included the African Steamship Co., the
British and African Steam Navigation Co., the Elder Line and
the Imperial Direct West India Mail Service Co. Ltd. In 1911,
he took over Lamport & Holt which included the Liverpool Brazil
and River Plate Steam Navigation Co. Ltd. In 1916 the Moss
Steam Ship Company was absorbed into his empire, in 1926 he
bought the White Star Line and several smaller companies were
also involved. The Kylsant empire was, however, built on in-
secure foundations. Losses of shipping during the first world
war were made good immediately afterwards at very high prices
and in addition Kylsant bought some 77 ships from the government. By 1920 he had a very large fleet which he could not
operate profitably during the adverse commercial conditions
ruling during the 1920s with intense foreign competition and
excess shipping capacity throughout the world. During the
1920s dividends were often paid out of reserves and by 1930
the Royal Mail Group's fleet, which had cost £106 million, was
worth less than £30 million.[9] Gradually public confidence was
undermined as the group's real financial position became clear
and in 1930 Lord Kylsant lost control of the group. Eventually,
Lord Kylsant himself was accused of improper commercial behaviour and in 1931 he received a gaol sentence for producing
misleading accounts and for issuing a fraudulent prospectus.

The collapse of the Royal Mail Group was a severe blow to
Liverpool shipping interests. Confidence was badly shaken because of shareholders' heavy losses and during the 1930s it was
more difficult to raise new capital for other shipping ventures
and for technological improvements in shipping. The component
companies of the group were not however all lost: although
the group was broken up many of the companies survived being
reorganised and regrouped in new ways. Of the Merseyside
components the Moss Steamship Company amalgamated with
Hutchison in 1934; White Star merged with Cunard in the same
year and in 1936 Elder Dempster became Elder Dempster Holdings
Ltd.

Such reorganisations were one way of dealing with excess
capacity by reducing competition and cutting management costs
and some mergers placed Merseyside in a strong position. During
the war, for example, coastal shipping companies had faced
grave difficulties. In 1917 several British lines merged to create
Coast Lines with their headquarters in Liverpool. After the war
this concern absorbed less efficient rivals and moved into a
dominant position in Britain's coasting trades extending its
interests to Scotland, Ireland and Wales as well as round the
coast to London. By offering new standards of comfort on
coastal ships it also attracted a good deal of new passenger
traffic as well as cargoes.

On the whole however the inter-war years were not happy ones
for Merseyside shipping companies fighting as they were against
excess capacity and low freight rates. What did all this mean for

the docks? During the inter-war years the tonnage of shipping
entering the Mersey and paying tonnage and harbour rates did
not change spectacularly. It fluctuated between 16.5 and 21.7
million tons compared with 19.1 million tons in 1914.[10] Although
there was not therefore a major increase in tonnage, the Mersey
Docks and Harbour Board considered that further expansion of
its facilities were needed to reduce congestion. More land was
acquired, more quay space made available, a new oil jetty was
built at the Dingle and work proceeded on the Gladstone Dock
complex: the latter, opened in 1927, added a further 58 acres
of new docks. In 1933 another new dock (Bidston) was opened
on the opposite side of the river. By 1938 the accumulated cost
of investment had reached some £45 million.

Although the picture is not wholly black during the inter-war
years it was becoming clear that the Liverpool/Birkenhead docks
had passed their peak relatively to other ports: between 1913
and 1938 their overall share of Britain's trade had fallen from
28 per cent to 21 per cent. Of other Merseyside ports, Runcorn
also suffered as a result of the depressed industrial hinterland
and Garston, taken over in 1922 by the L.M.S. Railway, could
not fail to be affected by the depression in the coal trade during
the inter-war years. Oil refining on the other hand expanded:
an oil dock was built at Stanlow, near to Ellesmere Port. Started
in 1916 it was fully operational in 1922 and during the next ten
years some six companies established storage, blending and
distribution depots. A larger oil dock was opened in Stanlow in
1933 the year in which Lobitos built the first refinery there.

Another inter-war development was the building of Bromborough Dock by Unilevers to facilitate the delivery to their
works of bulk oils and oil seeds. They received authority to
build the dock in 1923 but it was not officially opened until
1931. Later it became an important channel of communication for
other manufacturers on the Bromborough Pool Industrial Estate.

Trade, shipping and docks therefore still occupied a prominent
place in Merseyside's economy. Canals and river navigation, on
the other hand, struggled hard during this period to retain
their viability apart from the Manchester Ship Canal. Throughout
the country the building of railways had posed a serious threat
to canals and river navigations in the mid-nineteenth century.
Although railway rates were relatively high because of heavy
capital charges, inland water transport had not successfully
held its own. Many canals had been taken over by railways by
1870 and this trend continued despite the 1873 Regulation of
Railways Act which tried to control such takeovers. In any event
many canals were already old and their facilities were unsatis-
factory - they varied in width, they did not provide through-
services, and many could not accommodate the most efficient
barges. In Merseyside some attempts were made to remedy such
faults: from 1860 the Weaver Navigation had been improved by
rebuilding the entrance locks, by increasing the size and reducing the number of locks and by the installation of a boat lift

to enable traffic to pass to and from the Trent and Mersey
Canal. The principal traffic on the Weaver was still salt: in
1880 over 1.2 million tons were carried. A further advance on
some canals was the use of steam barges.

In 1909 a Royal Commission spelled out the measures necessary
for the widespread modernisation of England's inland waterways
but little progress had been made by 1914. During the 1914-18
war those canals belonging to railway companies passed straight
into government control and the independent ones came within
the Board of Trade's control from 1917. Attempts to utilise
canals more fully during the war to compensate for congestion
on the railways were not very successful. The volume of canal
traffic actually fell during the war and they reverted to private
ownership in 1920. Another enquiry in 1920 failed to lead to any
general improvements and many inland waterways fell into a state
of disrepair.

Many of the canals' troubles (and some of those afflicting the
docks) can be laid at the feet of the railways; but did the railways themselves provide a highly efficient transport system
to compensate for the damage they inflicted on other forms of
transport? Liverpool had, of course, helped to pioneer railways
partly in order to break the stranglehold of canal interests, but
it was soon clear that the monopolistic canal interests had been
exchanged for an equally uncomfortable stranglehold by railway
companies over the region's communications: and to add insult
to injury the services provided were far from satisfactory for
many users. By 1870 there were lines radiating from Liverpool
eastwards to Manchester, north-east to Wigan and Preston, north
to Southport and south to Warrington and there were several
short lines on the Wirral. Through these various lines it was
possible, by linking with other lines, to transport goods and
passengers throughout the country but Merseyside's network
was not yet complete. New lines were opened after 1870 to serve
the expanding dock estate; the Cheshire Lines Committee even
introduced some measure of competition by opening a second line
from Liverpool to Manchester (1873) with an extension to Southport (1884). The opening of the Mersey railway bridge at Runcorn
in 1869 gave Runcorn itself access to the rail network and also
greatly shortened the L. & N.W.'s route between London and
Liverpool. Nearer home, there was a service from Liverpool to
Maghull, Aughton and Ormskirk, new lines in the Wirral met the
demands of its rapidly growing dormitory areas and the Great
Central Railway extended its services from North Wales and
Chester to the Wirral.

Despite this proliferation of lines the railways retained something of a stranglehold particularly over Liverpool. There were
serious limits to the building of competitive lines. Geographical
constraints made railway building costly. Tunnels had to be cut
through the high ground east of the city and the Cheshire Lines,
when extending their network from Garston to central Liverpool,
had to construct costly tunnels to Central Station. Although this

line was completed in 1874 it did not compete vigorously with
the L.N.W.R. which, to the bitter annoyance of merchants,
shippers and manufacturers, charged discriminatory rates. It
cost as much, for example, to carry a consignment from Liverpool to Manchester as to carry the same cargo from Manchester to
London. Liverpool in fact suffered in railway terms from being
at the end of the line. Unlike such cities as Manchester and
Birmingham it was a terminus - competing lines did not pass
through it on the way to other termini. It has also been sug-
gested that the existence of the dock monopoly (the Mersey
Docks and Harbour Board) sparked off retaliatory monopolistic
railway activities: and, of course, the Manchester Ship Canal
was intended as a challenge to both the dock and railway
monopolies.

There were therefore many complaints about the railways'
high and often discriminatory charges and about inadequate
long distance services but within Merseyside railway technology
brought some novel solutions to some of the region's internal
travel problems: namely the overhead railway and the underground railway. The overhead railway was partly the brainchild
of the Mersey Docks and Harbour Board though the idea of an
'elevated' railway along the Liverpool docks had been discussed
as early as the 1850s. The subject was raised again in 1878 but
Parliamentary authorisation only came in 1887 and the actual
operation was not in fact carried out by the Mersey Docks and
Harbour Board but by the newly created Liverpool Overhead
Railway Company. The initial stretch opened in 1893 ran between the Alexandra and Herculaneum docks; in 1894 the line
was extended to Seaforth and in 1896 to Dingle. In 1901 the
first railway escalator was installed at Seaforth and in 1905 a
further short extension linked the railway to the Lancashire
and Yorkshire Railway Company's line from Liverpool to Southport.

This overhead railway, carried on a steel viaduct built on
concrete foundations, was the world's first elevated electric
railway with the first automatic electric signalling system. Apart
from providing transport for the docks the long viaduct became
known as the 'Dockers Umbrella' and because of the excellent
view of the docks the railway soon became an important tourist
attraction. Unfortunately after the second world war it failed
to pay its way and was closed down on 30 December 1956.

The underground railway was one attempt to deal with the
problems posed over the centuries by the physical difficulty
of bridging the Mersey near Liverpool. During the nineteenth
century serious studies had been made to try to find ways of
bridging the river without obstructing shipping but construc-
tional problems prevented the implementation of such ideas.
Early in the nineteenth century various proposals had been
made for a road tunnel to link Liverpool and the Wirral but these
too had failed to materialise. In 1866 came the first serious
proposal to build a railway *under* the Mersey but there was a

lack of capital and work did not start until 1880. The line
between Liverpool and Birkenhead was eventually opened in
June 1886. The construction of the tunnel was regarded as a
great feat of engineering but the operation of the railway itself
was fraught with difficulty. Trains were drawn by steam locomotives. Failure to overcome ventilation problems satisfactorily
meant that passengers, plagued by smoke and soot, did not
regard the line as a popular alternative to the healthier ferries.
The underground did, however, become an important transport
link after it had been electrified in 1903. It then became possible
greatly to extend the development of the Wirral as a dormitory
area for Liverpool particularly when the underground was linked
into the existing network of lines on the Wirral. It also greatly
facilitated travel between Liverpool, Chester, North Wales and
South West England.

Electrification played an important part in the success of both
the overhead and underground railways. Other commuter lines
also electrified early in the twentieth century were the lines
between Liverpool and Southport and between Liverpool and
Ormskirk but the Wirral lines were not electrified by the L.M.S.
until 1938. Meanwhile, however, electric technology was also
causing something of a revolution in one form of road transport
and further increasing the short-distance mobility of population.
This was the electric tram.

During the earlier nineteenth century public transport had
been developing in towns especially through the use of horse-
drawn omnibuses. An important extension of this type of service
in which Birkenhead and Liverpool were U.K. leaders was in
the building of tramways on which horses drew vehicles. One
of England's earliest tramways operated in Birkenhead in 1860.
In 1868 the Liverpool Tramways Company was incorporated to
build a line from the centre of the city to the south end. The
1870 Tramways Act authorised local authorities throughout the
country to finance and own tramways and to offer twenty-one
year leases to private companies to operate within their boundaries. In 1876, through the amalgamation of the Tramways
Company with the Omnibus Company the Liverpool United Tramways and Omnibus Company came into being to operate both
tram and omnibus services, its system eventually being bought
by Liverpool Corporation in 1897. Many other towns followed
suit replacing omnibus services by tramways on their main routes.
In 1879, for example, the St Helens and District Tramways
Company Ltd. was formed. Its first service was to Prescot but
this was soon extended to Denton's Green, Peasley Cross and
Haydock.

Trams offered considerable advantages over omnibuses: each
car could carry more passengers, they were cheaper to operate
and because they ran on fixed rails, they reduced traffic confusion. All in all they allowed existing roads to carry a greater
volume of traffic. Further advantages could be gained by replacing horses by new forms of traction. In 1889 steam cars were

used in St Helens but the greatest advance as the conversion
to electric traction. This idea swept America from 1888 but it
was only slowly adopted in Continental Europe and even more
slowly in England. In this century electrification occurred
gradually - electric trams arrived in St Helens in 1899, in Southport in 1900 and between 1898 and 1903 Liverpool's tramways
were electrified: by 1914 the city had a ninety-mile system
powered by five power stations fuelled by public refuse. From
1900 the Liverpool Overhead Railway Company also operated an
electric tramway between Seaforth Sands and Great Crosby.

In Merseyside, as in other regions, trams made a major
contribution towards increasing mobility especially by allowing
workers to live at considerable distances from their work places.
As with most new forms of transport, however, many people were
also quick to recognise a new form of leisure activity. Guides
were published advertising tours by tram: the *Liverpool Official
Handbook* for 1909 contained a whole chapter on tram tours
including a 23½ mile ride from the pierhead to Garston returning
via Aintree for 11d and a 17 mile tour to Knotty Ash, Knowsley,
St Helens and Prescot for 12d. Between 1908 and 1923 Liverpool
also pioneered the idea of first class trams so that middle and
upper class travellers could, if they wished, be segregated from
working class passengers.

During the inter-war years trams continued to operate though
they now began to suffer renewed competition from their old
rivals, omnibuses - but the latter were no longer horse-drawn;
they were now motorised. Certainly by 1939 tramways had passed
their peak and the internal combustion engine was beginning to
dominate road transport and even to challenge the railways.

During the canal and railway ages road transport had played
a restricted though important role: horse-drawn carts had acted
as feeder services to canals, railways and docks; over short
distances passengers had travelled on horseback or in horse-
drawn buses or carriages and carts of various sorts. The
development of new forms of road transport during this period
considerably changed the balance of power between roads and
other forms of travel. There were electric trams, bicycles and
petrol-driven cars, lorries and buses as well as various types
of steam-propelled commercial vehicles. This growing use of
roads created new demands for road building and for new Mersey
crossings for road users. It was possible to take motorised and
horse-drawn vehicles of all sorts on the ferries but this was slow
and inconvenient especially in bad weather so two new road
crossings were devised in this period - the Runcorn Transporter
Bridge and the first Mersey road tunnel.

As we have seen until the opening of the Widnes-Runcorn
railway bridge in 1869 the nearest point to the sea at which the
Mersey had been bridged was Warrington. The railway bridge
was an important advance but no help to road travellers so a
novel solution was devised at the beginning of the twentieth
century, namely, the Transporter Bridge opened in 1905. This

linked Runcorn and Widnes and enabled road vehicles and
pedestrians to cross the river in a cage, provided the wind
was not too strong. Although it was slow and cumbersome it
saved road users a long journey and it came to carry as many
as two million passengers in a year as well as 150,000 private
vehicles and a further 100,000 commercial vehicles. It lasted
until the opening of the new road bridge in 1961.

Even with the railway bridge, the transporter and the underground railway there was still a serious gap in facilities for
crossing the Mersey. What was increasingly needed was a
crossing for road vehicles between Liverpool and Birkenhead.
Viability studies had indicated that the engineering problems
involved in building a road bridge would be virtually insuperable because of the nature of the estuary, the very high
tides and the need not to impede shipping: on the other hand
the building of the rail tunnel had shown that a tunnel could
be constructed at a reasonable cost without too many engineering problems.

After several abortive attempts to promote such a venture,
the decision to build a road tunnel was eventually taken and
work began in 1925. The tunnel, running parallel to the rail
tunnel, was just over two miles long with four traffic lanes
and two branches to serve the docks. At the time it was the
world's longest underwater tunnel. It cost nearly £8 million of
which the government contributed £2½ million and it was opened
in July 1934. In the following year some $3\frac{1}{4}$ million vehicles passed
through it. Contemporaries regarded it as one of the wonders of
the age but its defects soon became evident – in particular the
fact that its entrances were right in the centre of Liverpool and
of Birkenhead greatly added to traffic congestion at both ends.
It was not, however, until after the second world war that this
built up into an intolerable problem calling for drastic action in
the form of the construction of a second road tunnel.

Apart from the urgent problem of Mersey crossings, the
growing volume of road traffic necessitated the building of more
and better main roads and, at the same time, the extension of
built-up areas resulted in a growing network of subsidiary roads.
Merseyside had not been blessed with a good road system in
earlier years. Although some turnpike roads formed a basis for
a main network, as late as 1914 there was no satisfactory highway linking Liverpool and Manchester and no commercial highway
between Merseyside and Yorkshire until well after the second
world war. In 1913 there were eight main roads radiating from
Liverpool through the region and they carried some 884,000 tons
of traffic a year. By 1922 the same roads had to cope with
9 million tons a year and by 1927 with over 15 million tons.

Such increased road usage was due both to private cars and
commercial services. To the first world war private cars were
not very numerous. The use of petrol driven buses and commercial vehicles was patchy but growing. London led although in
the north west bus services were operated by both the Crosville

Motor Services Ltd. and the Lancashire United Transport and
Power Company. It was, however, the experience gained in the
first world war that led to a more rapid proliferation of both
private and commercial vehicles: immediately after the war large
numbers of ex-army lorries were sold to private owners and
motor lorries increasingly ousted horse-drawn vehicles both for
local delivery services and for longer distance services. In order
to avoid the need to run empty vehicles on one leg of a journey
a committee was set up by the Liverpool Chamber of Commerce to
co-operate with the Manchester Chamber and as early as 1919 a
Motor Haulage Clearing House was created to arrange return
loads between Merseyside and London, Bolton, Leicester,
Nottingham and other towns. For passengers, bus services also
grew in number as municipal authorities began to develop their
own within towns to supplement or replace trams.

In the country as a whole there was growing pressure for new
trunk roads and it seemed logical to use the increasing proceeds
of motor taxation (the Road Fund) to build the roads needed
for the increasing number of vehicles. Merseyside joined the
chorus of demands for a share of the Road Fund. Many possibilities were considered on Merseyside including one modern sound-
ing proposal in 1926 for the building of a 'motorway' (excluding
horses and pedestrians) between the Mersey and Birmingham
partly financed by charging tolls based on mileage. The main
achievement, however, in this period was more modest: it was
the important East Lancashire road opened in 1933 to provide
faster transport between Liverpool, Manchester and inter-
mediate towns. The intention was eventually to continue the
road to Yorkshire but this did not materialise at the time.

In the same way that new forms of road transport were given
a boost by the first world war, air transport also became commercially viable as a result of war-time developments. After the
war the number of air services within Britain and between Britain
and other countries began to multiply. In Merseyside air services
were started between Liverpool and Belfast and the Liverpool and
District Aero Club was agitating for the building of a large new
airport. In this it received support from the Liverpool Chamber
of Commerce and the Shipowners Association. In 1930 a new air
service linked Liverpool and London and through this passengers
could gain access to continental and world routes. Early in the
1930s Liverpool Corporation bought Speke Hall estate and
allocated part for use as an airport - the airport was opened
in 1939 and during the war additional runways, hangars and
workshops were built. By 1939 there were air services from
Liverpool to the Isle of Man, Belfast, Glasgow and Birmingham
as well as the main route to London. In addition there was a
privately owned aerodrome at Hooton and during the war military
aerodromes were built in the region.

The growth of communications was therefore somewhat uneven
during this period and in some cases it was fraught with bitter
rivalries. Despite such difficulties the transport industries

struggled to cope with the growing volume of goods and passenger traffic by a multiplication of the same types of services
and, with the help of new technology and imaginative enterprise,
by finding interesting new solutions both to long-standing
problems and to new needs.

The development of Merseyside was still closely bound up with
its communications. Increased mobility for passengers allowed
the spread of dormitory suburbs by greatly extending the travel-
to-work areas. At the same time some forms of transport contributed to improved health and to new leisure activities. Those
industries needing bulky raw materials and producing bulky
finished products still frequently clung closely to docks or
clustered along rivers and canals (including the Manchester
Ship Canal) but during this period the extension of railways
and the growing use of road transport (especially after the first
world war) considerably extended the potential locations available
for new or growing industries and it is with the fortunes of the
region's industries during this period that the next chapter is
concerned.

NOTES

1. For a history of the Chamber of Commerce see W.A.
Gibson-Martin, *A Century of Liverpool's Commerce* (Charles
Birchall, Liverpool, 1950).

2. F.E. Hyde, *Liverpool and the Mersey. The Development
of a Port 1700-1970* (David and Charles, Newton Abbot, 1971),
p. 14.

3. For a discussion of the importance of agencies to Liverpool shipping businesses see ibid., pp. 59-63.

4. A general survey of Liverpool shipping lines can be found
in G. Chandler, *Liverpool Shipping. A Short History* (Phoenix,
London, 1960).

5. S. Mountfield, *Western Gateway. A History of the Mersey
Docks and Harbour Board* (Liverpool University Press, 1965),
pp. 203-5.

6. D.A. Farnie, *The Manchester Ship Canal and the Rise of
the Port of Manchester* (Manchester University Press, 1980),
p. 34.

7. G.C. Allen *et alia*, *The Import Trade of the Port of
Liverpool* (Liverpool University Press, 1946), p. 20.

8. Ibid., pp. 20, 22.

9. P.N. Davies and A.M. Bourn, 'Lord Kylsant and the
Royal Mail', *Business History*, vol. XIV no. 2 (July 1972),
p. 117.

10. S. Mountfield, *Western Gateway*, p. 205.

Chapter 7

FORTUNES AND MISFORTUNES OF MERSEYSIDE'S INDUSTRIES
1870-1939

Many of Merseyside's social and economic problems are blamed
on its lack of a sufficiently varied range of non-service industries
and to counteract this intensive efforts have been made from the
1930s to diversify the industrial base. If one defines Merseyside
in such a way as to exclude the obviously manufacturing centres
of Widnes, Runcorn and St Helens then clearly by 1939 the
region had a greater proportion of workers employed in transport and distribution than the norm for the U.K.

Table 7.1: Relative Importance of Industry Groups on
            Merseyside, 1939.

Industry Groups	Percentage of Insured Workers Employed in:	
	Merseyside	United Kingdom
Food, Drink and Tobacco	8.4	4.3
Textiles and Clothing	3.9	11.1
Metals and Engineering	13.6	19.1
Fishing, Mining and Quarrying	0.0	6.5
Other Manufacturing Industries	14.7	12.7
Transport	15.0	6.1
Distribution	19.1	14.9
Other Services	25.3	25.3
	100.0	100.0

Source: W. Smith, *The Distribution of Population and the
Location of Industry on Merseyside* (Liverpool University Press,
1942), p. 42.

If, however, we keep to the wider definition of Merseyside
there is a very considerable range of occupations, in addition
to transport and distribution, including agricultural pursuits
which still maintained their importance despite damage in some
parts of the region from pollution and despite the relentless
encroachment of houses, factories, roads etc. into agricultural
land. In many parts of Britain there was a swing away from
arable farming during the last quarter of the nineteenth century
but this did not happen in Merseyside. On the contrary the
arable acreage, fertilised by ample supplies of town manure,

increased in response to the pressing demands from the urban areas. Wheat and rye were produced for human consumption and oats, hay and straw for urban horses and cows. In the twentieth century as the towns' animal populations began to decline in response to transport changes farmers in Lancashire and North Cheshire increasingly used the oats and hay to feed dairy cattle and meat animals.

In the production of potatoes south-west Lancashire was the largest growing region next to Lincolnshire and on both sides of the Mersey considerable quantities of other vegetables were produced - turnips and swedes, cauliflowers, peas, celery, brussel sprouts etc. Market gardening also became widespread to supply town-dwellers with tomatoes and other salad produce - south-west Lancashire became known as the Salad Bowl of England, and, inland from Southport, asparagus became an important speciality.

Cultivation of the land was not therefore destroyed by the rapid growth of the manufacturing centres which by 1870 were producing an expanding range of chemicals, soaps, metallurgical and engineering products, leather, glass, ships, processed foodstuffs and drinks. Between 1870 and 1939 new industries came into being and older industries experienced far-reaching changes. New technology, developed within Merseyside or imported from outside the region, revolutionised some industries. In some cases new technology combined with the need to tap economies of large scale caused the concentration of production as happened in flour-milling and brewing. In other cases the use of new methods and new raw materials broke the traditional links between industries and caused long-established firms to venture into the production of a diversified range of commodities. The soap industry, as we have seen, had played a key role in the creation of the chemical industry through its urgent demand for soda. After 1870 soap manufacturers still needed soda but the growing use of imported vegetable oils in place of tallow inevitably linked the industry's fortunes more and more closely with the production of margarine and animal feeding-stuffs. At the same time the hitherto vital links between chemical and copper production were temporarily weakened.

Another very noticeable feature of the more successful Merseyside firms was the adoption and development of much more aggressive marketing methods. Increasingly products were branded and sold in distinctive wrappings so that customers could easily recognise them and retailers could more easily handle them. These methods inevitably necessitated extensive advertising campaigns and it was by such means that rapidly growing firms like Beechams, Lever Bros. and Henry Tate rose from obscurity to become industrial giants.

To some extent Merseyside's prosperity followed the cyclical upswings and downswings common throughout Britain and it was equally affected by war-time stimuli and dislocations but, in addition, the fortunes of Merseyside's component parts fluctuated

relatively to each other: some older industries declined or concentrated in fewer districts and new industries developed. Very
importantly in this period some of Merseyside's firms or even
whole industries were irresistibly swept into the mainstream of
national and even international influences. Through natural
growth, through horizontal and vertical integration, through
mergers, amalgamations and takeovers, some formerly independent
concerns simply became parts of massive corporations so that it
becomes more and more difficult to talk about them in regional
terms. At the same time, the switch of economic power to the
south-east of England meant that even those giants originally
conceived in Merseyside frequently switched their head offices
to London. Vital policy decisions were, therefore no longer taken
in the region, nor were they even necessarily closely relevant to
the interests of Merseyside: they related to national or international strategies and responded to the national and international
environment. In the process of rationalisation after mergers it
was often necessary to reduce the number of manufacturing
units: many hitherto independent businesses were closed in
Merseyside for this reason.

Nowhere were all these general trends more evident than in
the rapidly growing and equally rapidly diversifying chemical
industries which, by 1939, were dominated by the massive
Imperial Chemical Industries (I.C.I.). By 1870, Britain's earlier
Industrial Revolution based on cotton, iron, coal, steam power
and railways had largely run its course. Of greater importance
on Merseyside was the 'chemical revolution'. It became increasingly
clear as industrialisation progressed in the more advanced
countries that chemical production must occupy a key position
as the foundation for many other industries. Merseyside's
chemical industries therefore became of crucial importance
(nationally as well as regionally) as developing technology swept
them into the production of a growing range of heavy chemicals
as well as leading to diversification in the production of consumer
goods such as pharmaceuticals, man-made fibres and dyestuffs.

Before 1870 the products of the chemical industry had, as we
have seen, been crucial for a narrow group of producers
especially soap-makers, glass-makers and bleachers. Apart
from the dependence of such firms on the supply of soda and
bleaching products, chemical production mostly attracted public
attention because of devastating pollution of the environment.
Public resistance to pollution had led to intensive research to
isolate the pollutants, to convert them into by-products and to
find new methods of production which did not have such serious
side effects. Between 1870 and 1914 this research bore fruit in
the application of two new processes to replace the Leblanc
process - the Solvay process and electrolytic decomposition of
salt.

The Solvay, or ammonia-soda process, patented in 1863, was
first applied in Britain at Winnington where, in 1872-3, Ludwig
Mond[1] and John Brunner established a partnership (converted

into the Brunner Mond Co. Ltd. in 1881) specifically to use the
Solvay process. They made the important decision that they
would work on the Cheshire salt-fields at Winnington instead
of operating in the established chemical areas of Widnes, Warrington or St Helens. The new firm expanded rapidly buying land to
acquire salt deposits and eventually absorbing other neighbouring producers. Winnington became the major new growth centre
for the industry leading to a proliferation of products and it
gradually undermined the industry in the older centres.

Firms still using the Leblanc process were not, however,
prepared to give up without a struggle. Pressure on their soda
markets was largely counterbalanced by the thriving demand
from the textile industries for their chlorine by-products for
bleaching during the 1870s. Early in the next decade, however,
pressure exerted by Solvay production at home was greatly
reinforced by foreign competition, particularly by a decline in
one hitherto very profitable trade as the U.S.A. raised tariffs
and began to make its own ammonia soda. In 1883, Merseyside
Leblanc producers tried to control prices by forming the Lancashire Bleaching Powder Manufacturers Association. This afforded
them a very temporary reprieve but it quickly became apparent
that a closer and stronger association was imperative. In 1890
forty-eight factories in England, Scotland and Ireland formed
the United Alkali Company with the not inconsiderable share
capital of £5 million. This first large national merger in the
chemical industry was of both immediate and of longer-term
significance. It included the whole of St Helens' chemical industry
and a major part of the Widnes industry in a national merger.

This move enabled some of the older producers of heavy
chemicals to survive by rationalising their organisation but the
very process of rationalisation was not an unmitigated blessing.
Some units had to be closed and between 1900 and 1930 St Helens'
chemical industry was largely phased out. The surviving components of the United Alkali Company were eventually switched
either to the ammonia soda process or to another new process -
the electrolytic production of soda and chlorine: this had been
devised and developed during the 1890s by the Castner-Kellner
Alkali Company which produced both caustic soda and bleaching
powder at Runcorn.

Salt, soda and bleaches were still, therefore, of major importance in chemical production and, fortunately, there were still
plentiful supplies of the major raw material, salt: in fact during
the 1860s output had outstripped demand leading to falling
prices. Some sixty-four salt producers formed a merger in 1888,
the Salt Union Limited, to try to control prices. This Union,
with a nominal capital of £4 million, claimed control of ninety
per cent of the U.K.'s salt output. Supply still far exceeded
demand and the salt producers' efforts to control prices were
further seriously undermined by chemical producers' increasing
use of brine in place of rock salt.

Meanwhile the range of products of the chemical industry was

continually increasing: by its very nature it was an industry
in which there was continuous research and development to find
new ways of making traditional products and new by-products
and this inevitably opened up new fields for enterprise. Although
research in coal-tar distillation and dyestuffs was centred in
Germany before 1914 (and there were two German firms in
business in Merseyside), British chemists were also beginning
to move into this field. In Widnes, the Alumina Co. Ltd. was
created in 1908 to make alumina, paints, soap and various drugs
and, in 1915, it was taken over by the British Alumina Co. Ltd.
Other firms (e.g. Bowmans of Warrington) made such products
as lactic acid, sulphated oils and materials for the tanning
industry. At Runcorn Castner-Kellner made solvents for engineering and increasingly for dry-cleaning. In Widnes the production
of zinc white thrived supplying new products to local and
national manufacturers of paint, linoleum and rubber. Chemical
fertilisers, sulphuric acid and copper products were still in
great demand and, to meet the ever-widening range of chemical
producers' needs for equipment, the development of chemical
engineering was essential.

Also in evidence was pharmaceutical production and this
eventually was to become a very important part of the industry.
Especially notable was the thriving young business set up to
produce Beechams Pills. Thomas Beecham had started to sell
his pills in Wigan in 1847 and when he moved to St Helens he
experienced rapid growth associated with his famous advertising
slogan 'worth a guinea a box'.[2] By 1866 he already had wholesale
agents in Liverpool, Manchester, London, Leeds, York and
Wolverhampton. From the 1880s he launched a national advertising campaign that successfully established the business as a
national concern.

If anyone had harboured any doubts about the chemical
industry's vital role in a modern economy, they were finally
dispelled by the 1914-18 war. The country's dependence on
chemical production gained government recognition and led
eventually to protective tariffs and other measures to encourage
the production of key commodities in order to reduce dependence
on imports. Guaranteed markets and high prices during the war
encouraged rapid expansion and changing organisation in the
industry especially amongst the largest firms. Under the pressure of war-time demand the United Alkali Company completed
its switchover from the Leblanc process to the electrolytic
process. The Castner-Kellner works at Runcorn expanded its
output of chlorine, caustic soda and hydrogen, Brunner Mond
made ammonium nitrate for explosives as well as producing a
wider range of industrial chemicals.

The war gave a further impetus to mergers in the industry -
both Brunner Mond and Castner-Kellner absorbed small firms
but, more significantly, in 1916 they exchanged shares to bring
their organisations closer together, a move which proved to be
a prelude to Brunner Mond's takeover of Castner-Kellner in

1920. The creation abroad of massive corporations such as Du Pont, I.G. Farben, the Union Carbide and Carbon Corporation and the Allied Chemical and Dye Corporation, put increasing pressure on the British industry. If it were to compete on equal terms with such giants it had to be organised in a similar way. In 1926, therefore, Imperial Chemical Industries was formed by merging Brunner Mond, the United Alkali Company, Nobel Industries of Ayrshire and the British Dyestuffs Corporation Ltd. (itself a large merger centred on Manchester in 1919).[3] Britain's new national corporation, I.C.I., chaired by Sir Alfred Mond, had a share capital of £65 million. Much of Merseyside's chemical industry was now only a division of this mammoth concern: In Merseyside production was particularly concentrated on traditional products, especially alkali, mineral acids, chlorine and nitrogen fixation. In 1937 the Salt Union also became part of I.C.I. with its headquarters at Winsford.

As with the rest of the chemical industry the production of proprietary medicines was also marked by natural growth, mergers and product diversification. Beechams, in particular, underwent a series of reorganisations and expansion throughout the inter-war years. Beechams Estates and Pills Ltd., formed in 1924, was broken up in 1928. Beechams Pills Ltd. was then created to absorb other producers of proprietary medicines - Veno Drug Ltd., Sherley, Prichard and Constana and Lintox. In the 1930s further acquisitions included Yeast Vite Ltd., Iron Jelloid Co. Ltd., Macleans Ltd. and Eno Proprietaries Ltd. and new companies were formed such as Phensic Ltd.

During this period, the very strong links that we examined in Chapter 4 between soap and chemical production weakened somewhat. Chemical producers now had many more interests and so were less dependent on the soap industry for the sale of their products. At the same time soap producers' orientation changed as the growing use of vegetable oils instead of tallow linked their fortunes more closely with the production of margarine and animal foods (although the links with the chemical industry were later to be greatly strengthened again as changing technology created detergents derived from petroleum). The difficulties involved in ensuring adequate supplies of vegetable oils at a reasonable price inexorably forced soap producers into operations abroad and contributed to the fact that soap, like many other industries, was increasingly subjected not only to national but also to multi-national influences.

In 1870 Merseyside's important soap producers such as Hudsons of Liverpool, Crosfields of Warrington, Gossages of Widnes and Hazelhursts of Runcorn were selling unbranded soap in a slowly growing market in competition with producers in other ports, especially in Bristol, London and Newcastle. Prices were falling throughout the century: Gladstone's repeal of the excise tax on soap in 1853 had given a notable boost to demand. Consumption per head in Britain had risen from 7.1 lbs per head per year in 1851 to 17.4 lbs by the end of the century[4]

and this combined with increasing population to ensure that
demand was buoyant.

The nature of the industry changed very radically during
this period with the entry of a newcomer who shook the long-
established producers to their very foundations. In 1885,
William Lever, a wholesale grocer, started a soap factory in
Warrington. So successful was he that in 1889 he moved to a
tract of land on the Cheshire side of the Mersey where he built
Port Sunlight. His methods seemed revolutionary to the traditional producers: by using more copra oil and palm kernel oil
and less tallow he created a more attractive kind of soap. Enclosed in a distinctive wrapping and branded 'Sunlight Soap'
it was advertised on a massive scale to the chagrin of the rest
of industry whose soaps were unbranded. In 1894 William Lever
added 'Lifebuoy' and in 1899 'Monkey Brand' to his brands and
in 1900 he launched Lux flakes. [5]

William Lever's new methods of production and marketing
took the industry by storm and he spectacularly shot into the
position of leading producer: by the mid-1890s he was already
controlling about a fifth of the U.K.'s total output. Within four
years the private company he had formed in 1890 with a nominal
capital of £300,000 was converted into Lever Bros. Ltd., a
public company with a nominal capital of £1.5 million. Well before
William Lever's entry into the industry a Soap Makers Association
had been formed in 1867 and attempts had been made to divide
up the British market on a regional basis. This Association was,
however, relatively weak and its members were soon badly hit
by Lever's methods. Some tried to meet him on level terms by
branding their own products but they lacked both Lever's outstanding flair for marketing and his entrepreneurial abilities
and they found it hard to survive despite the growing consumer
demand to 1900 which was fuelled by rising real incomes and
population growth. After 1900 there was some slowing down in
the growth of demand and at the same time foreign competition
(especially from Dutch firms) became intense but Lever remained
very much the market leader not only in Merseyside but throughout Britain and he demonstrated this by buying up older producers. By 1914 Lever Bros. controlled some 61 per cent of
Britain's output and by the 1920s this concern controlled 70 per
cent of domestic consumption and 90 per cent of Britain's exports.

Meanwhile the battle for raw materials had been exerting a
growing influence over investment and development policies.
The use of imported vegetable oils in place of tallow had
significant effects by bringing soap and margarine producers
in Britain and on the Continent into conflict in their efforts to
control world supplies which were increasing at a slower rate
than demand. William Lever tried various strategems: he began
to develop palm culture in the Belgian Congo and built up a
group of African trading companies to supply oil seeds. He
acquired oil mills in America and Australia before eventually
building one at Port Sunlight which inevitably took him into

the animal feeding stuffs industry. Both soap and margarine
producers also became increasingly interested in the possibility
of using whale oil: a new process, hydrogenation, which would
have rendered whale oil a suitable substitute for vegetable oils
became the subject of bitter patent battles. Eventually in 1913
the leading European soap and margarine producers established
a Whale Oil Pool to regulate and distribute supplies. For a few
years Levers' links with chemical producers were further weakened. He had become concerned about his supplies of caustic
soda and bought up a salt estate on which he could produce
his own soda and so free himself from the monopoly now exercised by Brunner Mond. The latter replied by buying up two
soap producers - Crosfields and Gossages.

Such tests of strength between the growing industrial giants
were interrupted by the first World War. Competition from the
important Dutch margarine producers, Jurgens and Van den
Berghs, was temporarily removed and there was an urgent demand
in Britain for soap and margarine leading to a sellers' market
protected from foreign competition. After the war Dutch competition revived. William Lever expanded his margarine production
and tried to ensure sales by acquiring his own retail outlets,
namely the chain of food shops. Once he owned these retail
shops he diversified further buying up Walls sausages and ice
cream to supply his retailers. He also launched into a further
programme of takeovers of firms producing soap and other
products including Crosfields, Gossages, Watsons, D. & W. Gibbs,
John Knights and Prices Patent Candle Co. In 1923 the Bromborough Dock Act allowed Levers to build their own private dock
(opened in 1931) to handle bulk oils and oilseeds, raw materials
for their traditional products.

Lever's business had, of course, long since outgrown its
regional basis and with increasing diversification the head office
was moved to London, but the boom of the early twenties quickly
ended. With the post-war collapse of prices markets shrank and
competition between British and foreign producers intensified.
In 1925 Lord Leverhulme died and eventually in 1929 Lever Bros.
and their Dutch competitors accepted the inevitable: continuing
competition would very likely destroy them all whereas cooperation could be fruitful. They decided to create two concerns -
Unilever Ltd. in Britain and Unilever N.V. in Holland. This
merger coincided with deepening world depression. Excess
capacity had to be mercilessly eradicated by rationalisation to
cut costs and reduce competition. In 1931 Unilever included some
forty nine soap producers: several were closed including
Gossages of Widnes. Unilever's African interests also had to
be pruned: the capital of its United Africa Co. was halved in
1931.

So another of Merseyside's most successful and rapidly growing concerns was converted first into a national and then into a
multi-national enterprise engaged in oil-seed crushing and
refining edible oils, and producing such commodities as cooking

fats, margarine, soap, oleochemicals and fatty acid derivates. By the early 1930s some of the manufacturing units that had formerly been independent businesses had been eradicated but the 1930s were not wholly gloomy: between 1929 and 1939 Unilever's sales of washing powders rose from 200,000 tons to 900,000 tons; the 1930s also witnessed an expansion in the output of toilet soap and, even more importantly, there was the beginning of what was to become the massive new business of soapless detergents.

The process of crushing seeds to obtain oils for soap, margarine etc. leaves behind valuable oil-cake for animal feeding stuff and Lever's oilseed crushing mill inevitably brought them into this industry too but this was a competitive industry including many other well-known firms such as Bibbys, Ranks, Silcocks, Spillers and Calthrop. In fact Merseyside became the largest producer of animal feeding stuffs in the country - about thirty per cent of the labour engaged in producing feeding stuffs in England and Wales was located in Merseyside.

Like soap, glass had been one of the industries whose demand for raw materials had stimulated chemical production and like the soap industry it too outgrew its humble origins. By 1870 Merseyside's glass production was concentrated in St Helens where local coal supplies and Shirdley Hall sand were still plentiful. Local chemical producers could still supply alkali but in addition in the 1860s Pilkingtons had created their own Mersey Chemical Works to supply saltcake for their own needs. By the 1870s this works was already selling bleaching powder and nitrate of soda to other customers.

The potential market for window glass had been expanding since the removal of the excise duty in 1840 and the repeal of the window tax in 1851. Population growth meant a large demand for houses and changes in technology made it easier to satisfy this and other growing markets especially the demand for plate glass which Pilkingtons started to produce in the 1870s. During the late nineteenth century many British glass producers especially in N.E. England failed to keep abreast of technological changes and consequently they fell by the wayside so reducing competition within Britain. At the same time, however, foreign competition became increasingly severe especially from Belgian firms and, during the 1890s, from America.

In the twentieth century Pilkingtons experienced somewhat mixed fortunes but the long-term trend, as in so many other progressive industries, was towards larger scale, mergers and takeovers and diversification of products.[6] Heavy investment in research and new technology such as high-speed grinding machinery for plate glass, continuous production and electrification greatly increased the volume of output. Cooperation with Ford at Detroit to develop plate glass for cars at the end of the 1914-18 war gave Pilkingtons an international advantage and their very effective marketing organisation developed sales at home and opened up wider markets abroad.

During the inter-war years Pilkingtons fell behind in the production of window glass but the development of plate glass and
other products more than compensated. The building boom
created opportunities for the sale of new types of glass such as
glassbricks and wired glass. Another new product was the high
voltage toughened glass insulator. Expanding car production
opened up new possibilities in the market for safety glass and
a start was made on the development of what was to become a
very important new commodity - fibre glass.

Throughout the inter-war years Belgian competition remained
fierce but Pilkingtons commitment to research and to investment
in new technology allowed them to hold their own against Belgian
firms. Meanwhile they embarked on a policy of expansion by
absorbing more firms at home and abroad to reduce competition
and to secure both materials and marketing outlets. They had
marketing subsidiaries and warehouses in such countries as
Canada, Australia and China. By 1936 Pilkingtons owned Sheet
Glass Ltd., the British Vitrolite Co. Ltd. and the Anglo-Belgian
Silver Sand Co. Ltd., the Société Industrielle de Grimberghen
and O.C. Hawkes of Birmingham (a furniture and mirror manufacturer). They had investments in such concerns as Rockware,
Chances, Joblings, N.V. Hollandsche Maatschappij Voor de
Vervaarding Van Glas. They also owned the Greengate Brick
and Tile Works Ltd.

Their introduction into brick production had been a natural
development stemming from their involvement during the nineteenth century in coal production. It was common for collieries
in the S.W. Lancashire coalfield to use the clay brought from
underground to make bricks. Pilkingtons had therefore been
drawn into brick production as a result of their decision in the
mid-nineteenth century to produce their own coal through the
Ravenhead Colliery Co. Ltd. and the St Helens Collieries Co.
Ltd. In this way they could obtain their own coal at favourable
rates as well as earning profits by selling coal to customers.
The former was a major consideration because by the 1870s
Pilkingtons were consuming some 75,000 tons of coal a year and
subsequently their consumption rose even higher.

For many other industries too coal was still the main fuel and
source of energy despite some growth in the use of gas and
electricity. The South-West Lancashire coalfield which pene-
trated into Merseyside in the St Helens/Prescot district therefore retained its great importance for the region's industries.
The 1870s had opened with a boom in coal prices which lured
many speculators into the industry and even during the so-
called Great Depression this industry continued to grow. In
the St Helens district alone employment in coal production rose
from 3,000 in 1881 to around 6,000 in 1901. By 1939 pits in this
district were employing about 6,500 miners and 1,500 surface
workers but during the inter-war years the coal industry's
general decline had set in and employment slumped partly due
to the general industrial depression even though coal was the

source of other forms of energy - first of all gas and then increasingly electricity. Initially the gas and electricity industries were operated by private companies. During the late nineteenth and early twentieth centuries, however municipalities increasingly became responsible for the operation of a wide range of trading services including not only gas and electricity but also water, tramways and later bus services etc. So such industries as electric supply became public undertakings and then in the 1920s the whole country's electricity supply began to be linked together through the National Grid.

Copper like glass had been very closely linked with chemical production but again after 1870 the ties between these two industries were weakened, although copper remained an important component of Merseyside's metallurgical and engineering production. We have already seen that Merseyside was not in the mainstream of the metallurgical innovations associated with the Industrial Revolution and yet metals and engineering products were by no means an unimportant part of the region's industrial structure. Both the raw materials and many finished products were heavy and bulky and Merseyside's good water communications enabled industries to obtain supplies of coal, ore and metals and to move their finished products. Consequently there were firms scattered throughout the region producing a wide range of metal and engineering products.

At Runcorn and Widnes copper was still smelted, refined and converted into such products as rods and plates for locomotives and rollers for calico printing. The St Helens sector of the industry, however, experienced a serious decline. Along the banks of the Leeds and Liverpool canal in north Liverpool tin was smelted and in Widnes the smelting of lead and refining of silver continued; there were also foundries and sheet-iron works and the production of galvanised iron sheets was of growing importance. This was an industry particularly suited to ports: by 1890 six galvanised corrugated iron works were operating in Liverpool, one in Ellesmere Port and another in Birkenhead. Sheets were either produced locally in Warrington, Stalybridge, Huyton Quarry, Bolton and Manchester or brought by water or rail from Staffordshire. A high proportion of the finished produce was exported.

The early 1900s witnessed an important expansion in steel production when John Summers established a large new works at Hawarden Bridge at the entrance to the Dee estuary (although the original intention of using water transport for materials and products had to be abandoned in favour of rail transport). This became a major new area of steel production and during the 1914-18 war output was further expanded by government assistance and the ploughing back of high war-time profits. By the 1920s John Summers ranked as Britain's chief producers of steel sheet although this was a position they were soon to yield to Lysaghts because of their failure to recognise the significance of the newly developing market for motor-body sheet.

During the 1930s they tried to remedy this: in the mid-1930s work started on a new strip mill which was in operation just in time for the second World War.

Many other parts of the region were also important in the production of metal goods and engineering products – one very important centre being Warrington where the most important products were nails, tubes for all sorts of purposes (tubular bridges, scaffolding, clothes posts etc.) and an endless range of wire products – netting, colliery ropes, springs, torpedo nets for the Admiralty. All sorts of metal products were also made in St Helens and in Widnes – the Widnes Foundry and Engineering Co. Ltd. for example produced materials for Victorian piers, it supplied the shell for London's Underground and countless miles of iron pipes to carry water from Lake Vyrnwy to Liverpool and from Thirlmere to Manchester. Widnes High Speed Steel Alloys Ltd. was formed during the first World War to supply special grades of steel. In the St Helens district metal-working also continued especially for the production of nails.

Aluminium was a somewhat newer metal produced and processed in the region in increasing quantities and from 1914 this became an important industry in Warrington where a new works was opened to produce sheet aluminium and to roll, draw and extrude it. On the other hand some of the older metal-goods industries experienced a fairly rapid decline. Watch and clock production rapidly died out: by 1890 it had gone altogether from Liverpool. In Prescot some parts and tools were still made and from 1890 one watch factory tried to compete with mass-production methods abroad but eventually this too succumbed in 1910. Some other branches of engineering, however, thrived and some new products began to be made. There were, for example, plants scattered through the region producing various types of steam engines and gas engines and in the inter-war years some aircraft production began. The production of scientific apparatus for the chemical industry expanded after the establishment of J.W. Towers and Co. Ltd. in Widnes in 1882.

Marine engineering continued to occupy a place in the region's economy although shipbuilding had largely moved across the Mersey from Liverpool to Birkenhead. In 1903 Lairds amalgamated with Charles Cammell & Co., steelmakers of Sheffield, so creating one of the most up-to-date shipbuilding concerns in the country, but this was by no means Merseyside's only shipyard. In Birkenhead all types of ships were produced and repaired ranging from naval and passenger vessels and naval craft to dredgers and ice-breakers. H.M.S. *Rodney* and H.M.S. *Prince of Wales* and two *Ark Royals* were built there. In other parts of Merseyside along rivers and canals smaller boats were built and repaired. At Runcorn the Bridgewater Navigation Company's boats were built and repaired and large numbers of coastal vessels were constructed. There were also boat-building and repair yards around the coast and estuary at Hoylake,

Bromborough Pool and Ellesmere Port. On the other hand, the foreshore between Tranmere Pool and Rock Ferry was used, not for building, but for breaking up vessels including the *Great Eastern* in the 1880s. Although Merseyside was by no means one of the U.K.'s major shipbuilding areas by the twentieth century, this industry was still an important part of the region's industrial structure.

Advances in technology opened up opportunities for the manufacture of many new engineering products including a wide range of electrical goods. A notable development was the Automatic Telephone and Electric Co. Ltd. formed in Liverpool in 1912: this company began by making telephone apparatus but went on to produce other things such as traffic signals, equipment for metering electricity, gas, water and oil, and remote control switches for street-lighting. At Prescot British Insulated Cables became a large producer of electric cables and overhead transmission systems. Marconi established the first marine wireless service depot in Seaforth as early as 1903. Much of the equipment for major electrification schemes was, however, produced outside the region. For example, the Preston firm, Dick Kerr, supplied the traction motors and control gear for Liverpool's Overhead Railway and equipment for Liverpool's electric tramway system and for the electrification of the Southport-Liverpool railway in 1904.

As we have seen earlier, textiles did not play an important role in Merseyside's industrial structure although there were still some scattered producers. In Warrington the defunct sailcloth industry had given birth to the production of tents and marquees and the wire industry (wire springs) gave rise to furniture production which in turn needed upholstery materials. Clothing manufacturers were scattered through the region: some were to be found in Warrington and Widnes, others in the salt-fields especially around Winsford. In Liverpool some employment was found in making hosiery, overalls and millinery and in tailoring and dress-making. Towards the end of this period the production of rayon began to grow in the region no doubt due to this new industry's need for close links with the chemical industry.

Many of Merseyside's traditional industries had grown up on the basis of local supplies of raw materials but some now depended increasingly on imports. Tanning was one such industry. Originally engaged in processing home-produced skins and hides with local tanning materials, this industry now imported both tanning materials and hides especially from South America. It thrived in Warrington, Runcorn and Liverpool to the 1920s producing leather for boots and shoes, harness, saddles, upholstery, bags etc. but after the first World War production was increasingly affected by competition from substitutes, especially rubber and later plastics.

Milling had also developed to process locally-produced grain but increasingly imported grains were fed into the mills through docks specially equipped with bulk-handling facilities, massive warehouses and floating elevators. The number of mills continued to decline but those still operating grew into large mechanised concerns driven by steam power or gas engines and fed by travelling belts from the holds of ships or from elevators. With such well-known millers as Applebys, Rank, Vernon and Wilson Merseyside became the leading milling area in Europe with Birkenhead and Wallasey occupying first place within the region, Liverpool the second place and other large steam driven mills in Warrington, Runcorn and Ellesmere Port.

Other industries concerned with the processing of foods and drink also continued to thrive and to grow in scale. Although there were still some small breweries (e.g. in 1916 there were still some thirteen breweries in Liverpool alone), brewing like milling was increasingly concentrated in large concerns such as Greenall Whitleys, Whitbreads, Bents, Tetley Walker and Higsons. This industry was not so dependent on importing raw materials from abroad: it still drew some from the hinterland and the rest from farther afield in Britain. By contrast another traditional industry, sugar refining had always been largely dependent on imported materials which were processed by the use of local coal and water. It was not until the twentieth century that intensive efforts were made to cultivate beet sugar in Britain and even then the growing areas were distant from Merseyside. Sugar refining was another industry dominated during this period by giants and by national and international considerations rather than regional ones. Already in the 1860s Macfie & Sons of Liverpool was the U.K.'s largest producer of soft sugar. In 1873 twelve of the U.K.'s fifty refineries were located in the centre of Merseyside with another large one, Sankeys, nearby at Earlestown; the main competing centres were Glasgow and London. By 1900 this industry had experienced a rapid reduction in the number of producers and an equally notable increase in scale. Between 1880 and 1900 two new firms had come to dominate the industry: Henry Tate of Liverpool who started business in 1870 and Abraham Lyle of Greenock and Plaistow. By 1900 these two concerns controlled some $62\frac{1}{2}$ per cent of the U.K.'s sugar production. They had achieved this dominating position by adopting new technology, by producing specialised types of sugar (syrup, cubes and high grade crystals), by branding, by the use of distinctive packaging and by vigorous advertising and sales compaigns.

By the early twentieth century many inefficient firms had been driven out of business or absorbed by the industry-leaders and the Liverpool firm, Henry Tate & Sons, was already extending its operations to the south, opening a refinery at Silvertown. After the first World War Tates and Lyles started to talk about the possibility of a merger and this materialised in 1921. Despite some personal difficulties, the merger proved a success allowing the two U.K. giants to combine their technical expertise, to rationalise their plants and to refrain from compe-

tition in the market place. As in other such mergers, Merseyside's interest now took second place to national interests and
this reinforced Liverpool's loss of locational advantage as beet
sugar from the continent and eastern England increasingly
replaced imported cane sugar. London now offered greater
advantages for the industry although some cane sugar was still
imported into Liverpool from Jamaica and Trinidad and in fact
Tate & Lyle formed the West Indies Sugar Co. in 1937.

Because of the ample supplies of sugar and flour and the
local production of fruit and vegetables other food processing
activities were able to thrive including the production of biscuits (e.g. Jacobs, Crawfords), jams (Hartley), canned foods,
bread, sweets (e.g. Everton mints), confectionery, chocolate,
cocoa (supplied by the West African trade), fruit preserving
and fruit canning. Although Liverpool was no longer very
important as a fishing centre, both trawling and shell-fishing
were still valuable occupations in other parts of the region such
as Crosby, Formby, Rock Ferry, New Ferry, Tranmere, Egremont and New Brighton. From Hoylake and Parkgate a fine fleet
of smacks fished in the Irish Sea landing their catches at
Liverpool. Within the estuary flat fish abounded, around the
coast Leasowe, Formby and Southport were well-known for their
cockles and shrimps and there were extensive mussel beds at
Hoylake. As an adjunct to fishing many boatmen still supplemented their incomes by running trips for tourists.

An industry that tended to decline during this period was
the processing of tobacco. Among several factories in Merseyside was Ogdens, a branch of the Imperial Tobacco Co. but
during the inter-war years Merseyside began to lose its hold on
the trade. By contrast oil refining was a relatively new industry
that was to gain a considerable foothold in the region. As early
as 1879 the Herculaneum Dock had special storage facilities in
caves cut in the rocks for barrels and tins of paraffin. During
the first World War refining was developed at Stanlow and after
the war Shell Mex started refining there. So the foundations
were laid for the later development of a large refinery.

Rubber too was a growing industry. Between 1875 and 1914
Liverpool was the chief import port for raw rubber from the
Americas and Africa. After 1918 supplies from the Far East were
increasing in importance these were often directed to London.
The availability of raw rubber had, however, already led to the
production of rubber goods before 1870: for example the first
U.K. manufacturer of rubber footwear was the Liverpool Rubber
Co. formed in 1859 and the range of rubber products grew
steadily. In 1925 the Liverpool Rubber Company was taken over
by Dunlops who also established other factories to produce
footwear, tyres, sportsgoods, and general rubber goods at
Bidston, Garston, Speke and Walton.

The range of miscellaneous products and services to be found
in Merseyside is too great to be covered exhaustively but in
addition to the industries already mentioned there were large

numbers of laundries, firms distilling tar and making asbestos, cement, paints, gelatine, glue and linoleum. There were the Bowater Group's large newsprint mill at Ellesmere Port, Bryant and Mays Match Works, Hornby trains and Meccano, printing and book-binding firms, football pools, makers of musical instruments and workers in marble. Most industries and trades needed containers of some sort for their produce and these were produced in large quantities in a seemingly endless range of forms - barrels, packing cases, cardboard, wooden and tin boxes, drums and kegs, canisters, baskets and hampers, sacks and paper bags. There were also many industries still devoted to supplying the needs of the building industry. Quarrying continued in many areas and brick-making was to be found in every part of the region. New technology brought into operation firms producing pre-cast concrete. Pottery production had largely died out by the mid-nineteenth century but some was still produced in Runcorn, Rainford and St Helens especially to provide builders with drainpipes, tiles and stoneware.

Building itself remained a very important industry though subject to severe fluctuations in prosperity as the demand for its products alternately boomed or slumped. Continuing population growth and obsolescence of the housing stock created a pressing demand for houses which was largely met by small builders and in the Liverpool area particularly by Welsh builders who had migrated to the city. By the inter-war years large contracts available from local authorities for housing estates encouraged the creation of large contractors but such jobs were put out to tender and many contracts were won by the national civil engineering and contracting firms that sprang up after the first World War. For example some forty per cent of Liverpool's local authority housing between the wars was built by Unit Construction, a subsidiary of Alfred Booth & Co., a shipping and leather company originally Liverpool-based that had moved to London. Some large local contractors developed such as Tysons and Williams but most large contractors had a national network of interests such as Laing, Henry Boot, Sir Robert McAlpine and Richard Costain.

The building industry did not have to confine itself to housing. Large areas were covered with industrial and commercial buildings, factories, offices and warehouses and during the inter-war years new activities demanded the services of builders and civil engineers - there was a rush of cinema-building, large numbers of electric sub-stations were needed for the National Grid, there was the building of many more roads, of Speke aerodrome, of the Mersey tunnel and during the 1930s a new source of industrial demand was created with the beginnings of the industrial estates designed to introduce new manufacturing industries to the region. In view of all the industries already mentioned it may seem perverse to say that Merseyside had too narrow an industrial base. It was, however, agreed both locally and nationally that more diversification was needed and indus-

trial estates were intended to promote this but they only began
to have a really important impact after the second World War
so consideration of them will be deferred to a later chapter.

NOTES

1. Mond's biography is available in J.M. Cohen, *The Life of
Ludwig Mond* (Methuen & Co., London, 1956).
2. Anne Francis, *A Guinea a Box. A Biography of Thomas
Beecham* (Hale, London, 1968).
3. The story of the creation of I.C.I. is told in W.J. Reader,
Imperial Chemical Industries: a history, 2 vols, (Oxford University Press, London, 1975).
4. A.E. Musson, *Enterprise in Soap and Chemicals. Joseph
Crosfield & Sons Ltd. 1815-1965* (Manchester University Press,
1965), p. 64.
5. William Lever's history is told in C.H. Wilson, *The History
of Unilever: a study in economic growth and social change* vol. I
(Cassell, London, 1954) and the creation of Unilever in ibid.,
vol. II and in W.J. Reader, *Unilever, a short history* (Unilever
House, London, 1960).
6. Pilkington's development is well-documented in T.C. Barker,
Pilkington Brothers and the Glass Industry (Allen and Unwin,
London, 1960) and T.C. Barker, *The Glassmakers: Pilkingtons,
the Rise of an International Company 1826-1976* (Weidenfeld and
Nicolson, London, 1977).

Chapter 8

THE MANAGED ECONOMY POST 1945

During the twentieth century Merseyside has been plagued by many seemingly intractable economic problems. The picture has not, of course, been uniform throughout the region but most of its constituent districts have been harassed by one or more of the endemic disadvantages. In most parts there has been an imbalance in the job opportunities for men and women: some districts suffering serious shortages of male employment, others lacking openings for women. Central Merseyside has particularly suffered from higher than average dependence on employment in the service, dock and transport industries compared with manufacturing, a dependency leading to chronic unemployment as these traditional industries have declined. This state of affairs has been compounded by rapid population growth which has increased the overall size of the labour force relatively to job opportunities. Consequently Merseyside has suffered persistently higher unemployment rates than national averages. In 1939 for example the percentage of unemployed in Merseyside was 18.8 compared with the national average for Great Britain and Northern Ireland of 9.6 per cent.

Efforts to counteract these tendencies encountered serious obstacles. New firms have frequently been deterred from moving into Merseyside by shortages of modern factory buildings, by the relative scarcity of skilled labour (compared with national averages) and by Merseyside's very bad public image (not wholly justified) in terms of strikes, vandalism, dereliction, pollution and high crime rates. Some of the new industries that have been attracted are capital-intensive, contributing only small numbers new jobs. Even worse, the opening of new factories has frequently coincided with or even been preceded by the closure of old ones. A continuous supply of new openings has therefore been needed simply to maintain the same total number of jobs.

It would seem obvious that the only viable solutions to such widespread problems must involve vigorous government intervention and, fortunately, there were precedents for such assistance well before the second world war. During the 1914-18 war the government had gained experience of intervention in the economy through the Ministry of Munitions and the widespread control and manipulation of all aspects of the economy. National Factories and new Royal Ordnance Factories were created and the government planned and directed private industry, shipping, railways, docks, imports and exports, and the capital markets. Merseyside had been intimately involved in

these government activities: Cammell Laird's, for example,
turned over to naval work, the docks were government-
controlled, railways were taken over, and the region's chemical
industry was wholly geared to war production. Additional works
were set up such as the one to produce synthetic phenol at
Ellesmere Port. National Factories in the region included one in
Liverpool to make cartridges and fill shells, a T.N.T. factory
at Litherland and an ammunition factory at St Helens. There
was a National Aircraft Factory at Aintree and nearby in
Cheshire, at Queen's Ferry, a very large T.N.T. factory and
nitrate plant.

After 1918 the government quickly disengaged itself throughout the country, allowing the reinstatement of private enterprise
but during the inter-war years chronic problems emerged both
nationally and locally. Many of Britain's staple industries were
declining against a backcloth of world depression. A new form
of government intervention was devised: namely the designation
of 'depressed areas' urgently in need of assistance. Under the
Special Areas (Development and Improvement) Acts of 1934 and
1937 financial provision could be made for building factories,
and for creating trading estates.

Merseyside, however, was in an ambiguous position: despite
chronic problems the region had a share of expanding industries.
Although unemployment for the region was at or above 18 per
cent it could not be claimed that Merseyside was a wholly derelict, hard-core, depressed area and so it did not qualify for
'depressed area' status. A unique solution was therefore needed
and initially it came through local initiative rather than from
central government. By the inter-war years local government
participation in economic matters was already extensive, including
the provision of gas, electricity and water, tramways and buses,
houses, roads and other transport facilities such as tunnels
and airports. In 1931 the Lancashire Industrial Development
Corporation was formed to look into the problems of finance for
new industries and the provision of marketing facilities and
labour: it served the interests of many Lancashire towns (inside
and outside Merseyside) including Liverpool and Manchester,
Bolton, Burnley, Oldham, Preston, Stockport, Widnes and
Wigan. [1]

In 1936 came a novel attempt to diversify the industrial base
of the very heart of Merseyside: in an act of Parliament powers
were given to Liverpool City Council that were unique at the
time although the same principle was subsequently applied elsewhere. [2] Previous development had used up the best building
sites in the city centre, along the docks and on other convenient
lines of communication. The Corporation was therefore given
powers to buy land on the outskirts of the city for industrial
estates to supply new jobs. On these estates the Corporation
could either build factories itself or provide inducements for
industrialists to build. Corporation-built factories could either
be leased or bought. A would-be purchaser could pay as little

as ten per cent repaying the remainder of the building's cost over twenty years at $4\frac{1}{2}$ per cent interest. Those wishing to build their own factories could obtain leases for 999 years and mortgages for up to 30 years for a maximum of two-thirds of the market value of each building.

The corporation immediately started two estates in 1936: one of 341 acres at Speke and the other of 300 acres at Fazakerley (renamed Aintree in 1952). Both enjoyed good communications: Aintree was close to the Leeds-Liverpool Canal and the new East Lancashire Road, and Speke was near to the port of Garston, it had adequate road and rail links and was located on part of the estate from which land was also allocated for the Liverpool Airport. A third estate was projected at Kirkby (which also enjoyed proximity to the East Lancashire Road) but the outbreak of war occurred before the conclusion of negotiations to buy the land.

By 1939, some factories were already operational at Aintree and Speke. At Aintree the aim was to develop clean industries - light engineering and food processing (e.g. jam-making, biscuits). At Speke there were firms concerned with light engineering, plywood and paper-bag making and manufacturing chemists. Some of the new factories were taken by existing firms attracted from the congested older industrial areas by better amenities - these of course did not bring new jobs to the region. There were, however, also some new developments: one potentially large employer was the Government's Shadow Aircraft Factory which was expected eventually to employ some 3,000 workers.

The outbreak of war in 1939 interrupted these developments but wartime production, including the building of some 15 Royal Ordnance Factories, was deliberately directed in such a way as to promote post-war development. In 1940, for example, a Royal Ordnance Factory was sited at Kirkby so that it could form the nucleus for a new industrial estate after the war. Another R.O.F. was built at Fazakerley and the Speke aircraft factory was greatly extended. These and other developments including the expansion of motor vehicle production in the region enabled the local labour force to acquire new engineering skills which could be redeployed post-war. As in the 1914-18 war, the chemical industry was mobilised for war and Cammell Lairds turned out a wide variety of battleships, submarines, aircraft carriers, cruisers, destroyers, tankers and cargo vessels as well as repairing and refitting merchant ships and naval vessels.

During the war the government attempted to assess the nature and extent of the problems likely to appear post-war after urgent wartime demands subsided. As early as 1940 the Barlow Report on the national distribution of industrial population drew attention to the imbalance arising from the southward drift of population and industry. The Employment Policies White Paper (Cmd. 6527, 1944) reiterated the problem and the 1945 Distribution of Industry Act empowered the Board of Trade to schedule 'development areas' in which land could be acquired and financial inducements could be provided to encourage new industrial development. At the local level in 1944 the *Merseyside Plan* was produced in consultation with a Technical Committee of the Merseyside Advisory Joint Planning Committee at the request of the Minister of Town and Country Planning.[3] This plan categorically asserted that the solution to congestion, slums and dilapidation in Merseyside was decentralisation: in the process of upgrading the central areas at least a quarter of a million people would be displaced. They should be resettled in other parts of the region and new jobs would have to be provided for them.

Certainly the war had by no means solved Merseyside's long-term problems. The devastation caused by bombing led to large rebuilding programmes. In Liverpool, for example, one third of all dock installations had been destroyed and another one third seriously damaged. They had to be rebuilt together with large areas of destroyed and damaged housing, commercial and industrial property. Despite the pent-up demand for rebuilding, unemployment, virtually obliterated during the war, quickly reappeared. Even the conversion of government factories to peacetime production could not fully compensate for both the decline in wartime employment and the rapidly growing population. Merseyside's unemployment figures soon reached two or three times the national average although the picture was by no means consistent throughout the region. As early as 1946 St Helens was detached temporarily from Central Merseyside and included with parts of South Lancashire in a development area to try to overcome serious economic and social problems: three years later, in 1949, Central Merseyside was similarly scheduled.[4] This development area included Liverpool, Bootle, Birkenhead, Wallasey, Bebington, Litherland, Huyton, Netherton, Aintree, Kirkby, Halewood and Simonswood. Such districts as Ellesmere Port and Runcorn were, at this juncture, regarded as potential growth points and were not included despite certain specialised needs such as a serious shortage of job opportunities for women. By comparison in much of central Merseyside, despite serious male unemployment, there were much better opportunities for women. In 1950 in central Merseyside the ratio of female to total labour was 36 per cent compared with the national average of under 34 per cent.

Taking the region as a whole, the wide range of problems and the varied fortunes of different parts of the region called for an equally wide range of solutions. Some efforts were concentrated on taking work to the worker by establishing new works in areas of high unemployment and regenerating run-down areas (e.g. Widnes); others involved moving blocks of population to new industries established in new towns (e.g. Runcorn and Skelmersdale) and in overspill areas (e.g. Ellesmere Port). The agencies for implementing these processes were also varied, including local authorities (e.g. Liverpool's Speke, Aintree and Kirkby Industrial Estates), private enterprise (e.g. Unilever's

Bromborough Industrial Estate) and central government (e.g.
Board of Trade estates and factories and from 1960, intensive
activity to expand the motor industry in the region). The Lancashire and Merseyside Industrial Development Association con-
ducted industrial surveys to provide information as well as
fostering the development of trade, industry and commerce.

The success of any such efforts to encourage industrial
expansion and diversification in order to reduce Merseyside's
dependence for employment on the transport and service industries depended in some measure at least on concomitant developments in communications - so that almost perversely, transport
facilities had to be extended and updated. Such developments
depended in turn on several different types of decision-making
bodies: local and central government, nationalised industries
and private enterprise. The Mersey Docks and Harbour Board
was still in the private sector and it launched into a great post-
war rebuilding programme to make good war-time devastation
and to create a highly mechanised, capital-intensive system
including the Royal Seaforth Container Dock. The container
terminal was computerised and there were special facilities
for handling grain, meat and timber and mechanisation slashed
the labour requirements of the docks. To reduce delays due to
fog a radar station was built. The fleet of dredgers, hopper
barges and floating cranes was also strengthened. These
developments were particularly concentrated on the north side
of Liverpool near to the sea so that large areas of older docks on
the south side further inland became derelict including the famous
Albert Dock.

The Manchester Ship Canal and its subsidiary the Bridgewater
Canal were not included in the nationalised waterways system
and their traffic increased for a time after the war though there
was a decline later and much of the Bridgewater Canal's inland
traffic came to be carried by road in its own fleet of lorries which
had steadily grown since the 1920s.[5] The Weaver Navigation, by
contrast, *was* included in the British Waterways Board's system
and underwent further modernisation including the construction
of new warehouses and a new depot at Anderton.

Ferry services across the Mersey gradually declined but
throughout the region road traffic boomed to carry both produce
and passengers, especially commuters. National and local
authorities had to undertake extensive work to cater for the
increased demand. The number of vehicles travelling through
the Mersey Tunnel rocketed from $3\frac{1}{4}$ million in the mid-1930s to
nearly 19 million in 1967-8 - little wonder a second tunnel had
to be constructed. This second tunnel emerged on the Wirral
side at Wallasey to join up with the mid-Wirral motorway (M53),
one of several motorways running through or near to Merseyside.
The M53 runs to within a few miles of Chester and links with the
M56 to give access to the M6 and the outskirts of Manchester. The
M6 running north/south just east of Merseyside can also be
reached from north Liverpool by the M58. From the outskirts of

south-east Liverpool the M62 runs near to Manchester and
thence across the Pennines to Yorkshire – giving Merseyside
its first really good road link with Yorkshire.

Rapid passenger travel to Yorkshire was also provided by
the railways' fast diesel trans-Pennine service. Merseyside's
railways were, of course, taken over by British Rail and pruned,
streamlined and modernised. Some lines were closed – the
Cheshire lines to Southport from Liverpool, the Southport/
Preston line, the West Kirby/Hooton service and Birkenhead's
rail links to London, but many passenger and freight services
were greatly improved. Freight depots were built (especially
to handle bulk products such as ores, steel, coal and chemicals)
adjacent to the docks on both sides of the Mersey with links to
the Mersey Docks and Harbour Board's internal rail and road
systems. Special bulk traffic services were also created to meet
the special needs of the Ellesmere Port refineries and of Ford
Motors. In 1969 responsibility for all local passenger transport
within the central conurbation was vested in the Merseyside
Passenger Transport Authority: the M.P.T.A. aimed to over-
see and co-ordinate local bus services and rail facilities and
it included a very important new commuter service – the new
underground system. This was built to link together under the
centre of the city the formerly separate rail services between
Liverpool and Southport, Ormskirk, Kirkby, Garston and the
Wirral. For long distance passengers the London/Liverpool line
was electrified for use by diesel electric locomotives which cut
the normal journey from about four hours to two and three
quarter hours.

Air transport could also be important to a developing region –
Speke airport had been taken over by the government during
the war and was only handed back to the city of Liverpool in
1961. Thereafter a new 7,500 foot runway was built and the
terminal buildings and freight facilities were modernised. The
airport has never, however, really thrived. Many airlines give
preference to Manchester's Ringway Airport, Speke was never
fully supported by the government, and it became a political
football kicked around by local government representatives and
rate payers who have resented subsidising it. It has therefore
had to struggle hard simply to survive.

Taken as a whole, communications both for passenger and
freight movements were sufficiently improved as not to act as a
brake on economic development in the region. It was therefore
possible for local governments, for the central government and
for private enterprise to launch into intensive development programmes to try to overcome some of Merseyside's long-standing
economic problems.

If we look first at local government initiative we find that it
became much more extensive after the war. Liverpool's Speke
estate had been rapidly expanded for war production. The
area developed to produce air frames during the war was subsequently taken over and extended by Dunlops. After the war

other firms also moved into the estate and by 1951 Speke's
population reached some 27,000. Speke was later to receive an
even greater boost during the 1960s with the development of
motor production. The Aintree Estate had also been stimulated
by war production especially by the building of a Royal Ordnance
Factory which was later taken over by Joseph Lucas. After the
war the estate was extended from Fazakerley and Aintree to
include Netherton where, in the early 1950s, English Electric
built a large new factory to produce a range of electrical goods:
in 1942 English Electric had already taken over the factory built
in Merseyside for D. Napier & Son to produce aero engines so
the Netherton works supplemented this. Other industries
established on this estate included artificial silk, the making of
tin canisters and drums and Schweppes large new factory for
making minerals and cordials. (Schweppes had been producing
mineral waters in Liverpool since 1836).

Merseyside's largest and best-known industrial estate was,
however, Kirkby: the attention both of the media and of academic
researchers has been irresistibly attracted by its serious social
and economic problems.[6] As we have seen the negotiations to buy
land for the estate were broken off by the war but during the
war a Royal Ordnance Factory, built on some 750 acres, was
intended to become the nucleus for the post-war development of
a 2,000 acre estate - one of the largest in Britain. At the time
the prognosis seemed favourable: there were good communications - an internal railway system built for the R.O.F., a link
to the Liverpool-Preston railway and, even more importantly,
proximity to the East Lancashire Road and eventually to the
M6 and the Runcorn road bridge. A wide range of factories
was built to accommodate firms of varying size producing goods
ranging from chemicals, photographic equipment, building
materials, wood, metal and engineering products to food processing; also included were service firms such as wholesale distri-
butors and transport depots. The local population grew apace
from 1,151 in 1931 and 3,078 in 1951 to 52,000 in 1961 and
58,000 in 1971. Unfortunately the estate proved unsuccessful
both economically and socially with very high closure rates,
unemployment rising to over 30 per cent, high crime rates and
social unrest.

Other areas within Merseyside also looked to industrial estates
to solve their difficulties. Birkenhead had its traditional industries - Joseph Ranks flour mills, tanning, brewing, mechanical
engineering and shipbuilding and ship-repairing. In the 1950s
Cammell Laird's had started an £18 million modernisation programme and there were also some thirty firms engaged in ship-
repairing but Birkenhead suffered some decline which needed to
be counteracted to maintain employment. After the war the
Tranmere Oil Jetty was built to supply Stanlow from large tankers
and in order to bring in light industries two small areas were
designated for industrial development at Arrowe Brook Road
and Prenton Dell - the mix of new industries included printing,

clothing and electrical engineering. Despite these efforts
Birkenhead's population declined from 151,000 in 1931 to just
over 141,000 in 1961 and to under 138,000 in 1971.

Another old area in desperate need of regeneration was
Widnes with its serious problem of pollution, dereliction and some
decline in traditional industries combined with rapid population
growth from 40,619 in 1931 to 52,168 in 1961 and to nearly
57,000 in 1971. This population growth was partly due to plans
to transfer some 15,000 surplus population from Liverpool to
Widnes but Widnes's inherited industrial base was fairly narrow
with chemical and metal production predominating. Amongst the
leading chemical producers were I.C.I.'s General Chemical
Division, Albright and Wilson, the Alumina Co. Ltd., Peter
Spence & Sons, Barium Chemicals Ltd., and the United Sulphuric Acid Corporation. To supply these chemical producers
laboratory equipment was made and, in addition, metals and
engineering production still played an important role in Widnes's
economy: such firms as Thomas Platt & Sons, the Widnes Foundry
and Engineering Co., British Copper Refiners Ltd. and High
Speed Steel Alloys Ltd. Other industries included Asbestos
Cement Products, fertiliser production, animal feeding stuffs
and an extensive timber trade. There was clearly a need for
light industry and for female employment, and the district was
given a considerable facelift by new industrial estates in Widnes
itself and nearby at Ditton: these attracted firms making such
products as baby linen, rainwear, clothing, ice cream and
potato crisps. Widnes also benefited from better road communications with the opening of the new Widnes/Runcorn road bridge.

The main private industrial estate in the region, the Bromborough Port Industrial Estate, controlled and administered by
Unilever, was developed pre-war with good road and rail communications as well as the dock facilities. Many firms on the
estate were members of the Unilever group manufacturing soap,
detergents, oleo-chemicals, fatty acid derivatives, animal feed,
margarine and cooking fats but, in addition, some independent
firms moved in to the estate including Kelvinator domestic
appliances, Viota foods, Girling vehicle components and firms
producing hydraulic presses, electrical switchgear, oxygen
welding equipment and packaging. As early as 1952 some 10,000
people were employed by some thirty firms. The district received a further stimulus by the building of the Vauxhall estate
on its borders.

Private enterprise was also responsible for a good deal of
development in Ellesmere Port and Stanlow. As we have seen
Ellesmere Port was an important port for the Manchester Ship
Canal: it had docks, wharves, mechanical handling equipment
and reasonably good road and rail links. Before 1939 it had
grown rapidly, its population increasing from 4,194 in 1901 to
10,253 in 1911 and to 23,057 by 1931. Between the wars the
oil, flour and paper industries thrived there as well as the
production of corrugated iron sheeting, bitumen, dyes and

metal containers. During the war oil was of vital importance.
A pipeline was constructed to the Thames and eventually it was
linked to the famous Pluto line for the invasion of Europe. [7]
By the end of the war the region's oil industry held a pre-
eminent place in the national industry and it was therefore
well-placed to act as a growth node for Merseyside. Shell built
a chemical plant (1946-49) and a very large new refinery (1949-
51) at Stanlow and by the 1960s Stanlow had one sixth of
Britain's total refining capacity handling some $10\frac{1}{2}$ million tons
of petroleum a year.

Oil was of course a continually developing industry both with
regard to size and technology. The increasing scale of tankers
created handling difficulties: in 1949 the Manchester Ship Canal
Company started to build the largest oil dock in Britain nearby
at Eastham – the Queen Elizabeth II dock was opened in 1954.
As tankers grew even larger a six-mile pipeline was built between Stanlow and a terminal at Tranmere (nearer the sea) and
eventually a 100-mile pipeline was designed to bring oil to
Stanlow from the Anglesey oil terminal which could meet the
needs of the very largest tankers.

Closely linked to oil refining was the petrochemical industry.
Plants were set up to produce carbon black, detergents, etc.
by leading companies – Shell Mex, Esso, B.P., Total and Burmah
Oil. Bowaters also already had a pulp mill there and factories
built to make paper products began to produce containers for a
growing range of oil products and to produce fibre pipes. Flour-
milling still remained an important local activity and new firms
were attracted to make roofing and decking materials, metal
windows and prefabricated houses.

In the years after the war the prospects for the Ellesmere
Port district seemed very bright but gradually the position
altered: as the oil industry became more and more mechanised
employment began to decline and yet there were plans to transfer some 20,000 of Liverpool's overspill population here. From
23,057 in 1931, the population had risen to over 44,000 by 1961
and to over 61,000 by 1971. In 1960 Ellesmere Port was included
in Merseyside's Development Area. In an effort to stem rising
unemployment the Borough Council established an estate for
light industry in 1961 and also in 1961 came the location of
Vauxhall Motors on the former Hooton Park Airfield on the
boundary of Ellesmere Port as part of the government's intensive
drive to expand the motor industry in Merseyside.

Central Government involvement in Merseyside's problems had
occurred spasmodically between 1946 and 1960: throughout the
region there was a smattering of Board of Trade factories and
estates built by North West Industrial Estates - the Board of
Trade's agent. The aim was to reinforce other efforts to diversify
the industrial base. To this end factories were built in Fazakerley,
Bromborough, Widnes, Speke, Birkenhead and Kirkby and, to
bring more jobs to the environs of Liverpool, industrial estates
were developed at Huyton and Knowsley. Although St Helens

retained some production of beer, bricks, clothing and animal foodstuffs, its coal and chemical industries had declined rapidly leaving it heavily dependent on Pilkington's Glass so a Board of Trade estate was developed at Parr to provide new light industries and to diversify the industrial base.

Some Merseyside industries were also very much affected by national decisions to nationalise certain industries. Its gas industry was merged in the North West Gas Board set up in 1949 to operate in a large area covering Lancashire and Cheshire and parts of Cumberland and Westmoreland, Derbyshire, Shropshire and Yorkshire. Its electricity industry was vested in the Merseyside and North Wales Electricity Board; railways, parts of road transport and eventually ship-building have all been nationalised too so that many decisions are no longer made at a regional level. A rather different decision by the government was that to locate an Atomic Energy Authority plant for the enrichment of uranium at Capenhurst.

It is very difficult to assess the balance of gains and losses to the region from nationalisation but the effectiveness of the other measures by central and local government and by private enterprise was by no means uniform. Once the immediate post-war boom ended Merseyside began to fall behind - her unemployment figures again far exceeding national averages. There was a further decline in such staple industries as chemicals, wood, textiles and clothing and leather. The growth industries during the 1950s were food, drink and tobacco, vehicles and electrical goods, distribution and services such as insurance, banking, professional and scientific services. Table 8.1 shows the changing proportion of employment in Merseyside's main industries between 1953 and 1963. Although the industrial estates had provided some new jobs the opening of new factories was often counteracted by the closing of old ones - in the 1950s it was calculated that for every two new jobs one old one was lost. Furthermore the development of new estates was often at the expense of the older areas from which both population and firms were attracted by a better environment leaving behind much dereliction.

Nationally the 1958 recession led to the revamping of regional employment policies with the 1958 Distribution of Industry (Industrial Finance) Act and the 1960 Local Employment Act. So far as Merseyside was concerned it was clear by 1960 that even greater efforts were needed and these were directed in two main ways: firstly there were intensive efforts to expand motor vehicle production and secondly came the creation of whole new towns instead of more industrial estates located in or adjacent to existing towns.

The motor industry was already present and showing a small expansion but now came a concerted effort to bring in the industry on a large scale through the siting in Merseyside of large plants for Ford, Vauxhall and Standard Triumph. Ford's plant at Halewood was second only to its Dagenham works

Table 8.1: Employment in Merseyside Industries 1953-1963

	1953		1963	
Expanding Industries	000's	%	000's	%
Food, Drink, Tobacco	45.5	6.9	50.1	7.2
Metals, Engineering, Electrical Goods	63.5	9.7	75.0	10.8
Vehicles	8.5	1.3	15.0	2.1
Distribution	80.2	12.3	102.2	14.7
Insurance, Banking, Finance, Professional and Scientific Services	64.3	9.8	84.3	12.1
Other Services	103.0	15.7	103.4	14.9
Chemical and Allied Industries	45.6	7.0	46.4	6.7
Declining Industries				
Agriculture, Forestry, Fishing, Quarrying and Mining	6.7	1.0	4.3	0.6
Textiles, Clothing, Footwear	20.7	3.2	17.2	2.5
Shipbuilding and Marine Engineering	25.9	4.0	17.7	2.5
Other Manufacturing Industries	47.2	7.2	45.4	6.5
Construction	46.4	7.1	45.8	6.6
Transport and Communications	96.6	14.8	88.8	12.8
Total	654.1	100.0	695.6	100.0

Source: D.E.A., *The Problems of Merseyside* (HMSO, London, 1965), pp. 56-7. 'Merseyside' includes the main areas within the definition used in this book with the exception of Formby, Southport, St Helens and Omskirk.

covering some 346 acres with assembly, transmission, metal stamping and body plants. A liner train service linked Halewood and Dagenham to supplement the fleet of trucks acquired to move parts and components. By 1967 it employed some 16,000 persons and represented an investment of nearly £50 millions.[8] Vauxhall Motors' major development was on the former Hooton Park Airfield initially to supply components to other works but in 1964 a stamping and assembly section were added. By 1967 Vauxhall had invested over £66 million in the region[9] and by 1970 it gave employment to some 12,000 workers. Standard Triumph initially took over a 100-acre site at Speke to develop as a paint, trim and body manufacturing unit.

Meanwhile the other 1960s 'solution' to Merseyside's problems was believed to be new towns. Within the region two new towns were developed at Skelmersdale and Runcorn and more recently another new town has been created nearby at Warrington (though this is more closely linked to Greater Manchester than to Merseyside). Skelmersdale was a coal mining village some twelve miles north-east of Liverpool on the main Wigan-Southport road. In that year the population was around 6,000. During the war the population was stationary but new works were opened for producing potato meal and clothing. In 1961 Skelmersdale was designated a new town with some 4,000 acres of land between Ormskirk and Wigan. There were good communications – it was near the M6, it had reasonable rail facilities and fairly easy access to both Speke and Ringway airports. Its new-town status enabled industrialists to obtain substantial grants and allowances and it attracted a wide range of firms and industries including some large concerns such as Dunlops, Union Carbide and Vick International Ltd. The commodities produced included rubber goods, polythene containers, metal and engineering products, hosiery and clothing, timber products, road signs, polishes, car components and pharmaceuticals. Population was mostly drawn from North Merseyside and had risen by 1971 to over 30,000.

Runcorn was, as we have seen, an integral part of Merseyside's economy from the nineteenth century. After the second world war its position changed somewhat. The port experienced considerable fluctuations in prosperity – coal and salt were still important but the canal traffic eventually declined leaving both Runcorn and Weston Point Docks mostly handling coasters and providing some ship-repairing facilities. In the early seventies Runcorn docks handled around half a million tons of traffic. Runcorn's importance in Merseyside's transport network was, however, greatly enhanced by the opening of the new road bridge across the Mersey which, in conjunction with the rail crossing and water transport, and with eacy access to both Liverpool and Manchester airports, ensured excellent facilities for the district. Industrially its leather industry declined rapidly because of competition from synthetics, but the chemical and chemical engineering industries thrived employing some 35 per cent of the workers in Runcorn's Employment Exchange area.[10] I.C.I. confirmed the importance of Runcorn's heavy chemical industry by creating their Mond division there and by locating there a large administrative and research complex.

In the mid-sixties it was decided that Runcorn could well absorb surplus population from other parts of Merseyside but also that the industrial base needed diversifying especially to provide more jobs for women. So in 1964 an area of some 7,250 acres (including the whole urban district of Runcorn and some undeveloped land adjacent to it) was designated Runcorn New Town. The aim was to attract new light industries such as clothing and light engineering and it was intended that the population

should grow to 100,000. Progress was however slow. By 1971 the
population had only risen to 36,000. Extensive building however
took place in the seventies.

Clearly, considerable efforts were made to alleviate Merseyside's
long-term difficulties and there was a good deal of initiative and
flexibility in searching for and implementing new solutions but
unfortunately many solutions were less successful than expected
and some even created further problems. The impact of development policies was by no means uniform throughout the region
and even within each part of the region progress was far from
even and continuous. Despite some temporary amelioration in
some districts and even some localised prosperity, none of the
solutions has so far proved general or lasting. There was a considerable spurt in the early 1950s as development area policies
were first implemented but, far from leading to self-sustaining
growth, the impetus died away in the later fifties as many jobs
were lost by firm closures. Another surge forward in the early
sixties came with government determination to extend the motor
industry in the region. This generated such optimism that the
region's problems would at last be resolved that in September
1962 Merseyside was descheduled so far as the Local Employment
Act was concerned. Again the optimism was misplaced: after
only a few months (in January 1963) this decision was reversed.
During the sixties manufacturing grew in importance in the
region and it seemed that the economy might at last have been
sufficiently restructured to predispose it to further growth.
Certainly the excessive dependence on processing imports and
on marine and other dock-related industries was reduced, but
by the late sixties there was a further relapse and through the
1970s unemployment relentlessly climbed to very high levels
again, well above the national averages.

How could all the efforts made fail to overcome Merseyside's
intractable problems? There seem to be several explanations.
Since the beginning of the twentieth century Merseyside has
increasingly lost the great geographical advantage that had
contributed so much to her earlier growth. This advantage
increasingly passed to the Midlands and South East and Britain's
entry into the Common Market greatly enhanced the location of
these districts leaving Merseyside floundering on the periphery -
a western outpost of the E.E.C. Then too many of Merseyside's
traditional industries continued their decline and even some
former growth-industries such as chemical, food, drink and
tobacco production turned downwards. In the chemical industries
there was obsolescence and excess capacity and in these and
other industries such as the docks, transport, distribution and
oil increasing capital investment reduced the amount of labour
needed and left behind serious dereliction. For example, the
building of the new container port at Seaforth and of the new
grain terminal contributed to a rapid run-down in the dock labour
force and at the same time large areas of docks and warehouses
in South Liverpool became derelict wastelands though there have

been several plans to reclaim some by redevelopment and by
the opening of a Maritime Museum. Then, too, the very efforts
to help proved counter-productive in some respects. Merseyside has always suffered a relative shortage of skilled labour:
the motor industry competed for the scarce supplies with existing
firms, drew away their best men and forced up wage rates so
causing many older firms to close. It has been estimated that
during the sixties the motor industry brought 30,000 new jobs
to the region but may have caused the loss of up to 20,000
existing jobs. True some of the older firms may have closed
eventually anyway but it is undisputed that the rate of closure
was accelerated.

Unfortunately too many of the new firms attracted to Merseyside
did not provide thoroughly secure new jobs. Many were national
concerns which regarded their new plants in Merseyside as
secondary to their main works thus making them extremely
vulnerable to closure in the event of recessions or mergers.
Furthermore such firms often supplied their Merseyside works
with components etc. from suppliers near their main works so
that the expected growth in ancillary industries failed to materialise on the anticipated scale. Again in the seventies many Merseyside producers both new and old have proved very vulnerable
to foreign competition e.g. the motor industry, Dunlops, T.V.
tubes, man-made fibres etc., so that even relative newcomers
have joined the long list of closures.

The situation has been further exacerbated by the deliberate
sacrifice of some older districts. Until the late seventies it was
deliberate policy to redistribute population away from the older
areas by resettling people in new districts and new towns. Inevitably this left a bitter legacy as older industrial centres became blighted, derelict and partly depopulated. For those left
behind in areas such as Central Liverpool, Birkenhead and
Tranmere the prospects were indeed bleak. Between 1961 and
1971 for example the City of Liverpool lost some 80,000 jobs in
the manufacturing, distribution, transport and construction
industries. [11] The impact was particularly severe in the inner
city for unskilled male workers. By 1971 male unemployment in
inner Liverpool averaged eleven per cent at a time when the
rate for Britain was four per cent and by 1975 in some of the
very worst parts of the inner city one man in three was unemployed. Unemployment was also high for young people and
for the coloured population. Such a bitter legacy might have
been accepted as the necessary price for regeneration of the
region if the newly developed districts had proved successful
but they have not: Kirkby, for example, has come to be widely
regarded as a disaster area and the new town of Skelmersdale
developed unemployment problems as bad as those in the blighted
areas. In fact even before the international recession of 1980
Merseyside already had steeply rising unemployment in both
new and old industries and districts; with even its major new
industry - motor production - in serious trouble. Undaunted by

past failures yet another government initiative came in 1981 with the designation of Enterprise Zones where firms could not only obtain financial incentives but would also be free from many controls, local rates and other impediments to growth. Merseyside's Enterprise Zone is at Speke. Whether this will succeed only time can tell. Pessimists claim that at best there will be no increase in jobs – only a movement of existing employers leaving other parts of the region in difficulties. However, despite disappointments it does seem realistic to assume that without all the past efforts the decline of the region could well have been even more disastrous. It may therefore be that a series of further new initiatives will be essential to prevent further disastrous deterioration.

NOTES

1. Subsequently the Lancashire and Merseyside Industrial Development Association was set up and it published a series of reports on the region (see Bibliography: Post-1945 Developments).

2. The Liverpool Corporation Act, 26 Geo. 5 & 1 Edw. 8 cap CXXII.

3. F. Longstreth Thompson, *Merseyside Plan 1944* (HMSO, London, 1945).

4. For a fuller discussion see P.E. Lloyd, 'The Impact of Development Area Policies on Merseyside 1949-67' in R. Lawton and C.M. Cunningham (eds), *Merseyside Social and Economic Studies* (Longman, London, 1970) and W. Robertson, 'The Merseyside Development Area' in W. Smith (ed.), *A Scientific Survey of Merseyside* (Liverpool University Press, 1953).

5. For further details see D.A. Farnie, *The Manchester Ship Canal and the Rise of the Port of Manchester 1894-1975* (Manchester University Press, 1980), p. 163 and J.D. Porteous, *Canal Ports* (Academic Press, London, 1977), pp. 191-2.

6. See, for example, H. Gentleman, 'Kirkby Industrial Estate. Theory versus Practice' in R. Lawton and C.M. Cunningham (eds), *Merseyside Studies*, pp. 411-49.

7. D.A. Farnie, *Manchester Ship Canal*, p. 148.

8. P. Burford (ed.), *A Guide to Merseyside* (Pyramid Press, London, 1967), p. 120.

9. Ibid., p. 103.

10. J.D. Porteous, *Canal Ports*, p. 195.

11. Department of the Environment, *Inner Area Studies, Liverpool, Birmingham and Lambeth* (HMSO, London, 1977), p. 5.

Chapter 9

THE QUALITY OF LIFE FROM 1870

All the economic changes considered in previous chapters naturally reacted in many ways on the quality of life for Merseyside's population which continued to grow, albeit at a slower rate than before 1870. The problems of using census data have already been considered in chapter 5 and the same provisoes apply to this period. There were inevitably further boundary changes: older conurbations sprawled outwards, hamlets and villages grew into towns and gained the status of county or municipal boroughs or of urban districts. The whole picture is one of continual change and adaptation. The table for the period 1871-1911 shows the population for the same registration districts as for 1801-71 (chapter 5) apart from some boundary changes but, with growing urbanisation and deliberate redistribution of population it seems better to use administrative districts for the years 1921-71. The tables are not therefore strictly comparable. The most glaring difference is for the 'City of Liverpool' which in the second table includes, in addition to the Liverpool Registration District, much of the districts of West Derby and Toxteth. As already indicated, academic precision is not crucial for the purpose of a study such as this: the aim is rather to emphasise the most important developments, and for 1921-71 the trends show more clearly if administrative districts are used.

Between 1871 and 1911 total population continued to grow through natural increase and immigration though the *rate* of increase slowed down. Central Liverpool's steep decline in relative and absolute terms was inevitable as it was already overcrowded. Overwhelming numerical predominance passed to the suburbs - West Derby and Toxteth Park. The relative importance of the Wirral grew both with industrial development and with expansion of the dormitory area, and some industrial districts such as St Helens had high birth rates.

Between 1921 and 1961 overall natural growth continued. A few parts of Merseyside such as Southport, with a high proportion of elderly, retired people, had low birth rates but throughout much of Merseyside birth rates continued to be relatively high: this was to be expected in expanding districts such as Ellesmere Port, Formby and Kirkby which attracted young people but birth rates also remained fairly high in older districts such as Liverpool, Bootle and St Helens which had large Roman Catholic communities. The cosmopolitan character of Merseyside's population was still very much in evidence with some new

Table 9.1: Merseyside Population 1871-1911

Registration District[1]	1871	1881	1891	1901	1911
			Thousands		
Cheshire					
Runcorn	30.5	34.0	42.5	39.7	45.6
Wirral (incl. Birkenhead)	102.9	131.4	170.2	209.5	272.3
Lancashire					
Liverpool	238.4	210.2	157.0	147.4	128.7
West Derby (incl. Toxteth Park)	342.9	476.3	572.8	665.9	749.4
Prescot	92.6	118.0	140.9	153.6	170.9
Ormskirk	59.3	83.2	99.2	108.6	117.7
Total	866.6	1,053.1	1,182.6	1,324.7	1,484.6
Cheshire			Percentage		
Runcorn	3.5	3.2	3.6	3.0	3.1
Wirral	11.9	12.5	14.4	15.8	18.3
Lancashire					
Liverpool	27.5	20.0	13.3	11.1	8.7
West Derby	39.6	45.2	48.4	50.3	50.5
Prescot	10.7	11.2	11.9	11.6	11.5
Ormskirk	6.8	7.9	8.4	8.2	7.9
	100.0	100.0	100.0	100.0	100.0

Source: *Censuses of England and Wales* 1871, 1881, 1891, 1901 and 1911
1. For the constitution of each district see Table 5.2 Merseyside Population 1801-71.

immigrants coming from Europe, Russia, Asia, Africa and the West Indies. There was also a growing Jewish community. Despite such a racial mix there was little racial trouble apart from isolated cases such as anti-negro riots in 1919 and some incidents in recent years in the Edge Hill district of Liverpool. Numerically by far the most important sources of population were still other parts of England, Wales, Scotland and above all Ireland. Some of the Welsh retained their own language, many retained their own chapels and some even held their own Eisteddfods (e.g. in Widnes). The Scots were rather more diffused but the Irish still tended to congregate in large but separate Protestant and Catholic communities - the latter reinforcing both the earlier

Table 9.2: Merseyside Population 1921–71

Administrative Area		1921	1931	1951	1961	1971
				Thousands		
	Cheshire					
County Boroughs	Birkenhead	149.8	151.5	142.5	141.8	137.9
	Wallasey	95.1	98.4	101.4	103.2	97.2
Municipal Borough	Bebington*	22.3	31.9	47.8	52.8	40.8
Urban Districts	Ellesmere Port	16.4	23.1	32.7	44.7	61.6
	Hoylake	18.9	19.7	30.9	32.3	32.3
	Neston	7.0	7.9	9.7	11.9	16.9
	Runcorn*	21.4	22.6	23.9	26.0	36.0
	Wirral	5.9	9.6	17.4	21.9	26.9
Rural District	Runcorn*	25.2	27.6	35.6	40.0	44.9
	Lancashire					
County Boroughs	Bootle	76.5	76.8	75.0	82.8	74.3
	City of Liverpool*	805.1	856.1	788.7	745.8	610.1
	St Helens*	103.1	107.5	110.3	108.7	104.3
	Southport	76.6	78.9	84.0	82.0	84.6
Municipal Boroughs	Crosby	44.5	50.6	58.4	59.2	57.5
	Widnes	38.9	40.6	48.8	52.2	57.9
Urban Districts	Formby	6.3	8.0	10.4	11.7	23.5
	Huyton with Roby*	5.2	5.2	55.8	63.1	66.8
	Litherland*	16.4	16.0	22.2	24.9	23.7
	Ormskirk	16.8	17.1	20.5	21.8	27.7
	Prescot	10.6	11.4	12.5	13.1	32.9
	Skelmersdale	6.7	6.2	6.2	6.3	30.6
Rural Districts	West Lancashire	21.2	24.7	41.7	55.8	71.4
	Whiston	17.1	19.8	43.0	43.8	85.6
		1,607.3	1,711.2	1,819.4	1,845.8	1,845.4

Source: *Censuses of England and Wales* 1921, 1931, 1951, 1961, 1971.   *Denotes a boundary change.

Table 9.3: Merseyside Population 1921-71

Administrative Area		1921	1931	1951	1961	1971
				Percentages		
	Cheshire					
County Boroughs	Birkenhead	9.3	8.8	7.9	7.7	7.5
	Wallasey	5.9	5.7	5.6	5.6	5.3
Municipal Borough	Bebington	1.4	1.9	2.6	2.9	2.2
Urban Districts	Ellesmere Port	1.0	1.3	1.8	2.4	3.3
	Hoylake	1.2	1.1	1.7	1.7	1.7
	Neston	0.4	0.5	0.5	0.7	0.9
	Runcorn	1.3	1.3	1.3	1.4	1.9
	Wirral	0.4	0.6	0.9	1.2	1.5
Rural District	Runcorn	1.6	1.6	2.0	2.2	2.4
	Lancashire					
County Boroughs	Bootle	4.8	4.5	4.1	4.5	4.0
	City of Liverpool	50.1	50.0	43.3	40.4	33.1
	St Helens	6.4	6.3	6.1	5.9	5.7
Municipal Boroughs	Southport	4.8	4.6	4.6	4.5	4.6
	Crosby	2.8	3.0	3.2	3.2	3.1
	Widnes	2.4	2.4	2.7	2.8	3.1
Urban Districts	Formby	0.4	0.5	0.6	0.6	1.3
	Huyton with Roby	0.3	0.3	3.1	3.4	3.6
	Litherland	1.0	0.9	1.2	1.3	1.3
	Ormskirk	1.0	1.0	1.1	1.2	1.5
	Prescot	0.7	0.7	0.7	0.7	1.8
	Skelmersdale	0.4	0.4	0.3	0.3	1.7
Rural Districts	West Lancashire	1.3	1.4	2.3	3.0	3.9
	Whiston	1.1	1.2	2.4	2.4	4.6
		100.0	100.0	100.0	100.0	100.0

Source: *Censuses of England and Wales* 1921, 1931, 1951, 1961, 1971.

immigrant communities and also the indigenous Catholic families
in Crosby (the Blundells), Speke (the Norrises), St Helens,
Aughton, Hesketh, Scarisbrick and Ormskirk. Birth rates were
particularly high amongst Roman Catholics and they were at least
partly responsible for keeping the average size of Merseyside
families above the national average as late as the 1960s.

There was still, therefore, some inward migration but it was
now outweighed by emigration to Wales, the Midlands and southern England, hence there was a slight fall in total population
during the 1960s. The decline in Liverpool's population was
particularly steep due in part at least to deliberate overspill
programmes but also due to the fact that the more prosperous
classes voluntarily moved into more pleasant suburbs and
country districts: the rural districts of Runcorn, West Lancashire
and Whiston together accounted for nearly eleven per cent of
total population by 1971 compared with only four per cent in 1921.
There was a great deal of private development, too, in such
areas as Formby, Crosby, Hoylake, Maghull, Southport and
Ormskirk. 'New town' status brought similar growth to Skelmersdale and the town of Runcorn.

Such redistribution of population necessarily called for new
house-building. At times in some parts of the region there were
surpluses - e.g. it was estimated that in 1898 nearly one-tenth
of Widnes's houses were empty because of a recession in the
alkali industry and in Liverpool in 1909 there were some 7,606
empty houses. More usually, however, there were severe shortages of certain types of houses. In the words of the Honorary
Secretary to a Commission of Inquiry into Liverpool's Unemployed[1] 'The erection of houses suitable for the labouring and
artisan classes, that can be rented at a reasonable rate, appears
to be, as yet, an unsolved problem, but is one deserving of the
attention of all municipalities, as well as individuals'. One of the
first 'municipalities' to take the problem seriously was Liverpool.
In 1869 Liverpool Corporation had built St Martins cottages, some
134 tenements, that are believed to be the first municipal flats
in Britain. By 1914 Liverpool had built some 2,824 dwellings
but in addition it had cleared away some 10,000 insanitary houses
and a further 11,000 had been destroyed by commercial developers
leaving serious gaps to be filled by 'individuals'. Furthermore
much of Merseyside's housing stock was old and of poor quality:
for example, in 1898 of Widnes's 5,902 houses some 4,789 were
only equipped with open privies and ashpits.[2] As new houses
were built older areas became very rundown. For example, in
the 1880s many dock workers moved into new houses near the
Bootle and Seaforth docks leaving houses empty between Nether-
field Road and Great Homer Street: landlords tried to find new
tenants by reducing rents but they only succeeded in attracting
a very bad class of tenant 'such as chip merchants, donkey
owners, pigeon breeders and all kinds of ruffians. . . . In some
streets doors, stairs and floors became the spoil of the chip
merchants, lead piping and iron were removed to marine store
dealers'.[3]

New houses were built by speculators and private investors and also by employers. We have already seen that it was common for employers to provide at least some housing for their workers especially in order to attract labour to new or expanding factories and works in districts where the local supply was inadequate. Canal companies would provide houses for lock keepers and later most railway companies built houses for their employees. Some employers went so far as to create model villages, an early example in Merseyside being that at Bromborough Pool where Prices Patent Candle Company built their works. The firm started the model village in 1854: by 1857 there were 76 cottages and after further building the number eventually reached 140 by 1905.[4] An important aspect of this scheme was the inclusion of community facilities - a school, church, hospital as well as the establishment of a Mutual Improvement Society (1854) through which most social life was gradually focused - a reading room, lectures, indoor games, cricket matches, a brass band etc. Similarly the more famous Port Sunlight started in the 1890s by William Lever included, in addition to some 140 houses, several community buildings - a church, a temperance hotel, hostels, men's and women's clubs and dining rooms.

Other employers continued to lay greater emphasis on simply housing their workers. In 1888 work began on building Hartley Village at Fazakerley to house the employees of Hartley's factory. Again the Wolverhampton Corrugated Iron Co. Ltd. moved from the Midlands to Ellesmere Port in 1905. At that time Ellesmere Port was about to become a boom town but lacked both skilled labour and housing. The firm brought many workers with it but houses had to be provided for them. In 1908 it is said that as many as 19 people lived in some of the available houses.[5] The company therefore built 40 new houses and one of its executives Mr E.P. Jones built a further 137. Similarly as late as 1919 Pilkingtons, suffering a severe shortage of skilled workers, began to build Eccleston Hall Estate Garden Village which, by 1923, consisted of some 100 houses and bungalows: the company also provided lodging houses for apprentices.

Many of Merseyside's inhabitants had, however, to find their own accommodation, by purchase in the case of many of the middle and upper classes or by renting for most of the working classes. In the late nineteenth and early twentieth centuries working class rents varied from around 2s 3d a week for extremely poor accommodation (such as the Birkenhead Dock Cottages), to 5s for poor houses and to 6s or 7s for more respectable ones. Between 1900 and 1914 many new small terraced houses were built for about 8s a week in Liverpool although away from the city in, for example, Wallasey, Birkenhead and Waterloo, the same type of house cost 10s to 11s 6d. Homes for the middle classes cost upwards of £30 a year rental though in addition of course many of the middle classes bought their own. By comparison even the more skilled members of the working classes seem to have been relatively reluctant to embark on house ownership. This was emphasised by the manager of the Liverpool Building Society in July 1918:[6] he refers to the reluctance of Merseyside's working classes 'to observe thrift to anything like the extent that it is found in other places' and to the fact that this was combined with 'a disinclination on the part of the working classes to become possessors of their own houses'. He contrasted 'Liverpool and south west Lancashire with the West Riding of Yorkshire where normally higher wages were obtained and the population was of a more stable and provident character'. He attributes this partly at least to Merseyside's 'migratory and largely hand-to-mouth industrial population' which offered 'a marked contrast to the more settled and thrifty population to be found in Yorkshire and East Lancashire'.

The inter-war years were characterised by great activity in house building - partly by private enterprise but also in the form of large municipal housing schemes undertaken in order both to remedy shortages and to also rehouse people displaced by slum clearance. In Widnes for example between 1919 and 1939 4,692 new houses were built, 2,092 by the local authority the remainder by private enterprise.[7] In many parts of Merseyside new building sprawled outwards from older conurbations into the countryside, a process accelerated by better transport which reduced the density of population but which also led to large continuous ribbons of built-up area. As elsewhere in Britain this was partly due to the building boom in private housing on both sides of the Mersey; but there were still many low-income families unable or unwilling to buy houses or to afford private rents, and the most striking feature of inter-war housebuilding was the creation of large corporation housing estates. These appeared throughout the region even in the better-class districts in the Wirral and Southport but they were most noticeable in Liverpool. The way had been paved by the Liverpool City Engineer J.A. Brodie who had not only been concerned with housing but had also in 1904 planned Liverpool's ring road Queen's Drive which facilitated expansion, and his work was particularly continued between the wars by Liverpool's City Architect, Sir Lancelot Keay. Liverpool was amongst Britain's leading authorities in building houses.[8] New estates, some equipped with their own shopping centres, encircled the city - sometimes outside the city boundaries (e.g. the Norris Green estate in Sefton rural district) but mostly within three to six miles of the pier head. Between 1925 and 1938 the Corporation built over 22,000 dwellings in addition to those built under Addison's Act. By 1931 about one-eighth of Liverpool's population already lived in council houses.

Inevitably as the better-off moved into new private houses and as the working classes moved into the new corporation estates, old housing in the more central areas became neglected and dilapidated. Large old houses were downgraded into flats or bed-sitters and large numbers of smaller houses degenerated into

slums. By the early 1930s slum clearance had become the most
urgent priority especially in Liverpool. In 1933 according to
Liverpool's Medical Officer of Health some 13,000 dwellings were
unsuitable for habitation. During the 1930s some former slum
dwellers were rehoused in the city centre but most were moved
to the new estates on the periphery. A similar process was also
taking place in other parts of Merseyside though on a much
smaller scale. In 1935, for example, five areas of slums in
Widnes were cleared, the inhabitants being rehoused on the
new Halebank Estate.

During the second world war large areas of housing were
destroyed or badly damaged by heavy bombing and many more
deteriorated through lack of repairs. By 1945 a new programme
off housebuilding was needed throughout the region. Because
of shortages of materials and skilled labour building was initially
restricted to local authorities but as more resources became
available the rate of private building rapidly accelerated especially in dormitory areas. In 1961 the proportion of households
renting their accommodation from Councils was 18 per cent for
Sefton and the Wirral, 27 per cent in St Helens, 30 per cent
in Liverpool and 56 per cent in Knowsley. [9] In the same districts
the proportion of owner-occupiers was 48 per cent for Sefton
and the Wirral, 37 per cent in St Helens, 25 per cent in Liverpool and 27 per cent for Knowsley. In some districts quite a high
proportion of homes were rented privately - 34 per cent in
Sefton and the Wirral, 36 per cent in St Helens, 45 per cent in
Liverpool but only 17 per cent in Knowsley.

Liverpool continued to extend its housing estates largely in
tandem with the industrial estates. Bootle cleared large tracts
of slum property rehousing some of its inhabitants in West
Lancashire on the Sefton Estates. In and around Widnes especially at Ditton large new housing estates appeared; in fact
new municipal housebuilding took place throughout the region
on estates or in new towns. Unfortunately many of the so-called
'solutions' to poor housing created at least as many problems
as they solved. In many town centres slum housing was replaced by new shopping centres, car parks and commercial
buildings uprooting whole communities and many of the new
estates such as Kirkby failed to meet social needs and led to
serious discontent and social malaise. Even where people were
rehoused in the same locality, many were forced into high-rise
flats in Everton, Sefton Park, Croxteth and Birkenhead; this
gave rise to feelings of bitterness and isolation and to widespread vandalism - some relatively new blocks had even to be
abandoned or demolished. In some parts of the inner city of
Liverpool 'the most striking impression . . . is its physical
decay'. Decay was also seen 'in the neglect of council estates
and in the crumbling facades, broken down back lanes and
derelict houses in the terraced streets'. [10] Furthermore the de-
population of town centres began to threaten the viability of
public services as they catered for fewer people. Many inner

areas were also hit by 'planning blight' - there was little
incentive to repair and maintain old housing that might soon be
condemned and bull-dozed. It was therefore decided by the
1970s that no more high-rise blocks should be built; new houses
should be low-rise and considerable tracts of old housing were
to be renovated and upgraded, so preserving communities
intact.

The creation of new towns on the basis of small long-established
communities (Runcorn and Skelmersdale) seems to have been
more successful socially. In the new towns a mix of properties
was available catering for different needs - some for sale, some
to be rented. These houses were intended particularly (though
not exclusively) for people working in local industries so trying
to avoid an even greater build-up in commuter traffic in the
region such as that resulting from the new private housing
estates in Formby, Maghull, Southport, Ormskirk and much of
the Wirral. The occupants of these houses frequently have to
commute to central Liverpool, Birkenhead, Bootle, Ellesmere
Port, St Helens, Widnes and some of the industrial estates,
leading to uncomfortable journeys on crowded roads and trains.

Despite all the new building much of Merseyside's housing
stock still left a good deal to be desired. Over-crowding generally was reduced but many houses still lacked amenities. As late
as 1971, 23 per cent of Liverpool's householders lacked an
inside w.c. and so did 21 per cent of St Helens' compared with
an average for England and Wales of 15 per cent, and in 1973
it was estimated that up to 52 per cent of central Liverpool's
housing needed some form of treatment or improvement.[11] But
although some housing still needed attention at least the problems of air pollution had been considerably reduced. In the
nineteenth century it was normal for Britain's industrial districts and large conurbations to suffer from air pollution and
Merseyside was no exception. Even in the twentieth century
postcards were sold saying 'The Sun blushes at Widnes smoke'.
Some parts of Merseyside had, however, to contend with more
than smoke because of the nature of their industries, a particular culprit being the chemical industry which polluted not
only the air but also rivers and streams. Many unfortunate
workers both worked and lived in polluted atmospheres especially such as those working in factories producing bleaching
powder where exposure to large amounts of chlorine was a
serious health hazard.

As we have seen the government tried to restrict the amount
of pollution and there was research to find new processes and to
convert waste into commercial by-products. Although such
measures helped there was still a good deal of grime from the
burning of coal for domestic and industrial purposes and to
power transport. Pollution from this source was not controlled
in the nineteenth century but conditions for the residents were
much improved by the creation of parks throughout the region
which, in addition to providing pleasant recreation, also acted

as barriers between blocks of buildings and so diluted the
polluted air with fresher air. By the late nineteenth century
Liverpool was ringed with parks - Stanley, Newsham, Shiel,
Sefton and Princes Parks and, in 1895 Wavertree Playground;
Birkenhead had Arrowe and Birkenhead Parks; St Helens had
Taylor and Victoria Parks, Thatto Heath and the Queens and
Parr Recreation Grounds; Widnes had Victoria Park and Recrea-
tion Ground and so on. Even districts such as Southport that
did not really need additional open spaces had several parks.

After 1945 strenuous efforts were made nationally to deal with
smoke pollution. The 1956 Public Health Act required local
authorities to control factory smoke and in Merseyside as elsewhere smokeless zones reduced the amount of domestic smoke
in the worst areas. Although *all* the grime has not been removed
at least many of the public buildings cleaned during the 1960s
and 1970s have remained relatively clean - a proof of a cleaner
atmosphere generally. On the other hand river pollution has not
been so vigorously tackled. The Mersey still acts as a drain
for much untreated domestic and industrial waste and partly
because of this much of the coastline is also affected, despite
the efforts of some of the holiday resorts to keep their beaches
clean. Fortunately the region does not depend for its water
supply on the Mersey - that comes from North Wales, from
Rivington and from wells.

Housing, pollution, sanitation and water supplies play an
important part in public health so the efforts made in these
respects could be expected to lead to a healthier population.
In the mid-nineteenth century some parts of Merseyside were
still very healthy, especially the holiday resorts, rural districts
and better class residential areas but Liverpool, Widnes and
some of the other industrial towns were as we have seen
extremely unhealthy. All over the country efforts were being
made to improve public health by better water supplies, sewers,
the paving of streets and control of cemetries and abattoirs,
and certainly Liverpool was one of the country's leaders in this
movement. From 1847 it had been the duty of local authorities
to ensure adequate water supplies and Liverpool Corporation
did this by taking over the private companies formerly supplying
its water. Sewage, drainage and paving works were undertaken
and from 1867 the Corporation used its own staff for scavenging
and cleaning. As an extension of the work of Mrs Kitty Wilkinson
and the Rathbones many new corporation baths and washhouses
were built. Slowly Liverpool's death rate fell. Between 1847 and
1856 it had averaged 38 per 1000 of the population. By 1867-76
it averaged 29.3 per 1000 - still high but at least falling. Further
efforts were made: hospitals, training for nurses and surgeons,
hygiene generally and medical services gradually improved. In
St Helens after 1870 the death rate averaged 21 or 22 per 1000
only rising as high as 30 per 1000 in epidemics such as an outbreak of scarlet fever in 1874. Perhaps one of the unhealthiest
parts of Merseyside was Widnes. Even by the 1890s it was re-

ported that although the water supply was good there were
many dirty cowsheds and bakeries in the town. [12] Deaths occurred
due to smallpox, typhoid, diptheria, scarlet fever, lung diseases
and above all intestinal diseases. In 1892 there were over 100
cases of enteric fever and in 1893 the death rate was still over
24 per 1000. Infant mortality was particularly high - in fact
many people died young. In 1893 of 730 deaths only 57 were over
65 years old. In the twentieth century Merseysiders' health
improved greatly (by 1921 even Widnes' death rate was down to
11.3 per 1000) due particularly to improved child health, ante-
natal clinics, school medicals, better hygiene and better food.

Improved nutrition was possible in Merseyside as elsewhere
due to the import of large quantities of cheap food. In the early
part of this period there were steep price falls. Prices supplied
to the Commission on Unemployment in Liverpool show how some
food prices more than halved: [13]

	Bread per lb.	Tea per lb.	Sugar per cwt.	Beef & Mutton per cwt.
1874	2d	3s 4d	35s	53s to 68s
1894	1d	1s 7d	15s	36s to 38s

The supply of ready-made clothing also increased and the range
of choice widened. As communities grew covered market halls
began to supplement or even replace outdoor markets and in
addition the number of shops increased from small stores supplying groceries, confectionery, meat, fish and poultry to multiple
chains which began to appear even in suburbs such as Everton;
and of course Merseyside's neighbour, Rochdale, had played an
important part in the development of co-operative stores which
had rapidly spread through the region helping further to
reduce prices and improve the quality of food.

To be meaningful, prices, of course, have to be related to
incomes - in the 1890s it was estimated that a careful married
couple with four children could live respectably (by contemporary standards) on £1 10s per week - this allowed 6s for rent,
and just under 7d per head per day for food, clothing, coal etc.
and it seems that many of Merseyside's workers' incomes exceeded this. [14] Skilled workers could earn 6s to 7s a day with,
in some trades, overtime rates and special rates for Bank
Holidays. 'Superior men' (i.e. foremen) could earn £4 a week.
At the other end of the scale some girls and youths were paid
as little as 10s a week. In between unskilled men could earn
4s to 5s a day, but for them this was not always a reliable guide
to 'take home pay' because of casual employment. Working hours
varied a good deal. In St Helens, for example, many chemical
workers laboured in bad condition for eleven or more hours a
day. Cunard's working week for shore workers was 54 hours
(9 per day for 6 days) but many of their unskilled workers were
only employed for two or three days a week so their incomes

were unreliable. In some industries there was insufficient work
to keep all workers continuously employed: in other cases men
chose to work irregularly. One witness to the Commission on
Liverpool's unemployed told how many men simply worked long
enough to buy drink and then left their work to consume their
earnings. Others would choose to work for two or three days
and then 'if there is a football match on, they will run away from
their work, drawing what is due of wages to go there'. [15] In fact
it was claimed that most sober, steady men who were really
anxious to work could find employment but this is open to doubt
and Merseyside also had a large 'hard core' of permanently
unemployed people due to 'ill-health, intemperance, restlessness,
hereditary incapacity, imprudence, overwhelming misfortune,
orphanage and bad home training.' [16] Amongst this group must
also be included an army of tramps who congregated in towns
in the winter and roamed the countryside in summer.

This, however, is only one aspect of Merseyside's unemployment problem. For the period in the twentieth century for which
statistics are available Merseyside's unemployment rate has
usually been at least fifty per cent above the national average
and unemployment has been evident in all its forms - seasonal,
short-term, cyclical and long-term together with under-employment.
This was not, however, solely a twentieth-century phenomenon.
All these forms of unemployment were equally in evidence in the
nineteenth century, so much so that in 1894, in response to a
pressing request from a group of leading citizens, businessmen
and trade unionists, Liverpool City Council had instituted the
Commission of Inquiry already referred to above 'into the subject of the Unemployed in the City of Liverpool'. The report
began 'The problem of the unemployed is not a new one, nor
is it peculiar to Liverpool . . . in all large towns, but especially
in seaport towns, there is a tendency to attract surplus
labour . . . special prominence is now given to the subject
because the public conscience is now more sensitive than before
to the sight of human suffering, and because the Press and
other channels of information have brought it conspicuously
forward.'

Some of the explanations for Liverpool's unemployment problem
in 1894 equally apply to much of Merseyside though some are no
longer relevant, and the picture is not uniform throughout the
region - some of its component parts enjoyed considerable prosperity e.g. early in the twentieth century Ellesmere Port was
very much a boom town and skilled workers in particular were
in great demand, in fact as we have seen when the Wolverhampton
Corrugated Iron Co. moved there from the Midlands in 1905 it
had to bring some of its skilled workers. Then, too, boiler
makers in Liverpool commanded higher wages than those on the
Clyde, and joiners and carpenters were also in great demand.
In 1924 the Merseyside building industry precipitated a national
strike and lock-out because adhering to national wage agreements
would have forced down wages for Merseyside's skilled workers.

In fact one of Merseyside's long-term problems has been a
relative shortage of skilled workers and of apprenticeships.
This kept up skilled wages but deterred potential new firms
likely to need skilled labour.

Another group of workers who fared relatively well were women.
Openings for women, especially in domestic service, were good:
then too many employers substituted cheap female labour for
dearer male labour. Again in ports prostitutes were in demand.
There were, therefore, fewer unemployed women than men. The
group most vulnerable to unemployment or under-employment
were the large body of unskilled men working, for example, as
porters in warehouses and on the docks. Many trades such as
those in grain and cotton were necessarily seasonal and the
labour force invariably exceeded demand even in season. By
definition unskilled jobs can be done by anyone: large
numbers of casual workers kept moving into Merseyside from rural districts (even unskilled wages seemed attractive compared with
rural wages). Usually they were healthier than local labour
and worked better. Employers naturally chose the strongest
and often favoured non-local labour because such men were
willing to act as strike-breakers. Because labour was so plentiful employers had no incentive to keep on workers in slack
times so many labourers (including all those employed by
Liverpool Corporation) were paid daily, being hired and fired
according to need. Men desperate for jobs resorted to bribing
foremen, a procedure known as 'mugging'. [17]

Such conditions for the large body of unskilled workers had
unfortunate results leading to bad workmanship, lack of incentive, bad habits and bitterness which was further aggravated
by religious dissension between workers themselves and which
led to many strikes and lock-outs. Merseyside labour gained a
bad image for readiness to strike, low productivity and
absenteeism - a reputation deserved by some groups of workers
in some industries though by no means applicable to the whole
region. As early as 1894 this image caused many employers to
be unwilling to embark on new enterprises and the same bad
image has continued through the twentieth century. Why did
it persist for so long?

We have seen in Chapter 5 that Merseyside's labour history
broadly followed the national trends to 1870 with moderate
craft unions predominating. By the late 1880s, however, there
was a distinct change as unskilled workers, both male and
female, were organised into 'New Unions'. Some of these unions
were national or regional, others were still local. The National
Union of Dock Labourers, for example, which was operating in
Liverpool by 1889 had absorbed several small local unions such
as the South End Union (a dockers club since 1849) and the
North End Coal Heavers Society (formed 1881). It was claimed
in 1894 that some seventy per cent of dock workers belonged to
this union. Many Merseyside miners belonged to the Lancashire
Miners Federation formed in 1881 and then to the Miners Federa-

tion of Great Britain (1889). The National Union of Gas Workers
and General Labourers (1889) included amongst its members
many of Merseyside's unskilled workers in ship-repairing,
foundries and the construction industry as well as some semi-
skilled working for Milners Safes. Among the smaller local unions
were such organisations as the Liverpool Warehouse Porters
Union (1898), the Carters Union (1889), the United Plate Glass
Workers Society (formed in 1889 and strong in St Helens) and
the Chemical and Copper Workers Union (1889) which claimed to
include most of Lancashire's alkali workers.

These and other unions recruited dockers, seamen, chemical
and glass workers, workers making coats and cigars, books,
sacks and bags, upholstery workers, laundresses, agricultural
workers and many others. The dues for unskilled workers were
usually around 2d or 3d a week compared with about 1s 2d for
skilled artisans. Because of these very low subscriptions unions
for the unskilled could not provide much in the way of benefits:
by comparison those for the skilled provided some unemployment
and/or sick pay and/or pensions. For example in the 1890s the
Amalgamated Society of Engineers had about 2,000 members in
the Liverpool district and provided the following benefits: [18]

Out of work allowance full members of ten years standing 10s
per week for 14 weeks, 7s for 30 weeks and then 6s until
work was obtained but with a maximum per member of
£19 18s a year. Members of less than ten years standing
received 10s a week for 14 weeks, 7s for 30 weeks and then
6s for 60 weeks.
Sick benefit 10s per week for 20 weeks, 5s per week as long
as ill.
Funeral benefit £12.
Total or Partial Disablement £100.
Superannuation 7s to 10s per week according to length of
membership.

The unskilled unions helped their members to fight for compensation under the Employers Liability Act in the case of
injury but their particular concern was to fight for better wages,
better working conditions and shorter hours and this usually
involved strikes and lock-outs so they provided some strike pay.
For example the branch of the Gas and General Labourers Union
covering most of Merseyside paid 10s a week strike benefit to
members and during its first five years of life (1889-1894)
claimed to have paid out £1,800 strike pay.

There were many strikes and lock-outs in the late 1880s and
early 1890s in Merseyside as in the rest of the country. In 1888
boiler makers went on strike; in 1889 dock labourers and seamen
struck and there were further dock strikes in 1890 and 1893;
in 1892 book binders struck for reduced hours and tailors were
involved in a strike and lock-out; in 1893 there was a coal strike.
Some of these strikes were successful, others failed. Merseyside

seems to have been particularly vulnerable because of its high proportion of low-paid, unskilled workers and because of inter-union quarrels and religious divisions. Thus, for example, Liverpool was the one district where the seamen's strike failed because of the large number of blacklegs. Other workers too found that news of strikes quickly spread to surrounding districts and brought in a flood of unemployed workers ready to replace men on strike. When the strike was over the strikers frequently found that their jobs had been given to these new-comers and they were not therefore re-employed.

In order to try to consolidate and strengthen their position efforts were made to bring unions together into Trade Councils. In St Helens even this proved difficult - it took three attempts (1867, 1885 and 1890) before unions would co-operate. In Liver-pool, on the other hand, the Trades Council expanded rapidly in the late 1880s. By 1891 it had 47 affiliated trades including the Birkenhead Sausage Skin Manufacturers Union. It had grown into the largest provincial Council and was even beginning to rival London for size, but on the whole, Merseyside was not as yet one of the main springboards for the development of unionism - the lead was rather taken by London and the North East.

Parallel to the development of unions was the slow progress of socialism in Merseyside. The Liverpool Fabian Society was the first provincial Fabian Society and in 1892 it merged with the Liverpool Socialist Society. Both the Independent Labour Party and the Social Democratic Federation won some support in Mersey-side and efforts began to be made to achieve labour representa-tion on local councils and later in Parliament. Religious disputes, however, still seriously hindered the development of a united body of workers.

By the turn of the century, therefore, Merseyside still had a strong body of moderate unions, but also a growing cluster of 'New Unions' and an active, if relatively small, sprinkling of socialists. Merseyside workers were only marginally affected in the early 1900s by the syndicalist movement (the industrial unionists who aimed to destroy capitalism and who were becoming active both in Britain and abroad) and yet it was here in Mersey-side that an anti-capitalist revolution nearly occured in 1911 during a complex series of strikes. In May there was a seamens' strike backed by sympathetic strikes of dockers and carters - this was so successful that other unions decided to follow suit - tug boat crews, lightshipmen, workers in tobacco factories, brewery workers and above all transport workers. A small unofficial strike in Liverpool on the Lancashire and Yorkshire Railway escalated into a national rail strike. For once Merseyside workers at least initially overcame their sectional and religious divisions and even non-union workers refused to act as strike breakers. By August there was a general transport strike throughout the Liverpool area and the workers were in complete control of the distribution of food and other supplies. Sympathetic

strikes by scavengers and electric supply workers aggravated
the authorities' problems.

Both the local authorities and the central government became
alarmed. Police reinforcements were brought in from Leeds,
Bradford, and Birmingham. Seven thousand troops were moved
into Merseyside and two gun boats were anchored in the Mersey.
On 13 August (Bloody Sunday) a mammoth working class demon-
stration erupted into violence between the police and demonstra-
tors. Sporadic fighting went on for several days between
workers and the police and troops. Two workers were killed
by troops firing on a group trying to stop a prison van and
the fragile truce between the local religious factions was partly
broken as old grievances between Catholics and Protestants
exploded into street battles. Eventually the government decided
to try mediation rather than more force. The industrial disputes
were fairly quickly settled but the peace was uneasy. Throughout the years 1911 to 1914 a strong element of bitterness persisted with serious industrial unrest in some parts of Merseyside
although in other districts, such as Runcorn and Widnes, there
was much less militancy.

During the first world war some Merseyside workers followed
the national labour party's general lead in opposing conscription
and in 1917 in sending greetings to Russian revolutionaries but
also in 1917 many workers complained that the existing Liverpool
Trades Council was too pacifist and socialist so they formed a
rival Trades Council. The end of the war, however, signalled
further labour troubles throughout the country including some
angry disputes on Merseyside. In 1919 train services in Liverpool were paralysed by a strike and (perhaps with memories of
1911) during a national rail strike the government again dis-
patched a battleship to the Mersey and brought in the troops.
On 8 August 1919 Liverpool was one of several cities in the
country where great demonstrations were held to oppose any
declaration of war on Russia following the Russian revolution.
From the government's point of view, however, the most dangerous occurrence in Merseyside in 1919 was the Liverpool police
strike in August which left the area at the mercy of looters and
vandals. To try to combat this even greater naval and military
strength was sent into Merseyside - two destroyers joined the
battleship in the estuary and on land two and a half thousand
soldiers were equipped with tanks. The strike failed, the striking
policemen were dismissed and they lost their pension rights.
Although there were also partial police strikes in Birmingham and
London, Mr Lloyd George told Sir Archibald Salvidge (Liverpool's
leading conservative politician) that he regarded the quashing
of the one in Liverpool and Bootle as the crucial turning point
which diverted British labour away from Bolshevism and back to
unionsim. [19]

The collapse of the post-war boom brought escalating unemployment and further massive but abortive demonstrations in Liverpool's streets and around the Town Hall and St Georges Hall in

September 1921. In 1924 the national rail strike included Merseyside and also in 1924 Merseyside's building industry precipitated
a national strike and lock-out because of the refusal of both
workers and employers to adhere to national wage agreements.
A further dock strike in 1924 was followed in 1925 by an unofficial seamen's strike. When the General Strike came in 1926
workers from several parts of Merseyside were already prepared:
they had set up a 'Provisional Council for Action for Merseyside'
(defined as Liverpool, Bootle, Birkenhead and Wallasey). This
Council was ready to control proceedings and movements of
goods, and to print bulletins but the strike was far from
'general' throughout Merseyside industries. A higher proportion
of transport workers came out than the average for the whole
country but some trains, buses and ferries still operated and
the electric supply workers continued to work. Dockers and
printers mostly stopped work and so did seamen but, unlike
1911, the unions failed completely to control the movement of
essential supplies by a permit system and they had to abandon
the attempt. The police did not join in this strike and in several
parts of Merseyside work continued e.g. at Lever Brothers at
Port Sunlight; chemical and metal workers in Runcorn and Widnes
did not strike although iron workers at Ellesmere Port did join
in. The unions themselves managed to avoid inter-union disputes
and for once the usual religious conflicts did not flare up. There
was little violence in the region apart from a very few isolated
incidents but the government was not prepared to take any
chances: two battleships, three destroyers and several contin-
gents of troops were again despatched to the region.

After the strike there was a great deal of bitterness as many
employers took the opportunity to weed out troublemakers, giving
their jobs to those from the ranks of the unemployed who had
volunteered to work through the strike. The long-term effects
on industry were slight but the growth in unemployment at the
end of the decade led to further demonstrations by the unemployed in the early 1930s. The strike had unfortunate effects
on the public's attitude towards strikers. In general the public
and the press did not support the general strike regarding it
as an attack on the government. Nevertheless there was something of a political swing towards Labour in local government
elections though this was not sufficient in Liverpool to give it
control as in Birkenhead. In the longer term the series of
violent demonstrations before 1926, especially those in 1911 and
1919 resulted in Merseyside being branded as a militant and
strike-prone region, a reputation not wholly deserved after the
1939-46 war. True there have been strikes since 1945 but many
firms and industries have been strike-free and the media have
publicised those strikes that have occurred in such a way as to
perpetuate the bad image.

The aim of the trade unions was to improve their members'
living and working conditions and, as we have seen, some
unions did provide some financial help for their members; in

addition, many of the people who were temporarily or permanently unemployed together with all the unemployable and elderly needed some other form of assistance. Even when in work wages were not high enough for workers to save enough to maintain themselves in illness or old age though it was expected that members of families would help each other and, in particular, it was regarded as the duty of children to maintain elderly and infirm parents. But on the whole self-help does not seem to have been popular. Merseysiders have often been criticised for their lack of thrift and particularly for squandering their money on alcohol. Certainly visits to the pub were a favourite recreation throughout the region. In Widnes, for example, in 1892 there were 121 licensed houses - one for every 289 inhabitants (compared with one for every 864 in 1961). Pubs opened eighteen hours a day with beer costing 2d per pint, and both Irish whisky and rum cost 1s 6d a quart. There were many convictions for drunkenness - Widnes' record was held by Rose Kelly who was convicted for drunkenness 124 times before dying in the workhouse.[20] In Liverpool, too, much poverty was attributed to excessive drinking, which in turn led to inability to pay the rent and to maintain a family and the temptation to run into debt.

Before the institution by the government early in the twentieth century of old age, health and unemployment insurance and later the creation of the 'welfare state' the last resort for the poor was to apply for help to the Poor Law Guardians who were supposed to ensure that no-one actually died of starvation. During the second half of the nineteenth century the administration of poor relief was tightened up to deter scroungers and malingerers. In particular steps were taken to enforce the provision that the able bodied should only be given outdoor relief in exceptional circumstances: even then they were required to perform some task of labour to ensure that they could not earn a wage and claim benefit simultaneously. The 'pauper' stigma became so strong that many honest, self-respecting unemployed would suffer anything rather than apply for help: the workhouse was regarded as the ultimate form of degradation and it even included disenfranchisement. The Guardians were allowed little discretion in dealing with the able-bodied but they could give outdoor relief for the sick, the incapacitated, the aged, children and some widows. By the late nineteenth century such relief was designed simply to save them from starvation - allowances were around 2s 6d per week for adults and 1s for children. The aim was always to ensure that living on poor relief was less advantageous than earning one's own living - a principle applied even to those who could not in any event maintain themselves. So the genuine poor suffered to ensure that the idlers, drinkers and gamblers would have an incentive to maintain themselves. For children there were some industrial schools such as those set up at Kirkdale to teach trades and crafts. The Guardians could also find apprenticeships for pauper children and even place them in jobs - for example in the 1880s and 1890s some

destitute Liverpool children were apprenticed to fishermen in
Grimsby and other ports.

For the elderly the main relief, often bitterly resented, was
the workhouse. In most jobs there was no formal retirement age
and few people were eligible for pensions until the national old
age pension scheme started. The age at which people became
too old to work varied a good deal from job to job: in those
involving heavy work some men were too old at 50 and in any
event with plentiful supplies of labour employers naturally
chose strong young men. The Mersey Docks and Harbour Board,
however, reported in the 1890s that most of its men retired
between 65 and 70 but a few even worked at 80. From the point
of view of the Poor Law people over 60 were regarded as 'old',
even if still able-bodied. When old-age pensions were introduced
nationally in 1908 the qualifying age was 70. Gradually during
the twentieth century the forms of poverty stemming from unemployment and sickness were partly at least relieved by national
insurance schemes though many people were not covered until
the further development of welfare facilities after the second
world war.

Meanwhile, for those who were either not eligible for relief
under the Poor Law or who were too independent to apply for it
there were many private charities. In most districts there were
hospitals built and supported by private donations, such as
the Cottage Hospital opened in 1873 at Peasley Cross (St Helens)
through the combined efforts of several benefactors, and the
Borough Hospital, Birkenhead built in the 1860s by John Laird.
In Liverpool there were many charity hospitals including the
Hospital for Consumption, the Hospital for Women, the Eye and
Ear Infirmary and the Dental Hospital. Other hospitals were
provided by religious bodies e.g. Providence Hospital (St Helens)
opened in 1884 by a Roman Catholic order - the Poor Servants
of the Mother of God. Then, too, there was a very varied range
of other charitable activities. During the times of particularly
high unemployment a central distress committee in St Helens
distributed soup and bread to needy families. In Widnes in 1893
the Co-op gave away 200 loaves a week and in 1895 a free soup
kitchen opened at the Gospel Mission Hall to provide soup and
bread daily to some 150 people. Each Christmas Day in Widnes
at the Hartley Wesleyan schoolroom 150 needy children were
given a meal, an orange and a Christmas card. [21] In Liverpool
there were organisations such as the Town Mission, the Society
of St Vincent de Paul (which helped the unemployed), the Board
of Guardians for the Relief of the Jewish Poor, three Orphan
Asylums founded by Mr Harmood Banner, a Self Help Emigration
Society and a Central Relief and Charity Organisation Society
which helped the 'deserving' poor and even arranged for wives
and children of paupers to find jobs in manufacturing districts.
In 1893 alone this latter society gave assistance to some 5,000
people. [22] Later came national organisations such as the Salvation
Army and Dr Barnardos and both the R.S.P.C.A. and the

N.S.P.C.C. grew out of Liverpool initiatives.

Some of these and of the many other charities in the region sprang from or were intimately linked with the religious bodies and sects which proliferated throughout the region and which included Anglicans and Roman Catholics, Unitarians, Baptists, Quakers, Jews, a variety of Methodists etc.: there was even a Swedish Seamen's Church. Although there were strong concentrations of particular sects in some districts (e.g. Unitarians in South Liverpool and Roman Catholics in Bootle, St Helens and parts of Birkenhead) the more striking feature was the immense variety: for example in 1960 there were some eighty places of worship in Birkenhead alone catering for all tastes. Despite such a wide choice many Merseysiders did not practice any religion at all but nonetheless the many religious groups played an important role in the region's development affecting not only people's spiritual well-being but also their secular education, their social and political life and the local culture. True, strongly-held religious convictions led to dissensions the best known being the antagonism between Irish Protestants and Catholics which split many labour movements, found expression in societies such as the Fenians, the Home Rule Association, the Ribbonmen and Orange Lodges and which often escalated into violence, especially on St Patrick's days (17 March) and 12 July (when the Protestant Orangemen commemorate William III's victory in 1690 at the Battle of the Boyne) though fortunately the antagonism was somewhat reduced after the second world war. Less publicised were squabbles such as those in St Helens between Roman Catholics and Non-conformists, the many splits within the body of Methodists and, from 1902 (after the Education Act), bitter controversy in Widnes where Non-conformists refused to pay education rates to maintain Church of England schools and had their personal and household effects seized and auctioned each year to cover their unpaid debts.

Despite such occurrences members of all religious persuasions contributed in their own many and varied ways not only to Merseyside's character but also to its well-being. In central Merseyside there was a very strong body of Unitarian families (including the Booths, Rathbones, Holts, Mellys, Fletchers, Bowrings and Heywoods) and of individuals, e.g. William Roscoe, Sir John Brunner and Sir Henry Tate. Unitarians regarded social service as part of their religion and they played a key role, not only in the development of trade and shipping but also in education and philanthropy. Methodists and later Salvationists tried to carry both religion and comfort to non-church goers; Quakers helped to develop industry and to care for the moral and physical well-being of their workers; the Roman Catholics and Anglicans set up a wide range of charitable institutions, and most sects joined the battle to attempt to combat the social, legal and moral problems arising from drunkenness by encouraging total abstinence and the creation of Temperance Bands and by holding temperance meetings, providing non-alcoholic refresh-

ments. For the young people many of the Free Churches had
Bands of Hope; Liverpool's first Y.M.C.A. had started in 1846
and another youth movement actually originated in a Y.M.C.A.
building in Birkenhead: namely the Boy Scout movement. General
Baden-Powell launched it there in 1908 and came back in 1929 to
celebrate the twenty-first anniversary with a World Jamboree
in Arrowe Park, Birkenhead.

During the mid and late nineteenth century a great deal of
work was undertaken throughout Merseyside to build or renovate
churches, chapels, meeting halls, synagogues and other religious
buildings and this culminated in the twentieth century in the
building of two cathedrals in Liverpool. The Anglican diocese of
Liverpool dates from 1880. After a good deal of planning the site
was chosen in 1901 and a competition was held to choose an
architect. Giles Gilbert Scott was appointed and the work started
in 1904 taking some 75 years to complete. The Gothic, red sandstone cathedral is in sharp contrast to the concrete Roman
Catholic cathedral. The Catholic diocese dates from 1850 but it
took a long time to collect the necessary financial resources for
building and to draw up the plans for what was intended to be
one of the largest cathedrals in the world. Sir Edward Lutyen's
ambitious plans had, however, only resulted in a massive crypt
by 1939 and after the war it was decided to adopt a smaller and
much more modern plan. A competition was won in 1960 by
Frederick Gibberd, building was swift and the cathedral was
consecrated some seven years later. No other British city
could claim to have built two cathedrals in the twentieth century,
a bold statement of faith in the future despite all Merseyside's
long-term problems, a faith perhaps underlined by the fact
that the two cathedrals are joined together by Hope Street and
by improving relationships between Anglicans and Catholics in
the region. Since the second world war many other churches
and chapels have fallen into disuse or been converted for secular
purposes, but in areas of expanding population many new churches
have been built in ultra modern styles using modern materials.
The religious diversity of the region has also been intensified
by the immigration of more adherents of Eastern religions especially Sikhs, Muslims and Hindus.

There are also close links between religion and education. By
1870 schools had already been established throughout the region
by churches and school societies in addition to many private
academies and grammar schools. The year 1870 saw the passing
of the Education Act that aimed to ensure compulsory elementary
education. Under this Act local school boards were set up
throughout the region to supplement the existing educational
provision where necessary but schooling was not yet free and
it was difficult to enforce the compulsory requirement: in 1879
for example in Widnes some 5,858 children received elementary
education but its estimated that another 1,276 were still receiv-
ing no schooling at all. Gradually, however, elementary schools
increased in number and, more importantly, became free but the

provision of secondary and grammar education was still very
limited. Even before 1870 long-established schools such as
Merchant Taylors (Crosby) and the Blue Coat School had already
been supplemented by other schools such as the Liverpool
Institutes for Boys and Girls, the Liverpool Collegiate High
School, St Xavier's Roman Catholic Secondary School for Boys,
St Mary's College (Crosby) and Seafield Convent (Waterloo)
and early in the 1870s by Birkenhead School. There were also
other local grammar schools such as Farnworth Grammar School,
and the number of secondary schools slowly increased throughout the region through the efforts of local councils (e.g. in 1904
Widnes Council's own Secondary School replaced Farnworth
Grammar School) and by charities (e.g. in 1882 the Non-conformist
Cowley Charity in St Helens opened a 'Middle School' for boys
and girls aged 8 to 17). There was also in the 1890s a very
noticeable acceleration in the provision of technical education
following the Technical Instruction Act (1889) – to name but a
few examples in 1896 the Widnes and St Helens Technical schools
were both opened; in 1897 Northwich's Technical school started;
in 1898-9 Wavertree's Technical Institute was built; in 1896 work
started on Liverpool's College of Technology and in 1903 a
Technical Institute opened in Port Sunlight. In 1892 a Nautical
College was opened in Liverpool to give practical training to
officers and men in the mercantile marine.

Another Education Act was passed in 1902 and this replaced
School Boards by Local Education Committees; they continued
to work along similar lines, supplementing the work of religious
and charity schools where necessary by setting up their own
schools financed by local rates. In Liverpool for example in
1903 there were some 156 elementary schools of which 43 had
been set up by the School Board and 113 were voluntary. Of
the latter 65 were Church of England, 37 Roman Catholic, 7
Wesleyan, 1 Jewish and 3 non-denominational. There were also
5 industrial schools where the children of drunken and dissolute
parents were both fed and taught – 4 set up by the School
Board, 1 voluntary. There was also an increase in centres for
training teachers – by 1900 there were several Pupil Teachers
Colleges created by local authorities, by the Church of England
and by the Roman Catholic Church, and three training colleges
for elementary teachers – the Liverpool, the Edge Hill and the
University Day Training Colleges.

Both local authorities and some religious bodies also took an
interest in the developments that were taking place in the region
in higher education. In 1881 Liverpool followed the lead of other
civic centres such as Manchester, Leeds and Bristol by creating
a University College which incorporated the Royal Infirmary
Medical School (established in 1834); in 1884 it became part of
the Victoria University to which Manchester's Owen College
already belonged. Liverpool's College was set up on the site of
a disused lunatic asylum on Brownlow Hill, a gift from Liverpool
Corporation. The aim of the founders was to 'provide such

instruction in all the branches of a liberal education' as to
enable Merseysiders to qualify for both Arts and Science degrees
but it was also intended that there should be professional and
commercial training. Some twenty two years after its foundation
the College was granted its own Royal Charter to convert it
into the University of Liverpool. [23]

The links between the University and the region were strong
from the start. Much of its finance was provided by businessmen (especially Unitarians and other non-conformists) and later
by local authorities; many of its students were local though the
number of students from other regions gradually increased;
local businessmen and leading citizens participated in the government of the university and close ties were forged with the
professions, especially with medicine, law, veterinary science,
engineering, architecture, town planning and accounting.
Amongst the University's many eminent scholars have been
numbered Sir Oliver Lodge, Sir Charles Sherrington, Sir William
Herdman, Oliver Elton, Sir Charles Reilly, Lord Holford, Sir
Alexander Carr-Saunders, Sir James Chadwick and Lord Cohen
of Birkenhead.

Since the first world war general education provision in Merseyside has continued to develop in line with national trends -
namely increasing provision of secondary schools, technical
colleges, colleges of commerce, colleges of art, teacher training
colleges and since 1945 comprehensive schools and further
education colleges, mostly run by local authorities though also
in some cases in close conjunction with religious bodies. Many
of the 'independent' schools have become 'grant-aided', the
number of small private schools has declined though they have
not completely disappeared and the University has grown into
one of Britain's important red-brick universities.

In addition to formal education there was widespread provision
throughout the region of evening classes to promote both education and hobbies: these have been provided by the University
(Extra-mural lectures now called Extension Studies), by technical
colleges and by the W.E.A. The region also enjoys a fairly lavish
provision of public libraries and reading rooms, museums, art
galleries and record offices. In 1850 a general Public Libraries
Act was passed largely through the efforts of a Liverpool merchant, William Ewart. Two years later in 1852 Liverpool's own
museum, public library and art gallery were established by a
private Act of Parliament, the buildings being largely financed
by Sir William Brown, Sir James Picton and Mr A.B. Walker;
Southport's Atkinson Public Library and Art Gallery date from
1876; Widnes had a public library and reading room in 1887 and
this was moved into the same building as the technical school in
1896; St Helens' public library was also joined with its technical
school in 1896; Warrington's public library was built in 1902-3,
Birkdale's in 1905, Northwich's Brunner Library in 1909 and
both Ellesmere Port's and Wallasey's public libraries were built
in 1910. William Lever's memorial to his wife, the Lady Lever Art

Gallery in Port Sunlight was completed in 1922 and Birkenhead's
Williamson Art Gallery and Museum opened in 1928. Many libraries
collect documents as well as books but in addition since the
second world war specialised record offices have appeared to
preserve documentary, photographic, and other evidence of
local interest. Many Merseyside records are to be found in the
Lancashire County Record Office at Preston, in the Cheshire
County Record Office at Chester and in local offices such as the
Liverpool Record Office, but after the creation of the Metropolitan County of Merseyside, Merseyside also gained its own
county record office.

Merseyside is also rich in indigenous local cultures which are
frequently oral rather than in documentary form and which are
to be found outside the normal types of cultural and educational
institutions - especially in the pubs. In both the nineteenth and
twentieth centuries pubs have been the major recreational
centres for the working classes and in them have developed the
so-called 'pub-cultures' - the best known being in Liverpool
where local songs, poetry and art thrive, expounded by characters such as Adrien Henri, Roger McGough and Brian Patten
and by the artist Arthur Dooley who set up his studio in a
former pub; and not to be forgotten are Liverpool's famous
'Scouse' language and characters immortalised in Tommy Handley's
I.M.T.A.

Apart from such localised interests, Merseyside has continued
throughout this period to offer a wide and ever-growing range
of recreational facilities. For those interested in music the choice
has been extensive ranging from choral societies, concerts in
theatres, halls and churches and the Liverpool Philharmonic
Orchestra (and Widnes' Philharmonic and Symphony Orchestras)
to performances by visiting opera and ballet companies. Famous
conductors such as Sir Thomas Beecham (born in St Helens)
and Sir Malcolm Sargent have long been associated with the region.
In bandstands in parks and holiday resorts outdoor concerts
thrived. In the inter-war years halls for ballroom dancing
mushroomed throughout the region, and from the appearance of
the Beatles in the Cavern in the 1960s Merseyside became a world-
renowned centre for pop music of every sort. Theatres too
cater for most tastes producing plays, pantomimes and variety -
and endowing Merseyside with its priceless heritage of comedians
including Billy Bennett, Arthur Askey, Ted Ray, Billy Danvers,
Jimmy Tarbuck and Ken Dodd. The inter-war years brought a
rash of cinema-building and the post-war years saw the conversion of many of these cinemas into bingo halls, clubs, casinos
and amusement arcades equipped with a seemingly endless variety
of slot machines. In addition during the post-war years visiting
restaurants has become a favourite recreation; thanks to Merseyside's cosmopolitan population it is possible to eat the national
dishes and drink the national wines of most countries in the
world on such outings.

Merseyside has also acquired facilities for most sporting

activities and in some sports it has gained national or international repute. Its soccer teams, Liverpool and Everton, are
justifiably renowned and in addition Liverpool pioneered football pools, and yet some parts of the region such as St Helens
and Widnes are rugby rather than soccer enthusiasts. Equally
renowned is the Grand National first run as long ago 1839;
international motor racing was also introduced at Aintree by the
redoubtable Mirabel Topham in 1957 with the Grand Prix d'Europe.
In coursing the classic Waterloo Cup was named, not after the
district Waterloo, but after a pub in Ranelagh Street, Liverpool
owned by one William Lynn; greyhound racing is a popular sport
in the region. The region is also extremely well-endowed with
golf courses which frequently host national and international
tournaments. The 'Mersey Golf Club' was founded in Fidlers
Ferry in the 1890s but there are many others throughout the
Wirral and South Lancashire, Southport alone boasting five full
size golf courses including the famous Royal Birkdale. The
provision for many other sports is less lavish but nonetheless
there are thriving cricket and tennis clubs, bowling greens and
bowling alleys, badminton and squash clubs, ice rinks and halls
for snooker and billiards, and around the coasts a variety of
marine sports - yachting, water skiing, fishing and angling.
Sea bathing still occurs from the region's many beaches though
pollution has encouraged many swimmers to transfer their attention to bathing pools and indoor baths.

The region is also well-endowed with open country for walkers
and with a rich diversity of plants, birds and animals for nature
lovers. Its long coast line provides extensive beaches and
stretches of coastal hills; at Ainsdale there is a nature reserve
designed to preserve amongst other animals a unique species of
natterjack toad; at Martin Mere the Wild Fowl Trust has a sanctuary and in the Dee estuary Hilbre Island also acts as a bird
sanctuary; Knowsley Safari park provides entertainment for
those interested in larger, more exotic animals. For walkers
there are open spaces such as Thurstaston common, and the
former West Kirby-Hooton railway has been converted into a
linear park known as the Wirral Way which gives access to
stretches of cliff and shore along the Dee estuary.

In the early part of this period the region's own holiday
resorts such as Southport, New Brighton, Hoylake and West
Kirby continued to provide all the seaside entertainments including piers, fairground amusements, paddling, bathing,
boating etc. More recently they have declined as residential
holiday areas but they still attract large numbers of day trippers
both from within the region and from other regions. With the
building of motorways, the availability of coach trips and more
extensive car-ownership many of the region's inhabitants now
also take advantage of the delightful country that is within easy
reach of the region - the Peak District of Derbyshire, the North
Wales coast, Snowdonia and the Lake District.

The picture of life in Merseyside is not therefore one of un-

relieved gloom despite the many problems and despite 'inner
city' studies which invariably emphasise dilapidation, vandalism,
illegitimacy, truancy, overcrowding, bad housing, unemployment
and job-instability and which quote escalating crime statistics
such as the fact that between 1959 and 1968 the number of
indictable offences in Liverpool and Bootle nearly doubled from
20,000 to just under 40,000. [24] In terms of national income figures,
Merseyside tends to be at the lower end of the income levels and
in matters such as car ownership per 1000 of the population it is
well below the national average. The gloomy figures certainly
apply very strongly to a few areas, particularly to central Liverpool and to a lesser extent to some declining districts such as
Birkenhead and Kirkby. The impact of unemployment has also
been particularly severe in inner city areas. In 1971 male unemployment in inner Liverpool averaged eleven per cent compared
with four per cent for Britain. By the summer of 1975 probably
one in three men were unemployed in the worst areas and a high
proportion of school leavers were unable to find work. [25]

Public attention has been concentrated on such phenomena by
sociological studies and by the media; the *Guardian* (9 Feb. 1977)
counted some 107 separate projects designed to help the sector
of Liverpool known as 'Liverpool, 8' and concluded that they had
achieved virtually nothing, and it was here that some of the worst
inner city riots occurred in 1981. Planners have indulged in
hectic activity to 'redevelop' some of the worst areas by sweeping
away homes, removing cherished landmarks such as the 'Cavern'
and infecting large areas with 'planning blight'. Even some newly
developed areas have already become slums again. There have
been all sorts of ambitious plans (so far largely abortive) to
replace Liverpool's derelict south dockland with marinas, housing
and recreational facilities and the world's largest office block:
to date they have only resulted in the creation of a maritime
museum on a small portion of the site. Other plans have aimed to
develop Merseyside as a whole rather than in small sections
(e.g. the Merseyside Area Land Use Transportation Study of
1965) and others include Merseyside in plans for the whole of
the north-west of England: this sort of integrated approach,
much resented in Merseyside, was the reason for its inclusion
in the North-West Planning Council. Similarly in 1971 Merseyside
was included in the government's 'Strategic Plan' for the North
West.

Most of the ambitious plans have either failed to materialise
or failed to solve the most urgent problems, or have created
even more serious new problems, and most Merseysiders are
largely disillusioned by planning Utopias. Fortunately Merseyside still has many natural and even some economic advantages,
some thriving industries, extensive recreational facilities and
pleasant residential areas. Above all Merseysiders have managed
despite, or perhaps because, of their many tribulations and disappointments to retain their unique and infectious sense of
humour: this has always enabled them to make the best even of

the worst job and hopefully it will continue to sustain them
during future decades.

NOTES

1. *Final Report of the Commission of Inquiry into the subject of the Unemployed in the City of Liverpool* (J. Stack,
Liverpool, 1894), p. 99 (hereafter *Commission on the Unemployed*).
2. G.E. Diggle, *A History of Widnes* (Corporation of Widnes,
1961), p. 88.
3. *Commission on the Unemployed*, pp. 101-2.
4. J.N. Tarn, 'The Model Village at Bromborough Pool',
The Town Planning Review vol. XXV (1964-4), pp. 332, 335.
5. A. Jarvis, *Ellesmere Port - Canal Town 1795-1921* (N.W.
Museum of Inland Navigation, undated), p. 32.
6. J.D. Macphail's evidence to the Housing Committee of the
Ministry of Reconstruction 3 and 30 July 1918, PRO, RECO 1,
640.
7. G.E. Diggle, *History of Widnes*, p. 151.
8. For a fuller account see Liverpool Corporation, *Housing
Progress 1864-1951: City of Liverpool Housing* (Liverpool
Corporation, 1951).
9. A.M. Lees, *Merseyside Facts and Figures* (Merseyside
County Planning Department, 1974), p. 10.
10. Department of the Environment, *Inner Area Studies:
Liverpool, Birmingham and Lambeth* (HMSO, 1977), p. 4.
11. A.M. Lees, *Merseyside Facts and Figures*, p. 10 and
North West Joint Planning Team, *North West 2000: Regional
Policies for the Present and Future* (HMSO, 1974), p. 21.
12. G.E. Diggle, *History of Widnes*, pp. 89-90.
13. *Commission on the Unemployed*, pp. 98-9.
14. Ibid., passim.
15. Ibid., p. 103.
16. Ibid., p. xv.
17. Ibid., p. 87.
18. Ibid., p. 113.
19. S. Salvidge, *Salvidge of Liverpool* (Hodder and
Stoughton, London, 1934), p. 177.
20. G.E. Diggle, *History of Widnes*, p. 91.
21. Ibid., p. 85.
22. This organisation gave information about its activities in
evidence to the *Commission on the Unemployed*, p. 105.
23. For a detailed history of the University see T. Kelly,
*For Advancement of Learning. The University of Liverpool
1881-1981* (Liverpool University Press, 1981).
24. F.J.C. Amos, *Liverpool Prospects. Opportunities for
the Seventies* (Liverpool City Planning Department, 1970), p. 26.
25. Department of the Environment, *Inner Area Studies*, p. 5.

SELECT BIBLIOGRAPHY

REGIONAL AND LOCAL HISTORIES

Aspden, J.P. (ed.) *Warrington Hundred* (Warrington Corporation, 1947).

Bagley, J.J. *Lancashire* (B.T. Batsford Ltd, London, 1972)

Bailey, F.A. *A History of Southport* (Downie, Southport, 1955)

Baines, E. edited by Harland, J. *The History of the County Palatine and Duchy of Lancaster* vo. I (Longmans, London 1868)

Baines, T. *Liverpool in 1859* (Longman, London, 1859)

Barker, T.C. and Harris, J.R. *A Merseyside Town in the Industrial Revolution. St Helens 1750-1900* (Frank Cass, London, 1954)

Brooke, R. *Liverpool as it was during the last quarter of the Eighteenth Century 1775 to 1800* (J. Mawdsley & Son, Liverpool, 1853)

Carter, G.A. *Warrington and the Mid Mersey Valley* (E.J. Morten, Manchester, 1971)

Diggle, G.E. *A History of Widnes* (Widnes Corporation, 1961)

Ellison, N. *The Wirral Peninsula* (Robert Hale, London, 1955)

Harris, J.R. (ed.) *Liverpool and Merseyside. Essays in the Economic History of the Port and its Hinterland* (Frank Cass, London, 1969)

Hyde, F.E. *Liverpool and the Mersey, the Development of a Port, 1700-1970* (David and Charles, Newton Abbot 1971)

Lawton, R. and Cunningham, C.M. (eds), *Merseyside, Social and Economic Studies* (Longman, London, 1970)

Mercer, G. 'Speke as a New Town: an experimental industrial survey' *Town Planning Review* vol. XXIV (1953)

Mortimer, W.W. *The History of the Hundred of Wirral* 2nd edition (E.J. Morten, Manchester, 1972)

Muir, J. Ramsay *A History of Liverpool* (SR Publications, Liverpool, 1907)

── and Platt, E.M. *A History of the Municipal Government in Liverpool from the earliest times to the Municipal Reform Act of 1835* (Liverpool University Press, 1906)

Nickson, C. *History of Runcorn* (Michie, London, 1887)

Patmore, J.A. and Hodgkiss A.G. (eds) *Merseyside in Maps* (Longman, London, 1970)

Smith, W. (ed.) *Merseyside, a Scientific Survey* (Liverpool University Press, 1953)

Sully, P. *The History of Ancient and Modern Birkenhead* (W.M.

Murphy, Liverpool, 1907)
Touzeau, J. *The Rise and Progress of Liverpool from 1551 to 1835*
(Liverpoool Booksellers, Liverpool, 1910)

AGRICULTURE

Davies, C. Stella, *The Agricultural History of Cheshire 1750-1850*
(Chetham Society, Manchester, 1960)
Fussell, G.E. 'Four Centuries of Cheshire Farming Systems
1500-1900', *Transactions of the Historic Society of Lancashire
and Cheshire* vol. 106, 1955

TRADE AND SHIPPING

Allen, G.C. *et. al. The Import Trade of the Port of Liverpool*
(Liverpool University Press, 1946)
Anstey, R. and Hair, P.E.H. (eds), *Liverpool, the African
Slave Trade and Abolition* (Historic Society of Lancashire and
Cheshire, Occasional Series vol. 2, 1976)
Baines, T. *History of the Commerce and Town of Liverpool*
(Longman, London, 1852)
Barker, T.C. 'Lancashire Coal, Cheshire Salt and the Rise of
Liverpool', *Transactions of the Historic Society of Lancashire
and Cheshire*, vol. 103 (1951)
Chandler, G. *Liverpool Shipping a Short History* (Phoenix,
London, 1960)
Cottrell, P.L. 'Commercial Enterprise' in Church, R. (ed.)
*The Dynamics of Victorian Business. Problems and Perspec-
tives to the 1870s* (Allen and Unwin, London, 1980)
—— 'The Steamship on the Mersey 1815-30. Investment and
Ownership' in Cottrell, P.L. and Aldcroft, D.H. (eds) *Shipping,
Trade and Commerce* (Leicester University Press, 1981)
Davies, P.N. *The Trade Makers. Elder Dempster in West Africa,
1852-1972* (Allen and Unwin, 1973)
Hyde, F.E. *Blue Funnel* (Liverpool University Press, 1956)
—— *Cunard and the North Atlantic 1840-1973* (Macmillan, London,
1975)
—— *Shipping Enterprise and Management 1830-1939. Harrisons of
Liverpool* (Liverpool University Press, 1967)
Neal, F. 'Liverpool Shipping 1815-1835' Unpublished M.A. dis-
sertation, University of Liverpool, 1962
Parkinson, C.N. *The Rise of the Port of Liverpool* (Liverpool
University Press, 1951)
Poole, Braithwaite *The Commerce of Liverpool* (Thomas Baines,
Liverpool, 1854)
Williams, D.M. 'Merchanting in the First Half of the Nineteenth
Century: the Liverpool Timber Trade' *Business History* vol.
VIII (1966)
Williams, Gomer *History of the Liverpool Privateers with an*

account of the Liverpool Slave Trade 1744-1812 (Edward Howell, Liverpool, 1897)

TRANSPORT AND DOCKS

Barker, T.C., 'The Sankey Navigation' *Transactions of the Historic Society of Lancashire and Cheshire* vol. 100 (1948)

Box, C.E. *Liverpool Overhead Railway 1893-1956* (Longman, London, 1959)

Broadbridge, S.A., *Studies in Railway Expansion and the Capital Market in England 1825-1873* (Frank Cass, London, 1970)

Farnie, D.A., *The Manchester Ship Canal and the Rise of the Port of Manchester 1894-1975* (Manchester University Press, 1980)

Mountfield, S., *Western Gateway: A History of the Mersey Docks and Harbour Board* (Liverpool University Press, 1965)

Parkin, G.W. *The Mersey Railway* (Williams, Lingfield, 1965)

Pollins, H., 'The Finances of the Liverpool and Manchester Railway' *Economic History Review*, Second Series vol. V. no. 1 (1951)

Porteous, J. Douglas *Canal Ports: The Urban Achievement of the Canal Age* (Academic Press, London, 1977)

Thomas, R.H.G. *The Liverpool and Manchester Railway* (B.T. Batsford, London, 1980)

Willan, T.S. *The Navigation of the River Weaver in the Eighteenth Century* (Chetham Society, Manchester, 1951)

BANKING

Anderson, B.L. and Cottrell, P.L. 'Another Victorian Capital Market: A Study of Banking and Bank Investors in Merseyside', *Economic History Review* Second Series vol. XXVIII (1975)

Hughes, J. *Liverpool Banks and Bankers 1760-1837* (Hughes, Liverpool, 1906)

INDUSTRIES

Barker, T.C. *Pilkington Brothers and the Glass Industry* (Allen) and Unwin, London, 1960)

—— *The Glassmakers: Pilkingtons. The Rise of an International Company 1826-1976* (Weidenfeld and Nicolson, London, 1977)

Clow, A. and Clow, N.L. *The Chemical Revolution* (Batchworth Press, London, 1952)

Haber, L.F. *The Chemical Industry during the Nineteenth Century* (Oxford University Press, Oxford, 1958)

Hardie, D.W.F. *A History of the Chemical Industry in Widnes* (ICI, London, 1950)

Jones, J.R. *The Welsh Builder on Merseyside: Annals and Lives*
    (J.R. Jones, Liverpool, 1946)
Langton, J. *Geographical Change and Industrial Revolution:*
    Coalmining in South West Lancashire 1590-1799 (Cambridge
    University Press, Cambridge, 1979)
Musson, A. *Enterprise in Soap and Chemicals: Joseph Cros-*
    field & Sons Ltd 1815-1965 (Manchester University Press,
    1965)
Reader, W.J. *Imperial Chemical Industries: a History* (2 vols,
    Oxford University Press, Oxford, 1975)
—— *Unilever, a Short History* (Unilever House, London 1960)
Warren K. *The British Iron and Steel Sheet Industry since*
    1840 (G. Bell & Sons, London, 1970)
Wilson, C.H. *The History of Unilever* (2 vols, Cassell, London,
    1954)

POPULATION AND LABOUR HISTORY

Bean, R. 'Working Conditions, Labour Agitation and the Origins
    of Unionism on the Liverpool Tramways, *Transport History*
    vol. 5 no. 2 (1975)
Censuses of Population 1801-1971
Hamling, W. *A Short History of the Liverpool Trades Council*
    1848-1948 (Liverpool Trades Council, 1948)
Hikins, H.R. 'The Liverpool General Transport Strike 1911'
    Transactions of the Historic Society of Lancashire and Cheshire,
    vol. 113 (1961)
Molton, A.L. and Tate, G. *The British Labour Movement 1770-1920:*
    a History (Lawrence and Wishart, London, 1956)
Smith, W. *The Distribution of Population and the Location of*
    Industry on Merseyside (Liverpool University Press, 1942)
Taplin, E. 'Dock Labour at Liverpool: Occupational Structure and
    Working Conditions in the late nineteenth century', *Transactions*
    of the Historic Society of Lancashire and Cheshire, vol. 127
    (1977)
Report of the Commission of Inquiry into the subject of the
    Unemployed in the City of Liverpool (Liverpool, 1894)

EDUCATION

Kelly, T. *Adult Education in Liverpool* (Liverpool University
    Press, 1960)
—— *For Advancement of Learning. The University of Liverpool*
    1881-1981 (Liverpool University Press, 1981)
Ormerod, H.A. *The Liverpool Royal Institution* (Liverpool Uni-
    versity Press, 1953)

HOUSING AND SOCIAL CONDITIONS

Chalklin, C.W. *The Provincial Towns of Georgian England 1740-1820* (Edward Arnold, London, 1974)

Gauldie, E. *Cruel Habitations. A History of Working Class Housing 1780-1918* (Allen and Unwin, London, 1974)

Holt, R.V. *The Unitarian Contribution to Social Progress in England* (Allen and Unwin, 1938)

Kellett, J.R. *The Impact of Railways on Victorian Cities* (Routledge and Kegan Paul, London, 1969)

Jones, D. Caradog *The Social Survey of Merseyside* (3 vols, Liverpool University Press, 1934)

Liverpool Corporation *Housing Progress 1864-1951. City of Liverpool Housing* (Liverpool Corporation, 1951)

McCabe, A.J. 'The Standard of Living in Merseyside 1850-1875' in Bell, S.P. (ed.) *Victorian Lancashire* (David and Charles, Newton Abbot, 1974)

Moss, W. *The Liverpool Guide* (1796. Facsimile edition of City of Liverpool Public Relations Department, 1974)

Shaw, F. *My Liverpool* (Wolfe Publishing Ltd, London, 1971)

Simey, M.B. *Charitable Effort in Liverpool in the Nineteenth Century* (Liverpool University Press, 1951)

Walker, P.J. *Democracy and Sectarianism. A Political and Social History of Liverpool 1868-1939* (Liverpool University Press, 1981)

Second Report of the Commissioners for Inquiring into the State of Large Towns and Populous Districts with Minutes of Evidence, *Parliamentary Papers*, vol. XVIII (1845)

POST-1945 DEVELOPMENTS

Allen, E.C.W. *Post-War Industrial Development in Lancashire and Merseyside* (Manchester Statistical Society, Manchester, 1963)

Amos, F.J.C. *Liverpool Prospects. Opportunities for the Seventies. The 1970 Planning Report on City Objectives and Policies* (Liverpool Corporation, 1970)

Burford, P. (ed.) *Merseyside: An Industrial and Commercial Review* (Pyramid Press, London, 1967)

Department of Economic Affairs *The Problems of Merseyside* (HMSO, London, 1965)

Department of the Environment *Inner Area Studies. Liverpool, Birmingham and Lambeth* (HMSO, London, 1977)

Lancashire and Merseyside Industrial Development Association *Lancashire and Merseyside* (Manchester, 1952, 1956, 1961)

—— *Development of Lancashire and Merseyside, Past, Present and Future* (Manchester, 1963)

Lees, A.M. *Merseyside Facts and Figures* (Merseyside County Planning Dept., Liverpool 1974)

Strategic Plan for the North West, S.P.N.W. Joint Planning Team Report (HMSO, London, 1974)

agriculture 7, 9, 48, 57, 109-10
air transport 107, 131
animal feeding stuffs 117
Ashton, John 19
Aspinall, J. & Son 41, 42
Automatic Telephone & Electric
    Company 121

banking 41-2, 91
Bank of Liverpool 42
Baring Brothers 41
Bebington 10
Beecham, Thos. 78, 110, 113, 114
Bentley, T. 56
Berry, Henry 19, 31, 32
Bibbys 43, 44
Birkenhead 9, 34, 77, 132-3
Blackburne, John 19, 30, 51, 52
Bold, J. 41
Booth, Alfred 44
Booth, Charles 44
Bowater 124
brewing 9, 49, 67, 122
brickworks 67-8, 118
Brindley, James 32
B.I.C. 121
Brocklebanks 43, 44
Bromborough 10
Brown Shipley & Co. 41
Brown, W. & J. 41
Brunner, J.T. 60, 61, 111
Brunner Mond 61, 111-12, 113-14, 116
Bryant & May 124
building industry 64-5, 67-8, 124

Caldwell & Co. 41, 42
Cammell Lairds see shipbuilding
Canals 5, 19-22, 101-2; Bridgewater
    6, 20, 21, 27, 34, 130; Lancaster
    21; Leeds-Liverpool 6, 7, 21, 23,
    52, 63; Manchester Ship 4, 6, 20,
    97-8, 101, 130; Old Quay 34;
    Sankey 6, 19, 28, 52, 59; Shrop-
    shire Union 6, 28; Trent & Mersey
    6, 20, 21, 34, 102
Case, Jonathan 52
Castner, Kellner Co. 112, 113
cathedrals 2, 161
Chamber of Commerce, American 92

Liverpool 92, 107; Salt 91
charities 159-61
Chartism 82
chemical industry 10, 56-62, 111-14
Clarke, John 41
Clarke, William 41
Clayton, Sarah 52, 78
Coalbrookdale 54-5
coal, demand for 14, 51
coalfield, Lancashire 4, 6, 10, 51-2,
    63, 118
coal trade 18-20, 21, 22, 40, 63
coastal shipping 6, 21-2, 28
containers 124
copper 5, 52-3, 60, 63, 119
Cropper & Co. 41
Cunard, Samuel 44 see also shipping
    companies

Daltera, J. 41
Deacon, J. 60
Dempster, J. 44
Dennistoun & Co. 41
docks, Birkenhead 34-5, 95; Brom-
    borough 101, 116; Garston 96,
    101; Liverpool 5, 6, 22, 30-3, 35,
    94-6, 101, 129, 138; Runcorn
    96-7, 137; Stanlow 101
drunkenness 158
Duncan, W.H. 81
Dunlops 123

earthenware 5
Eastham 74-5, 77-8, 134
education 86-7, 161-4
Elder, A. 44
electrical engineering 121
electricity industry 119, 135
Ellesmere Port 10, 74, 97, 129, 133,
    146
engineering 55, 65, 121
entertainments 87-9, 164-5

ferries 17, 22-3, 76
Fisher & Co. 50
fishing 50, 123
food processing 123
Foster, John 32

Gamble, J.C. 58
gas industry 119, 135
Gaskell, Holbrook 60
Gladstone, John 43, 76
glass-making 5, 53–4, 59, 62, 117–18
Gossage, William 60, 61
Great Crosby 76
Greenall, P. 62
Gregson & Co. 41
Gregson, W. 41

Hadwen, J. 41
Harrison, T. & J. 44
Hartley, Jesse 32, 95
Hartley village 146
Heywood, A. & B. 41
Hind & Son 50
Holt, Alfred 44
Holt, George 44
Holt, John 44
Hornby 124
housing 72, 78–9, 81, 145–9
Hoylake 75
Humble and Hurry 50
Hutchinson, John 59, 61

immigrant population 2–3
I.C.I. 111, 114, 133, 137
industrial estates 127–8, 129–30,
   131–4; Aintree 128, 130, 132;
   Birkenhead 132–3; Board of Trade
   134–5; Bromborough 130, 133;
   Ellesmere Port 134; Kirkby 128,
   130, 132; Parr 135; Speke 128, 130,
   132; Widnes and Ditton 133
Ingram, F. 41
Inman, W. 44
insurance 91
iron and steel industry 54–5, 64–5,
   66, 119–20
Ismay, T.H. 44, 94

Jones, A. 44

Kylsant, Lord 100

labour organisation 82–4, 153–7
Laird, John 65–6
Laird, Macgregor 44
Laird, William 65–6, 77
Lamport, W.J. 44
Lancashire Bleaching Powder Manu-
   facturers Association 112
Lancashire Industrial Development
   Corporation 127
Lancashire and Merseyside Industrial
   Development Corporation 130, 140
Leather & Co. 50
Lever Bros. 110
Lever, William, 115–16
Leyland, T. 41

libraries 87, 163–4
linen 49
Liverpool Common Council 14, 19, 30,
   33
Liverpool, death rate 80, 150; growth
   of 7, 73, 74, 75–6, 78–9; housing
   73, 78–9, 81, 145–9; illegitemacy 80;
   Party 25; port of, 4, 5, 30–3; town
   dues 33, 35; water supply 78–9,
   81, 150; *see also* docks
Liverpool Rubber Co. 123
London, competition with Liverpool
   98
Lyle, Abraham 122
Lyster, G.F. 95

Macfie & Sons 122
MacIver, Charles 44
Mackay, John 52
Manchester, competition with Liver-
   pool 35, 97–8
Manchester & Liverpool District Bank
   42
Marconi 121
markets 47–8
Meccano 124
Mersey Docks and Harbour Board 35,
   95–6, 101, 130
Merseyside, definition of, 3–4
Merseyside Passenger Transport
   Authority 131
Mersey Tunnel 106, 130
metal goods industries 9, 54–5, 63–5,
   120
milling, 7, 9, 11, 48–9, 67, 121–2
Mond, Ludwig, 60, 61, 111
Morris, Thomas 32
Moss, James 44
Moss, John 41
motor industry 134, 135–6, 138, 139
Muspratt, James, 58, 60, 76

Neston 75, 78
New Brighton 75, 77

Ogdens 122
oil industry 10, 123, 134
overseas trades 5, 14, 36–40, 92;
   African 37, 38–9; Australian 39,
   40; cotton 39, 41, 92; emigrant 92,
   93; far east 39, 40; Irish 36;
   Mediterranean 35; Newfoundland 36;
   North American 37, 39; slave 37–8;
   Scandinavian 36; South American
   39, 92; tea 41; timber 92; West
   Indian 36, 29, 92

Parkgate 75
parks 149–50
Patten, Thomas 17–18, 53, 75
Pilkington 62, 117–18, 146

pollution 57, 58, 61-2, 73, 149-50
poor relief 84-5, 158-9
population 70-2, 141-5; Birkenhead
71, 77, 133; Ellesmere Port 134;
emigration 3; immigration 71, 80,
142, 145; Liverpool 14, 70-1, 72,
141, 142, 145; Runcorn 71, 72,
138, 142; St Helens 71, 72;
Skelmersdale 136; sources of 71;
Southport 74, 141; Warrington 71;
Widnes 71, 72, 133
Port Sunlight 10, 115, 146
pottery 54, 67, 124
Prescot 9
prices 151
Prices Patent Candle Co. 10, 78, 146
Priestley, J. 56, 87
privateering 37-8
pub. cultures 164

quarrying 68
Quirk, P. & W. 50

railways 6, 24-7, 101, 102-4, 131;
Cheshire lines 102, 131; Grand
Junction 26; Great Northern 27;
Great Western 35; Liverpool-
Manchester 6, 24-5, 27; London
and North Western 27, 28, 102;
Manchester, Sheffield and Lincolnshire 27; Overhead 103; St Helens
Railway and Canal Co. 28; Underground 103-4
Rathbone family 37, 41, 43, 44,
50, 87
religions 86-7, 160-1
Rendel, J.M. 34
riots 82
river navigations 5-6, 17-19; Douglas
6, 18, 19, 21, 52; Mersey-Irwell
6, 18, 28, 34; Weaver 18, 19,
33, 51, 59, 102, 130
roads 106-7, 130-1
road transport, bicycles 105; cars
105, 130; lorries 105, 107, 130;
Mersey tunnel 106, 130; omnibuses
17, 104, 105, 106-7; tramways 17,
104-5; transporter bridge 105-6;
wagon services 16, 28, 105
Roscoe, Clarke & Roscoe 42
Roscoe, William 37, 41, 87
rubber industry 123
Runcorn 4, 10, 33-4, 96-7, 101,
129, 137-8, 149

St Helens 12, 78, 80, 129, 150
salt 9-10, 18, 36, 40, 51, 52, 63
Salt Union 112, 114
Sankeys 122
Seaforth 76
shipbuilding 11, 43, 50, 65-6, 120

Cammell Lairds 11, 65-6, 77, 120,
127, 128
ship owning 42-3
shipping companies 92-4, 99-100;
African S.S. Co. 39, 100; Anchor
94; Bahr Behrend; Beazley 94;
Bibby 94; British & African S.
Navigation Co. 100; Brocklebank
94, 99; Canadian Pacific 94;
Clan 94; Cunard 92, 94, 99, 100;
Elder Dempster 94, 100; Ellerman
94; Furness Withy 94; Glen 99;
Glynn 94; Guinea 94; Guion 92, 93;
Gulf 94; Hall 94; Harrisons 94;
Henderson 94; Alfred Holt 94, 99;
John Holt 94; Hutchinson 100;
Inman 92; Lamport & Holt 94, 100;
Larrinaga 94; Liverpool Brazil &
River Plate 100; James Moss 94,
100; National 92, 93; Pacific S.N.
Co. 94; Palm Line 94; P. & O. 94;
Royal Mail 100; Shire 99; White
Star 92, 94, 100
Skelmersdale 7, 137, 149
soap industry 53, 58-9, 114-17
Southport 7, 73-4, 76-7
Speke airport 6, 107, 131
Staniforth, T. 41
Stanlow 101, 134
steam engines 55-6
Steers, Thomas 30, 32
Stephenson, Robert 34
strikes 153, 154-7
sugar refining 67, 122-3
Swire, J.S. 44

tanning 48, 67, 121
Tate, Henry 110, 122
Tate & Lyle 122
Tayleur, Chas. & Sons 43
Taylor, Potter & Co. 43
textile industries 4, 121; cotton 49;
linen 9, 49; rayon 121; sail cloth
50, 66, 121; silk 49;
timber trade 68
tobacco 56, 67, 123
Tobins 43
tools 55, 63-4, 120
trade associations 42, 91-2; African
91; Corn Trade 91; Jute Goods 91;
timber 91; West Indian 92; Wine
and Spirit 91
Trades Council 155
Tranmere 134
turnpike roads 5, 15-16

unemployment 12, 84, 126, 129,
135, 138, 139, 152, 156
Unilever Ltd 116-17, 133
United Alkali Co. 112, 113

wages 151-2
Warrington 5, 9, 64, 75, 80
Warrington Academy 57, 87
watchmaking 5, 55, 63, 120
Widnes 4, 10, 27, 33, 59-60, 74, 80,
　133, 145, 147, 148, 150-1

Wigan 4, 7
Williams, Thomas 53
wire industry 64
Winnington 111-12
Wolverhampton Corrugated Iron Co.
　Ltd. 146, 152